D1351981

Following football is strongly tied to notions of community and identity. But many supporters of Celtic FC have experienced a dilemma in having been regarded with hostility in Scotland because of their historic ethnic Irish and religious origins. Such antagonism, still prevalent today, is reflected in an ill-informed and sensationalist media. In turn, this works against the realisation of a plural and genuinely multicultural Scotland.

Over 20 contributors from Scotland, Ireland, North America and Germany, including Professor of English Literature Patrick Reilly, author and poet Des Dillon, Herald newspaper columnist Hugh MacDonald, composer James MacMillan, former players Tommy Gemmell and Andy Walker, and an appreciative Foreword by leading historian, Professor Tom Devine.

Dr Joseph Bradley is lecturer in Sports Studies at the University of Stirling. He has researched and published extensively in the sphere of sport, history, politics and society.

Celtic
Minded

essays on religion, politics,
society, identity . . . and football

JOSEPH M. BRADLEY

Argyll
publishing

© Joseph M. Bradley 2004

© The contributors 2004

First published in 2004 by

Argyll Publishing

Glendaruel

Argyll PA22 3AE

Scotland

www.skoobe.biz

The author has asserted his moral rights.

British Library Cataloguing-in-Publication Data.
A catalogue record for this book is available from
the British Library.

ISBN 1 902831 69 1

Origination: Cordfall Ltd, Glasgow

Printing: Bell & Bain Ltd, Glasgow

For the unheard, unseen and marginalised
For those who don't listen, don't look and don't care
For recognition, reconciliation and harmony
For the dead, the living and those to come

ACKNOWLEDGEMENTS

Among those to be acknowledged and thanked for their permission to reproduce images are Famine artist Rodney Charman, Celtic historian Tom Campbell, First Press/Daily Record, The Herald/Evening Times Newsquest Media Group, and SNS. Ricky Fearon provided the memorabilia for the front cover.

The author would like to thank the many people who have contributed to this book in so many different ways. Thanks to colleagues and friends who have provided numerous comments on drafts, and the numerous followers of Celtic and other clubs who have offered their wisdom, advice and support during this process.

Lastly, a word of appreciation to all the contributors who have made this work possible. Go raibh maith agaibh.

Contents

Foreword Tom Devine   11

Introduction Joseph M. Bradley   13

Celtic Football Club and the Irish in Scotland Joseph M. Bradley   19

ROOTS

Commemorating the Great Famine in song and deed Edward O'Neil 87

Celtic and charity Frank O'Hagan   93

The Case for Brother Walfrid Mark Burke   100

DIASPORA

Not a fan. I don't go. I don't like football. But! Des Dillon   109

The Scottish-born Irish and Celtic Joseph McAleer & Brendan Sweeney   115

Scottish-born, living in Canada and being Irish James Rooney   121

FANDOM

Living the dream Eddie Toner   129

The Celtic phenomenon Tom Grant   134

Why Celtic? Heiko Schlesselmann   141

Across the Irish Sea Jim Greenan   147

Social consciousness, class and political identity Frank Devine   151

Playing for Celtic: family and community Andy Walker   158

'Celtic minded': a Protestant view Tommy Gemmell   165

FACING PREJUDICE

Let the people sing Patricia Ferns 173

The wearing of the green Stephen Ferrie 181

See no evil, speak no evil, hear no evil Hugh MacDonald 189

'Shut Up' and 'Trouble': the nonsense over 'sectarianism' Willy Maley 195

FAITH AND SOCIAL CONSCIOUSNESS

Celtic and Catholicism Patrick Reilly 205

Worthy is the Lamb that was slain James MacMillan 212

An identity worth having Aidan Donaldson 218

Home, School and Church: for it's a grand old team?
Roisín Coll & Robert A. Davis 227

Contributors 235

Bibliography 241

Foreword

The sporting shelves in any bookshop are crammed with run-of-the-mill texts on football clubs, famous players and colourful incidents. The majority of these volumes have little lasting value and sooner or later mournfully sit among piles of remaindered and bargain books.

Celtic Minded is, however, a football book with a difference. At one level it is an impressive contribution to the remarkable history of one of the world's most famous clubs. But the book's true value lies elsewhere.

It addresses the subject from the perspective of football as an important social and cultural force in modern Scottish society. Celtic Minded is also a highly readable account of the Catholic Irish immigrant community which gave birth to the club and has sustained it for over a century. In its pages the reader will find impressive accounts of the relationship between Celtic FC and such varied and controversial topics as national identities, modern Scottish culture, Irish diaspora, racism, bigotry and sectarianism.

Much of what appears here is new and fresh, a recapturing of the hidden history of an immigrant group whose descendants have only achieved real social and economic emancipation in Scotland during the last few decades.

Every football fan, even if not Celtic-minded will enjoy this book. But it will also have much broader appeal because of the contentious and provocative issues dealt with here. Celtic Minded deserves a wide readership as a fascinating and intriguing examination of one of Scotland's great sporting institutions and also as a contribution to understanding some key aspects of modern Scottish society.

Tom Devine

Professor Thomas M Devine, FRSE, FBA, Research Professor and Director of the AHRB Centre for Irish and Scottish Studies at the University of Aberdeen. He is the author of the best selling 'The Scottish Nation 1700-2000' (1999) and 'Scotland's Empire 1600-1815' (2003)

IRELAND

Border	━━━━
County Boundaries	─────

DONEGAL

Derry

DERRY

ANTRIM

TYRONE

Belfast

LEITRIM

FERMANAGH

DOWN

SLIGO

MONAGHAN

ARMAGH

LOUTH

MAYO

ROSCOMMON

CAVAN

LONGFORD

MEATH

DUBLIN

GALWAY

WEST MEATH

Galway

OFFALY

Dublin

KILDARE

CLARE

LEIX

WICKLOW

CARLOW

LIMERICK

TIPPERARY

KILKENNY

WEXFORD

KERRY

WATERFORD

CORK

Cork

SHETLAND
Is.

ORKNEY
Is.

SUTHERLAND

CAITHNESS

SCOTLAND

showing main towns
of Irish immigration

ROSS &
CROMARTY

Inverness

NAIRN MORAY BANFF

OUTER HEBRIDES

INNER HEBRIDES

INVERNESS

ABERDEEN

Aberdeen

KIN-
CARDINE

ANGUS

PERTH

Dundee

ARGYLL

FIFE

STIRLING

2   3

Edinburgh

E.
LOTHIAN

Clydebank
Dumbarton
Greenock
& PortGlasgow

Paisley

Glasgow

Glenboig
Coatbridge
Airdrie
Hamilton
Carfin

5

1

4

MID-
LOTHIAN

BERWICK

LANARK

PEEBLES

SELKIRK

ROXBURGH

Motherwell

AYR

Ayr

1 DUMBARTON
2 CLACKMANNAN
3 KINROSS
4 WEST LOTHIAN
5 RENFREW

WIGTOWN

KIRCUDBRIGHT

DUMFRIES

ENGLAND

Introduction

Scotland has recorded some of the biggest football crowds ever witnessed, including 136,505 for the Celtic versus Leeds United European Champions Cup semi-final of 1970 and 147,365 at the Aberdeen versus Celtic Scottish Cup Final of 1937, both held at Hampden Park, Glasgow. On one evening in 1972, just ten kilometres apart in the same city, 155,000 attended two games: Celtic versus Inter Milan in the European Champions Cup semi-final and Glasgow Rangers versus Bayern Munich in the European Cup Winners Cup semi-final. By the new millennium Celtic and Glasgow Rangers respectively had 50,000 and 40,000 season tickets holders. In 2003, Celtic's appearance in the UEFA Cup Final attracted a reported 80,000 supporters from around the globe to attend festivities in the Spanish city of Seville.

Despite football's stature in Scotland as well the game's popularity around much of the world, the advent and growth of the mass media and the enormous increase in the flow of capital into the sport's upper echelons has in recent years changed the face of the game. Although this development emphasises the central place that football occupies in Scottish and other societies' cultures, at its highest level, it might also be argued that this shows that football is now firmly an aspect of global capitalism.[1] As such it can be viewed as being a sport less grounded than in the past and one profoundly influenced by powerful

Notes

1 R. Haynes and R. Boyle 'The grand old game: football, media and identity in Scotland' in Media, Culture and Society, 1996, Vol.18 pp.549-564

people who have little interest or appreciation of the factors that have made the game so appealing to the masses who have traditionally followed, supported and sustained the sport.

Nonetheless, outside of record crowds, winning trophies, famous players and who scored what and when, numerous observers have argued that football's importance has always lain beyond the football stadium and the mere kicking of a ball.[2] At least as far as the beginning of the twenty first century is concerned, despite its potential to implode as a result of serious economic and social changes, the game continues to hold its pre-eminent role in world sport.

A sports columnist reflected this reality, arguing that:

> History, tradition, rivalry, culture and habit are every bit as important to the game as any yardsticks set by the quality of players, teams and facilities . . . there is more to football than football.[3]

Speaking of the world famous Barcelona Football Club and its winning of the Spanish League Championship in 1985 for the first time in over a decade, an academic commentator recounted how a woman told him that:

> I detest football, but Barca is more than football. In the bad days, when we had nothing else, Barca meant Catalonia. People used to go to the stadium just to speak Catalan.[4]

Using an approach that reflects on the cultural, historical, social, religious, political and moral dimensions of soccer, this book is a study of one sporting institution that is based in the east end of Glasgow in Scotland. It is a reflection on the meaningfulness of Celtic Football Club in relation to its historic community of supporters. That these supporters are vital in any acknowledgement of the history and culture that is Celtic FC was stated by one of the club's players:

> I think the thing about Celtic is the supporters. The

2 For example, see R. Giulianotti & G. Armstrong, 2001

3 Tom Watt 'Raucous family fare at heaving Loftus Road is what it's all about miles away from hype' Scotland on Sunday 23/11/03

4 Lincoln Alison, 1986, pp.2-3

players come and go but the club and the fans are always there.[5]

A Celtic Supporters Association representative opined that:

> We are not customers despite a new language to describe us as such. Many of us have been supporting Celtic for longer even than our very admirable manager, certainly most of the players, and quite a few of our directors, including our biggest single shareholder. Add our fathers' and grandfathers' support for Celtic and you might come to the conclusion that we are the most important dimension of Celtic FC.[6]

Another fan expressed the view in a popular supporter's fanzine that:

> Celtic is a way of life! So many Celtic fans and generations of Celtic fans have been steeped in this tradition of being 'Celtic'! It is our culture, our history and our heritage! The tradition of music, banter and song . . . Celtic is in your heart and soul![7]

Former Celtic player and manager, Tommy Burns, encapsulated aspects of the bonding and relationship between the fans, players and club as well as its value, meaning and importance to its historic supporting community, when he stated:

> They [the players] have to remember it's more than just a football team they're playing for. They're playing for a cause and a people.[8]

Similar to the sentiment expressed by the female supporter of Barcelona, with specific regard to Celtic FC, Irish music star and writer Shane McGowan told an interviewer that his invitation to appear at the club's ground in 2002 was like:

> . . . going out on stage at the Barrowlands; it was the same crowd. Celtic are the only team I'm interested in apart from the Ireland team, but I'm not really a big soccer fan.[9]

5 Didier Agathe 'Coming Home to Boost' Sunday Herald 2/11/03

6 The Alternative View 'The article The Celtic View refused to let you read' Oct/Nov 2003

7 The Alternative View 'Alternative Fanzone' Dec 2003

8 D. Burdsey & D Chappell 2001

9 Richard Purdon 'The Rogue from the Pogues' Scotland on Sunday 5/10/03

Such discourses are evidence of the common perception that football goes beyond 'mere' sport and in fact, almost certainly finds its lifeblood in the extra-sporting passions and meanings that link it to everyday aspects of life, especially those involving social and community life.

This book is not a history of football, Celtic, Catholics, religion, or of the totality of the experience of being part of the historic Irish diaspora in Scotland. It is not a history of how the Irish have been received and how they have evolved. In Scotland and elsewhere, other immigrant experiences are similar as well as divergent. However, these themes are significantly meaningful and central to understanding Celtic Football Club and its support. In that context, this book endeavours to capture critical aspects of the story of Irish Catholics in Scotland. Such accounts are an indispensable feature of Catholic, Irish and Celtic narratives, but they are rarely relayed, addressed or represented in academic and popular works.

The social and community experiences of the Irish diaspora in Scotland, aspects of the socialisation that they have encountered and the contestation that 'their' club has been seemingly perennially involved in Scottish society are some of the issues explored here. The first part of this exercise provides some of the context for such an exploration. As part of the Irish diaspora in Scotland and using the medium of the football club this diaspora has founded, developed and supported, in the main this book is concerned with 'Celtic Minded' people reflecting upon their individual and collective Celtic-related experiences. Using the cultural focus of 'their' club, these writers seek to examine and express important aspects of the experience of the Irish Catholic diaspora in Scotland, features and accounts that have a history of being misrepresented and marginalised. Such narratives and cultures that the Irish diaspora have shared through this experience have often being rendered invisible. These essayists seek to remedy some of this exclusion through representing themes and experiences frequent and familiar within their community.

This book is partly about racism, bigotry, prejudice and 'sectarianism' in Scottish society. It also constitutes a reflection on Scottishness, varying versions of Scottishness and how people in Scotland become 'Scottish', specifically, how members of the Irish diaspora might have become Scottish.[10] This collection of essays is about those in Scotland whose parents, grandparents, great grand-parents and beyond, fled or departed their homes and communities in Ireland, to embark on a new life in Scotland. It is partly about how many of them have retained as fundamental their sense of Irishness and, of being Irish, despite being born in Scotland. The evidence demonstrates that for many supporters, Celtic Football Club can be individualised and personified as an Irish immigrant. Celtic Football Club was specifically born as an Irish institution in 1887/88. In the main it is the support that determines that this Irishness remains fundamental to their club and its community of supporters: despite the hostility towards that actuality.

This book of essays assists in an understanding of Celtic Football Club and its historic community of support-ers that in the main is constituted by the Irish diaspora in Scotland and elsewhere. It reflects on the roots and nature of the Club as well as the culture and identities of its support. It considers both the Club and its supporters in the context of Scottish society. This book adds to current notions of modern Scotland and how it manages and reflects its multicultural society.

Joseph M. Bradley

10 An understanding of this 'socialisation' process that most people take for granted is possibly best explored through Anderson's notion of the 'imagined community': a concept implicitly important to a contextual understanding of this work.

Detail from 'The Ford Family', a painting of
the Irish Famine by the marine artist Rodney
Charman. Leaving home has been a
common experience for many Irish in the
nineteenth and twentieth centuries

Background and context: Celtic Football Club and the Irish in Scotland

Joseph M. Bradley

Reliable estimates show that around 300,000 refugees migrated to Britain during 'an Gorta Mor', the Great Irish Famine of the mid-nineteenth century, with 100,000 arriving in Scotland. Throughout the post-Famine years of the mid-nineteenth century, during the first quarter of the twentieth, and more erratically for the rest of that century, substantial numbers of immigrant Irish entered Scotland, most eventually settling in the west-central belt in and around Lanarkshire and greater Glasgow. During this period, numerous areas in west-central Scotland changed in their religious and social composition as Irish Catholics in particular streamed in. Towns and villages such as Coatbridge, Carfin and Glenboig in Lanarkshire, areas of Glasgow like Calton and the Gorbals, and districts of Paisley, Port Glasgow, Greenock and Dumbarton, absorbed many Irish, thus assisting in the social and economic growth and development of these areas.

The 1851 census recorded 207,367 Irish born in Scotland: around 7 per cent of the population.[1] By this time McCaffrey estimates that there were around 150,000 Catholics in the country although the figure of 332,000 by 1878 may be a more accurate estimate and a better

Notes

1 J.E. Handley 1964, p.197

indicator of the number of Irish Catholics coming to Scotland during the period of the 'Great Famine' in Ireland and for several decades afterwards.[2]

Proportionately, in relation to the size of the Scottish population, more Irish emigrated to Scotland than to any other country. This factor is striking when one considers that the vast majority of Irish and their offspring eventually settled in a thirty mile radius around the greater Glasgow and Lanarkshire areas of the west-central belt. Collins estimates that around eight per cent of all Irish-born emigrants went to Scotland during the period 1841 to 1921 and most Irish immigration to Scotland took place during this time.[3] After 1921 Irish emigration continued, but Scotland declined as a significant focus of settlement. However, the post-World War II boom period in Britain once again increased migration from Ireland and resulted in thousands of Ulster and Donegal people in particular arriving in the Glasgow area. The Irish in Scotland are a multi-generational ethnic community.

REPRESENTATIONS OF THE IRISH IN SCOTLAND

For much of the nineteenth century, the Irish in Scotland huddled together in the worst parts of towns and cities. They came to Scotland with an alien and often detested Catholic faith and arrived in a land that had played a significant role in what they often perceived as the subjugation and division of their own country. They comprised amongst and often constituted the very poorest sections of Scottish society. They were labelled unskilled due to their limitation to mainly manual labour, although their presence was viewed as essential to the progress of the industrial revolution in Scotland and the development of the transport infrastructure, the coal industry and other economic concerns.

Many of the stereotyped attitudes that developed towards the Irish did so in this context and negative feelings amongst the native community towards the

2 J. McCaffrey 1983, p.276

3 B. Collins 'The Origins of Irish Immigration to Scotland in the Nineteenth and Twentieth centuries' in T.M. Devine 1991

increasing Irish Catholic influx emerged within various facets of Scottish life. For example, during Victorian times, 'No Irish Need Apply' notices were a common warning in the recruitment columns of the contemporary press and the walls and entrances of employment concerns. Pamphlets, lectures and tracts against Ireland, the Irish and Catholics, as well as their rudimentary schools, were common during these decades.[4] A cultural and ideological polemic was waged by many sections of society against Irish Catholic immigrants, thus demonstrating that the Irish were generally viewed with suspicion and hostility in Scottish society.[5]

Apes and Aryans? – an unflattering cartoon from *Scottish Referee*, 3 February 1905. An example of popular attitudes to the Irish in Scotland

Writing of the small Irish immigrant community in early nineteenth century Scotland, Handley reports that the Irish were subjected to all sorts of 'verbal abuse and mockery': local newspapers where there was an Irish presence often being among the chief purveyors of this denigration. Handley quotes a number of newspaper articles having such titles as 'gims of the Emerald Isle' and 'bhoys from the land of the bog and the shamrock'. In addition, 'ape-faced' and 'small headed Irishmen', 'a cruel Tipperary visage', 'a malicious-looking Irishman' and 'a blackguard-looking creature with a plastered face' are all cases from the North British Daily Mail during the nineteenth century.[6] When the comic reporting became exhausted it usually dismissed the incomers as the 'low Irish'.[7]

For Handley, the hostility faced by the Irish in Scotland stemmed from economic, political and religious reasons, all factors that shaped discourses in relation to Irish Catholic immigrants.[8] Commentators such as Finn and Curtis agree with Handley and consider this antagonism a form of racism.[9] Handley also argues that the chief reason for native animosity towards Catholics from Ireland was their faith, the fewer Ulster Scots Protestants of the north of Ireland who also arrived in Scotland in their thousands apparently assimilating easily with their former kith and kin.

4 T. Gallagher 1987, c.32

5 Some newspapers like The Scotsman in Edinburgh were occasionally more favourable towards the immigrants, but this was the exception rather than the rule

6 Handley p.249

7 Ibid p.133

8 Ibid p.131

9 Also, see Finn 1991 and Curtis 1984 and 1988

Close inspection of the columns of the North British Daily Mail, the Glasgow Courier, The Witness, the Bulletin, the Glasgow Chronicle, the Glasgow Constitutional, the Glasgow Herald, and the Scottish Guardian among others, reveals an abundance of animosity towards the Irish in Scotland. A discourse that constituted an ideology of superiority, domination and rejection was evidenced by the census report for Scotland in 1871.

> As yet the great body of these Irish do not seem to have improved by their residence among us; and it is quite certain that the native Scot who has associated with them has most certainly deteriorated. It is painful to contemplate what may be the ultimate effect of this Irish immigration on the morals and habits of the people, and on the future prospects of the country.[10]

One significant factor negatively used to distinguish the Irish from the native Scots and British population generally was their 'Celticism', defined as:

> Their religion and their perceived Irish nationalism. As 'white negroes', the Irish were regarded as 'dirty' and 'diseased', a contagion within Victorian [Britain] and a threat to it.[11]

Historically, such reporting on the Irish is fundamental to an understanding of how the wider society viewed the offspring of Irish Catholic immigrants, as well as in how they perceived themselves. This context is important in relation to contemporary Irish identity: that is, the Irishness of the progeny of Irish immigrants in Scotland. This is also crucial to a consideration of 'sectarianism' in modern Scotland as well as the position and role of Celtic Football Club in Scottish society.

Such reporting indicates that the Irish were largely seen and prescribed as a racialised minority. As this minority began to become a more permanent feature of industrial Scotland, its offspring began to be 'sectarianised' in a related racialised fashion. Amongst other things, this has subsequently meant that they have been identified not by their differing accent and place of birth but via

10 Handley, p.321
11 J. MacLaughlin 1999

their town or village of residence, some of their cultural tastes and practices, but primarily, identified via their Irish names, Catholic religion and support for Celtic. A number of authors allude to the resultant discrimination faced by this community.[12]

In Scotland, 'Presbyterianism was not just a state religion but, for more than three centuries, defined the Scots to one another and to the rest of the world'.[13] Additionally, Muirhead opines that 'in Scotland anti-Romanism had become a religion and a way of life'.[14] Although Protestantism in Scotland has long been multi-dimensional, involving social, political, moral, philosophical and spiritual aspects, it is the relationship between Scottishness and Protestantism, and the anti-Catholic dimensions of Presbyterianism, that have had a significant impact on relations between Protestants and Catholics in Scotland. Since the Reformation, a significant anti-Catholic culture has existed in Scotland, one that has varyingly infused many aspects of social and political life. Partly reflecting the significance of anti-Catholicism in Scotland prior to Irish-Catholic migration, two statistics singularly demonstrate this in the city of Glasgow in the 1790s. One commentator relays that at this time there were only thirty-nine Catholics in the city but forty-three anti-Catholic societies (Devine notes sixty anti-Catholic societies in 1791).[15]

Nonetheless, this complex culture has involved many different strands and dimensions over both time and place, and the arrival of Irish Catholic immigrants to Scotland during the nineteenth and twentieth centuries added ethnic and racial aspects to traditional anti-Catholic antagonism.[16] Anti-Catholicism, with a new potent ethnic element, subsequently became a framework for influencing many features of everyday life from employment and education, to sport and politics.

12 See Handley, p.357, T. Devine (ed) 1995 and, Gallagher 1987

13 Gallagher 'The Catholic Irish in Scotland: In Search of Identity' in Devine T.M. (ed) 1991 pp.19-43

14 I.A. Muirhead 1973

15 B. Murray 1984, p.93 and T.M.Devine 1988, p.154

16 See E.W. McFarland 1990, Gallagher 1987 and Devine 1991

THE IRISH FOOTBALL CLUB IN SCOTLAND

The origins and development of Celtic Football Club are embedded and intertwined in the history and evolution of the Irish Catholic community in Scotland. By the end of the 1880s, football was a popular game throughout Britain. In Glasgow, Brother Walfrid, a member of the Catholic Marist Order, and some of his Irish-Catholic immigrant compatriots, saw in the development of the game an opportunity to raise money and feed poor immigrant Irish Catholics in the east end of the city. Brother Walfrid's intention was to keep Catholics within the reaches of the faith (and therefore out of the reaches of proselytism), while also raising the confidence and morale of that community.

Like other commentators, Campbell and Woods argue that, at the time of Celtic's founding in 1887/88, the words Catholic and Irish were interchangeable in the west of Scotland. All the club's founders were expatriate Irishmen or from Irish stock, and the new club's support was drawn from the swelling Irish community in Glasgow. The donations to charity frequently included some to exclusively Irish causes such as the Evicted Tenant's Fund, then an important feature of Irish nationalist politics. In addition, if as Catholics the members were concerned about the plight of local charities, like many other members of their community, as Irishmen, they were also preoccupied with the perennial question of Irish politics, Home Rule.[17]

For example, John Glass, President and Director of the club in its foremost years, was an outstanding figure

17 T. Campbell and P. Woods 1986, p.18

Celtic FC in 1888 – the club's first ever team

in nationalist circles; he was prominent in the Catholic Union, a founder of the O'Connell branch of the Irish National Foresters and the treasurer of the Home Government Branch of the United Irish League. Another member, William McKillop, became MP for North Sligo in Ireland (holding this constituency for eight years before winning in South Armagh in 1908), whilst Michael Davitt (a former revolutionary/Fenian and founder of the Irish Land League) the celebrated Irish patriot, was one of the club's original patrons. Club officials, players and supporters alike, were often involved in politics; supporting Irish Home Rule, campaigning for the release of Irish political prisoners, opposing what they viewed as British imperialism in the Boer War in South Africa and supporting the contentious Catholic endeavour to have their schools brought within the state-funded system.

During the 1870s the Irish Home Rule movement had began to grow in Britain. Its branch in Glasgow, known initially as the Home Government Association, became the Irish National League after 1880. It was to develop into one of the strongest branches in Britain. The League was able to mobilise the bulk of votes in strongly immigrant neighbourhoods up until World War I.

> Its support was usually placed at the disposal of the Liberal party which introduced Home Rule Bills into parliament in 1886, 1892, and 1912.[18]

The political thrust involved in the establishment of Celtic is emphasised by Wilson who notes that although the decision to form Celtic is rightly identified with the needs of Catholic charity in the east end of Glasgow:

> the early nature of the club, and the direction it pursued, owe at least as much to the influence exercised by the political organisation which spoke for the vast majority of the Irish in Scotland in the 1880s, the Irish National League, and specifically one of its branches in Glasgow, known as the Home Government Branch. Among those involved in setting up Celtic, John Glass, James Quillan, the McKillops and the Murphys were heavily involved in the Home Government Branch. . . The influence which the leading figures in the Home Government Branch exercised in the founding of Celtic ensured that the primary aim would be to create a club that was outward-looking, proudly Irish and excellent. . .[19]

The outward looking nature of this Irish club in Glasgow is further noted by Wilson to be of a strong non-sectarian kind. After all, John Ferguson was a Belfast Protestant who founded the Irish National League in Glasgow in 1871. Amongst his closest colleagues were people like Glass, Murphy and Quillan. Although these men established a symbol of, and representation for, Irish Catholic migrants in the west of Scotland, the club incorporated no notion of excluding anyone on the basis of their religion or ethnic or national origins. The club's subsequent history has reflected this ethos and, it might be argued, this also reflects a long history of Protestant involvement in Irish nationalist political struggle.

18 Gallagher 1987, p.68

19 Campbell and Woods 1986, p.13

At an institutional level, Celtic's overt political symbolism remained evident until at least the 1960s when the club launched its own newspaper, The Celtic View. Prominent adverts were included for 'Irish Rebel Records' including 'The Merry Ploughboy' and 'James Connolly'.[20] Commemorative concerts for Irish patriots 'Sean South' and 'Kevin Barry' were also advertised, as was a Glasgow concert to celebrate the fiftieth anniversary of the 1916 Easter Uprising, which included the appearance of readers' favourite Celtic stars.[21] Such activities remain popular with Celtic supporters.

Apart from the Irish-born immigrant Walfrid, the club's first important Catholic patron was Archbishop Charles Eyre of Glasgow. Many cartoons of the time, in both the Catholic and the secular press, 'included sympathetic caricatures of priests among the crowds at Celtic games', whilst Campbell and Woods state that the Glasgow Observer, a Catholic newspaper catering to the Irish Catholic community, took a keen interest in Celtic's progress. Other Irish football clubs also existed at the same time, in Lanarkshire, Glasgow and Edinburgh, who with the same national and religious make-up as Celtic, made efforts to establish themselves. However, it was the remarkable competitive successes of the Celtic club, as well as good organisation, an apt location and a supportive community, which enabled it to prosper.[22]

Celtic was founded by and for Irish Catholics, though never exclusively so. The club has always included Scottish non-Catholics/Protestants amongst both its staff and its support, and by the 1990s others from outside of Britain and Ireland. Some like Johnny Thomson, Kenny Dalglish, Danny McGrain, Henrik Larsson and manager Jock Stein, have become legendary sporting icons within the Celtic community. Nonetheless, the club has been the cultural and symbolic champion of the Irish Catholic community in Scotland and its ethno-religious make-up, along with its early successes on the football field, helped attract crowds to football that had never previously been exper-

20 Celtic View, 9/3/66, 20/7/66, 19/4/67

21 Ibid, 6/4/66

22 Campbell and Woods 1987, pp.11-26, also J.E. Handley 1960

ienced in Scotland.[23] The club came into existence as the focus for much Catholic and Irish community activity, a setting for that community's broad social and political aspirations.

Although Celtic's uniqueness lay in its Irish and Catholic identity, in fact many football clubs grew out of pre-existing social contexts and relationships. Many had political, national and religious dimensions to them.[24] Sporting clubs require a base for both establishment and support and these things have made a crucial contribution to the very existence of sport and competition across the globe. In this context, Celtic's ethnic and religious origins are less unique than is often thought the case.[25]

Despite rising to become the most significant Irish team in Scotland, Celtic's presence and subsequent success, also caused it problems. For example, in 1896 Celtic and Hibernian (the Edinburgh side which had also emerged from the local Irish community) were top of the Scottish league. This prompted the newspaper, Scottish Sport, to note the dominance in Scotland of two Irish teams and asking where was the Scottish team that could challenge the incomers.[26] In fact, a few years earlier, Hibernian had been refused entry to the Scottish League on the basis of the club's Irish identity. Such newspaper comment was a refined example of the antagonism faced by Irish clubs in Scotland, but the challenge by Scottish Sport explicitly reflects the ethnic nature of the Scottish game from its earliest years and is also reflective of later discourses concerning the Irish and Celtic in Scotland.

The most noteworthy counter to the success of Celtic was Glasgow Rangers. Finn argues that, like many Scottish clubs, from its earliest days Rangers had a significant Protestant, Unionist and increasingly anti-Catholic and anti-Irish character.[27] Although Rangers had existed for around fifteen years before Celtic, its early years had not been marked by any significant degree of success. Nonetheless, steady advance in both winning trophies and improving finances meant that gradually, Rangers came

23 B. Murray 1988, p.19
24 See G. Finn 1991
25 See Murray 1984, 1988
26 Finn 1994b
27 Murray 1984 p.31

to provide an answer to the question asked by Scottish Sport. For many Scots, the task for defending native prestige eventually fell primarily to Glasgow Rangers.

Since the foundation of the club, Celtic and its supporting community's Irishness has been a focus for dispute for many people in Scotland. In 1952 the traditional flying of the Irish national flag at Celtic Park even came to threaten the place of Celtic in Scottish football. Celtic's official club historian in its centenary year, future British Government minister Brian Wilson, describes how:

> . . . an attempt was made to force Celtic out of business if they would not agree to remove the Irish flag from their home ground.[28]

This controversy arose after spectator trouble in the Celtic versus Rangers match in January of that year. After recommendations by the Magistrates' Committee of Glasgow Corporation in relation to future crowd disturbances, the Scottish Football Association (SFA) eventually decided that among other things, both clubs should avoid the display of any flag or emblem which had no association with this country or the game. In fact, Celtic was the only club that flew a flag that 'might' be construed as having nothing to do with Scotland. In addition, the shamrock was the central emblem of the club and Celtic supporters were also characterised by much Irish symbolism, visual as well as in chant, song and identity. Robert Kelly, the Chairman of Celtic, saw this as an attack upon the nature of the club as well as upon the Irishness of many Catholics in Scotland. In a speech to a lay Catholic organisation, Kelly stated:

> We have no need to be ashamed of our fathers, nor have we any cause to be ashamed that those founders [of Celtic] came from that country that has provided protagonists for liberty wherever they have settled.[29]

Celtic was ordered to take down the flag or be suspended

28 B. Wilson 1988 p.94
29 Wilson 1988, pp.97-98

from football in Scotland. The SFA adopted these recommendations by a vote of 26 to 7, showing the strength of feeling against the club. With the support of the Celtic followers, Kelly refrained from complying with the order, determined to protect the identity of the club: the Irish flag would remain or Celtic would indeed stop playing.

Nonetheless, the SFA lacked recourse to legitimate means of enforcing its demand. Most clubs eventually waned in their attack on Celtic recognising that the income generated by them was a major factor in Scottish football's vibrancy. The furore eventually died down and Celtic continued to fly the Irish flag, though numerous people and organisations have continued to disapprove of its presence at Celtic, both above the stadium and amongst Celtic supporters.

Although historically an Irish club, Celtic's involvement in football allowed its supporting Catholic immigrant community to integrate with and share in a popular cultural activity of many people in Scotland. Football and Celtic were avenues for interaction and co-operation with the host community, despite the ethnic competitiveness of the game itself. Nonetheless, numerous authors refer to widespread discrimination against the Irish Catholic community in the workplace up until at least this period and the episode over Celtic's flying of the Irish flag suggests that hostility extended to this community's sporting representatives and beyond.[30]

For many who followed the events surrounding the flag issue, this hostility seemed to be emphasised by the 1952 incident since no reference was made during the dispute to Rangers' policy of refusing to sign Roman Catholic players. Indeed, for some sections of the Catholic community, lack of attention to this matter indicated an endorsement or acceptance of the policy and was linked to similar practices on the part of the wider society.

30 See footnote 20

Celtic FC in 1908

CONFLICT AND DISCORD

Anti-Irish and anti-Catholic feeling in Scotland has rarely been uniform. For many individuals, organisations and communities, they form a complex and differentiated phenomenon. Although other factors are also crucial to assessments of historical Scotland, since the sixteenth century, these notions have had a varying but profound effect on social, economic, cultural and national issues. Although for other Scots, anti-Catholicism and anti-Irishness have had little or no part to play in their lives,[31] the history of ethno-religious cleavage in Scotland since the mid-nineteenth century has meant that opposition and prejudice towards the immigrant community has been widespread, and has clearly had a wide resonance in Scottish society.

Cooney writes that as late as 1938, the Church and Nation Committee of the Church of Scotland emphasised 'the elementary right of a nation to control and select its immigrants'.[32] The debate which had resulted in such a

31 J.M. Bradley, 1995 pp.83-94, also Devine 1996, pp.72-3

32 J. Cooney 1982, p. 19

way of thinking was conducted solely with Irish Catholics in mind. In fact, Brown, states that from around the time of the Education Act (Scotland) 1918, until the outbreak of World War II, there was an 'official' Presbyterian campaign against the Irish Catholic community in Scotland. This campaign was both institutional and popular, and is viewed by Brown as an attempt at 'marginalising, and even eliminating an ethnic minority whose presence was regarded as an evil, polluting the purity of Scottish race and culture'.[33]

The pre-World War II period seems to have been a fertile one for such activities as well as a time when they were acceptable to and supported by the wider society. Such sentiments found expression in popular literature, for example in the works of Andrew Dewar Gibb (later to become Regius Professor of Scots Law at Glasgow University) and of journalist George Malcolm Thomson.[34] Political activists, like Alexander Ratcliffe and John McCormick, gained success at the ballot by declaring similar anti-Irish and anti-Catholic opinions. Other significant political figures at the time reflected these widespread feelings regarding the Irish in Scotland. For example, Conservative Member of Parliament, Lord Scone, believed that:

> . . . culturally the Irish population. . . has not been assimilated into the Scottish population. It is not my purpose to discuss now whether the Irish culture is good or bad, but merely to state the definite fact that there is in the west of Scotland a completely separate race of alien origin practically homogeneous whose presence there is bitterly resented by tens of thousands of the Scottish working-class.[35]

Such attitudes recorded in the recent past also have contemporary manifestations and cases like these, which in themselves might be viewed as insignificant and normally unrelated comment, could in fact be repeated many times and reflect a widely held broad ideological and attitudinal position. For example, the unacceptability of Irish-Catholics to the Orange community in Scotland is

33 Brown 1991, p.21

34 Gallagher, 1987 pp.168-171

35 Hansard, 261, 22/11/32, p.245

one of the most perceptible contemporary manifestations of this attitude.

> Study the [Irish-Catholic] names of some of the 'Labour'
> candidates elected. . . What do Glasgow's Protestant
> clergymen think of this situation? What do the genuine
> patriots, in the SNP's rank-and-file, think about it?. . .
> There isn't a Scoto-Eirishman in Scotland, a Lally, a
> Murphy, or a Gaffney, who is not Eirish under his skin.
> Scratch them and their Eirish bit comes out. . .[36]

Similar sentiments have frequently been expressed by some of the Reformed Churches in Scotland. In 1986, the Moderator of the Free Church of Scotland addressed its annual Assembly. His speech included criticism of the Catholic and Irish nature of those of immigrant extraction:

> In 1755 there were no Roman Catholics in Glasgow, our
> largest city today. In 1786 there were about seventy and
> by 1830, they numbered 30,000, with 14,000 in
> Edinburgh. . . Today the Roman Catholic system is
> virtually triumphant in Scotland. Being allowed by its
> constitution to lie and cheat as long as its own ends are
> realised, its close organisation and its intelligence set-up
> has enabled it to infiltrate the whole educational
> framework of the land.[37]

In a secular society that inter alia involves popular conceptions of 'liberalism', and given the social and political progress made by the offspring of the Irish in Scotland, especially in recent decades, most of the overt statements and activities of half a century ago are unlikely to gain the currency they once had. Today, society in Scotland is more complex. For some sections of the population, ethnic and religious identity is less significant than in the past. The growth of a Catholic middle class, the effects of globalisation in Scotland, the decline of heavy industry and the development and growth of the mass media are only some of the factors that have given rise to change.

However, the publications and assertions of some organisations and individuals remain anti-Irish and anti-Catholic.[38] In contemporary society more subtle and

36 Orange Torch, June 1984

37 Moderator's address to the Church Assembly, Church Records, July/August 1986

38 Bradley 1995

recycled forms of antagonism persist and continue to have an impact on Irish, and arguably Catholic, identity in Scotland. This is evidenced in contemporary discourses surrounding matters 'Celtic' in the Scottish media and elsewhere. It might be argued that many of these previous discourses now manifest themselves in a recycled form while maintaining a similar range of sentiments and positions.

'RELIGION' IN SCOTTISH SOCIETY

Socially, politically and in relation to life chances, religion has had a varying effect in Scottish society over the course of at least a century and a half. It has traditionally been one of the most significant factors in Scottish life, though the influence of formal and institutional religion has been falling since at least the early 1960s, and rapidly so in the last few decades. Despite the importance of religious questions, it is clear that with respect to Church attendance and many of the dominant cultural features and mores of society, Scotland can be considered a secular country, though secularism varies in degree and depth across the country. It might even be argued that a dominant mode of thinking is apparent amongst significant and influential sections of the population in Scotland: one that believes religion is a private affair and should be restricted to the home or Church. For many religious people this is a curious philosophy in that faith can provide the very rationale for human existence and as such cannot be compartment-alised.

Nevertheless, it might also be argued that religious 'identity' as opposed to religious 'faith' and 'lifestyles' still have a significant role to play in Scottish life. Despite the decline in formal religious adherence in modern Scotland and the growth of a secular society, the capacity of 'religious' matters to dominate periods of news remains a feature in Scotland. The media attention and subsequent debates over Glasgow Rangers' Vice Chairman Donald Findlay singing sectarian songs in May 1999, composer

Celtic FC in 1930

James MacMillan's accusations of Scottish anti-Catholic bigotry in August 1999 and the controversy over the proposed unveiling of a national monument in Lanarkshire to the victims of the great Irish Famine of the mid-nineteenth century are a few occasions that have demonstrated the contentiousness of religiously related issues in Scottish society in recent years.[39] Likewise, it is commonplace for the popular media in Scotland to develop a 'religious' perspective when discussing matters related to Celtic and Glasgow Rangers. This attention has also attracted media focus from outside Scotland, though the depth of inquiry regarding this matter is similarly superficial and lacking in informed opinion and analysis, whilst ironically, it is often dependent on Scottish sources for information.

Ironically however, people in Scotland can often be seen to refuse to countenance interesting, informed discussions about religion and its significance to people and institutions: especially beyond the Church or Mosque.

39 Religously related in that they frequently do not address or debate serious religious issues in terms of the substance of faith itself. For examples of furore surrounding these events, for Findlay see Daily Record, 3/6/99, for MacMillan see Sunday Herald, 15/8/99, for the Irish Famine Memorial see Daily Record 9/2/01

Indeed, this raises a question over many people's capacity for informed and knowledgeable discussions concerning religious matters. This is one of the things Herald sports columnist Graham Spiers implied when he stated that mentioning Celtic in the same breath as 'Catholic', he is often viewed as breaking an unwritten rule amongst journalists. This rule, 'you just don't go there'.[40] Spiers asks why? Why does Scotland have a difficulty with this? In a related sense, fellow journalist Ian Bell also opined, 'sport is not immune to politics, nor is it divorced from reality'. In addition to these perceived 'realities', it might also be argued that 'religious' discourses in the Scottish media are characterised by an extensive ignorance and lack of penetrating and reflective exploration.[41] Although anti-Catholicism has been viewed as a characteristic common to Scotland for several hundred years it might also be argued that much of Scotland had become hostile not only to Catholics, but to many Christian beliefs, teachings and doctrines by the new millennium.[42]

Celtic FC in 1955

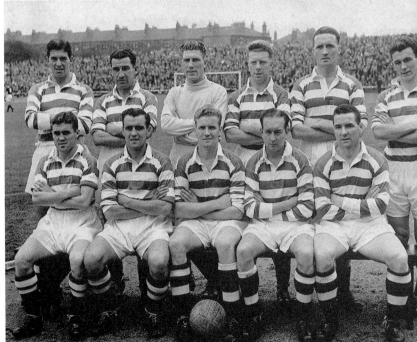

40 The Herald, 27/8/02

41 Sunday Herald, 25/8/02

42 See 'Christmas banned by Holyrood', Scottish Daily Mail, 22/11/03 and 'Church Storm over BBC Bias The Irish Post, 4/10/03

THE IRISH DIASPORA IN SCOTLAND

At a conference held at the University of Stirling in January 1997, consideration was given to a number of pertinent social and political questions that focused on the historical and contemporary position of Catholics in Scotland.[43] Apart from a small number of indigenous Scots, and several thousand with origins in countries such as Poland, Lithuania and Italy, Catholics in Scotland largely originate from Ireland and relevant issues were expected to be a part of conference proceedings. Nevertheless, during the discussion, two academic speakers expressed the view that the Irish in Scotland could be referred to historically but not contemporaneously. Only after a number of exchanges did one concede that discussants could talk about 'the ex-Irish' in Scotland. The Chair of the conference, as well as his supporting professorial colleague, offered a view that talk of the Irish in contemporary Scotland was illusory and that the greatest single immigrant grouping in society had 'ceased being Irish'.

This assertion is not surprising when you consider that comparatively few academic or popular books and articles address historical, cultural, economic and religious issues in relation to the Irish in Scotland, and that a significant amount of published sources do so only within the boundaries of a 'sectarian discourse'.[44] Devine states with some surprise that 'Irish immigrants in Scotland have not until recent years been effectively integrated into the wider study of Scottish historical development'.[45]

In a related sense, a member of the Irish diaspora, Scottish-born writer and novelist Andrew O'Hagan has lamented the dearth of reflective works on Catholic or

43 'Out of the Ghetto? The Catholic Community in Modern Scotland', University of Stirling, 24th January 1997

44 As is evidenced throughout this work such discourses characterise much Scottish press reporting regarding matters connected to the Irish in Scotland

45 Devine 1991, introduction

Irish Catholic life in Scotland in the 1970s. For him, this means that there are few realistic or supportive references which can assist the formulation and transmission of his ideas and experiences.[46] Likewise, a Dublin-based interviewee stated that at school he learned of the Irish in the USA, Australia and England. Until he became interested in Celtic Football Club in Glasgow, he was unaware that a significant part of the Irish diaspora existed in Scotland.[47] Such perspectives constitute a view that Irishness in Scotland has been pushed to the periphery of social, cultural and political narratives.

That textual, oral, historical, social and other such omissions apply in countless instances and accounts and across many time spans is unarguable. Nonetheless, the importance of such omissions cannot be underestimated. Devine makes the point regarding the building and exploitation of the British Empire that:

> The Scottish connection with the Caribbean colonies has, until very recently, rarely attracted much attention from Scottish historians.

As an example, he cites the Oxford Companion to Scottish History of 2001:

> The index contains only one reference to the West Indies, and that merely relates to the sale of Scottish coarse linen in the Caribbean. Slavery and the slave trade come off even worse. There is no index entry to 'slavery' and the single 'slave trade' reference is exclusively concerned with the campaigns of the Scottish missionary societies of the nineteenth century against the immoral commerce in human beings. The omission is surprising because the role of the Scots in the British Caribbean was deeply significant.[48]

Significantly, and with few exceptions, the Irish or Catholic experience in Scotland is largely absent from research, novels, histories and stories from Scottish life. MacMillan points out that the Collins Encyclopedia of Scotland:

46 M. Tierney on Andrew O'Hagan in 'Leaving Caledonia' The Herald Magazine, 9/10/99

47 Interview Mark Burke, secretary, Naomh Padraig Celtic Supporters Club, Dublin, 3/12/99

48 The Herald, Tom Devine, 'Scotland's dark trade in slavery', 18/10/03

. . . has no entry for the Irish in Scotland or the Catholic Church. Foreign visitors to Edinburgh attended an exhibition a couple of years ago at the Scottish Record Office, recounting the history of immigration to Scotland. Large displays set out the history of the immigration of Flemish weavers, Jewish traders, Italian peasants, Asian shopkeepers, Chinese restaurant owners, black bus conductors, and rightly praised the contribution they had all made to Scottish society. The massive Irish immigration in the nineteenth and early twentieth centuries was dealt with in something like three sentences as follows:

> 'in the mid-nineteenth century an increasing number of seasonal Irish farm labourers who worked in the summers in lowland Scotland stayed over due to poor economic conditions in Ireland. Many of them became a burden on the local Parish Poor Laws.'[49]

Scotland's role in the colonisation of Ireland (which contributed ultimately to the creation of the Northern Ireland conflict), the great Irish Famine, the massive economic contribution of the Irish to emerging industrial and then post-industrial Scotland, the Irish contribution to the advancement of the Scottish health services, to Christianity, to education provision, to political life (particularly through the Labour party) and of course to Scottish sport (particularly football) has simply been omitted in this important text. In addition, the sectarianism faced by many Irish in Scotland has also been silenced in this account.

The frequent omission of the Irish in Scotland's recent history is evident throughout literature, oral records, the contemporary media and other forms of communication and records. For example, with over one hundred thousand of a population, the area formally known as Monklands in the west central belt of Scotland, has served as an important industrial, social and economic centre for at least one hundred and fifty years. Until the creation of new administrative areas in the mid-1990s, it included the north Lanarkshire towns and villages of Airdrie, Coatbridge, Chapelhall, Glenboig, Calderbank, Plains and Salsburgh, among others. It is also an area that has

49 J. MacMillan 'Scotland's Shame' in 'Scotland's Shame' Devine, 2000, pp.13-24

attracted tens of thousands of Irish since the early and mid-nineteenth century. Indeed, per head of population, no area in Scotland or indeed Britain contains as many people of Irish descent as the former Monklands district. Nevertheless, in the Monklands Official Guide of 1989 containing several thousand words and pictures illustrating social history, environment, leisure, sport, housing, industry past and present, educational facilities and local businesses, there is neither historical nor contemporary references to the Irish in the area. In this account, the Irish presence in the area is rendered invisible: it is omitted.[50]

Such omissions are repeated in much of the contemporary Scottish media. Throughout Scottish education one can find numerous gaps in historical, political and sociological texts where references to the Irish in Scotland might be expected, indeed, where they might enhance an understanding of the relevant subject. For example, there is little reference in Scottish social, journalistic or academic circles concerning Famine in Ireland, its effects on the diasporic Irish and its impact on subsequent Scottish history, society and politics. This is despite an interpretation that might argue that Irish migration to Scotland from this period is in fact fundamental to understanding a variety of social, religious, economic, health and political issues in contemporary Scotland, particularly in the west-central belt.

Maley makes a general point regarding education stating that through the curriculum children should be encouraged to be aware 'of the cultural diversity of the society they will inherit'. In the Scottish context he believes that Catholics of Irish extraction should be allowed 'access to their own cultures and histories'.[51] The implication by Maley is that if they are not able to access this, then ignorance of their past and present constitution will dominate amongst Scotland's Catholic Irish while conceivably serving an assimilationist, acculturising or secularist agenda on the part of Scottish society and the British state more generally.

50 Monkland's Official Guide, published by Ed J Burrow & Co Limited, London, 1989

51 Glasgow Herald, Weekender, 29/6/91

Diasporic peoples are frequently cut off from representations of important strands of their histories by a series of absences from spaces of cultural reproduction, in education, memorials and popular culture more widely. The population who experience this disjuncture most sharply are often those born and raised in one society, but whose parents, grandparents and great-grandparents, originate from a different society. This generally equates with a largely differing socialisation process to that learned by prior family and community members in the ethnic and historical 'home'. At least some aspects of 'original' culture are passed on in privatised spaces and this may have a greater chance of occurrence in areas where large numbers of immigrants settled together and re-created numerous structures and cultural agents that promote reproduction of ethnic and religious identities.

Often however, diasporic offspring are thrust into public spheres where their culture is underrepresented, only partly visible or missing altogether. Immigrant practices, beliefs, attitudes and lifestyles, including those of subsequent generations, can also be viewed with varying degrees of hostility. This will invariably contribute to the context of second, third and subsequent generation identity formation: whether reproduction and sustenance of ethnic and religious identities takes place and in what form.

For colonised populations who emigrate to the former ruler state this may entail a more active suppression of dissident identities in order to avoid contestation and speed up the process of incorporation and acceptability into the national mainstream.[52] For example, Mary J Hickman[53] shows that Irish history has been conspicuously excluded from curricula throughout Britain since the nineteenth century, not only from non-denominational state schools, but also from the distinctive Catholic school framework that operates within the state system and where the majority of children of Irish descent are educated. Hickman argues that this has been a key element in the denationalisation of the Irish in Britain and their

52 See B. Walter, S. Morgan, M.J. Hickman and J.M. Bradley 'Family Stories, public silence: Irish identity construction amongst the second-generation Irish in England' Scottish Geographical Journal, Special Edition on 'The Fate of 'Nations' in a Globalised World' Vol.118, No.3, pp.201-218, 2002

53 M. Hickman 1990 & 1995. Much history teaching in Scotland has traditionally been centred on British and English characters and events

construction as good Catholic British citizens. As Doyle states:

> . . . the history curriculum has always held a primary position in the transmission of national identity and national values and the history textbook has been an important tool in this process.[54]

In simple terms, children whose origins lie elsewhere are taught histories often alien to their backgrounds. Indeed, sometimes they are oppositional to the histories of the nations and communities from where they originate. It is important to note that teaching history at school is only one – albeit a vital one in relation to age and the lifelong learning experience – of numerous important agents and sources of identity construction and socialisation. In this sense, the importance of Celtic Football Club to the Irish Catholic community in Scotland can be seen.

> There are many political, social and cultural forces which exert and have exerted an influence on the formation of national and cultural identities, such as religion, family, community, mass media, art and literature. . . [55]

Despite a denial of Irishness within the education system and in other spheres, research demonstrates that knowledge of their cultural background in Ireland cannot be erased from accurate reflections on the identities of the Irish diaspora and remains relevant. An Economic and Social Research Council (ESRC) funded undertaking in 2002, The Irish 2 Project, demonstrates that there remain second and third generation Irish in Scotland who consider themselves 'Irish', not Scottish or British.[56]

It should be noted that the term diaspora (as well as that of community) is used in this book more as a conceptual tool than an analytical device: one that enables a more fluid approach to identity – especially ethnicity.[57] Likewise, in relation to those accounts that seek or contribute to the sectarianisation, racialisation, marginalisation and invisibility of those of Irish descent in Scotland,

54 A Doyle, 2002

55 Ibid

56 This project was financed by the Government sponsored Economic and Social Research Council in 2001/02 and essentially looked at questions and issues of identity focusing on people born in Britain of at least one Irish-born parent or grandparent. Interviewees have been given pseudonyms for the purpose of reporting findings. The work was carried out by Dr J. Bradley, Dr S. Morgan, Prof M. Hickman & Prof B. Walter.

57 See Y. McKenna, 2003

it is important to note that as Walter points out:

> . . . diaspora is a notion which exposes the political agendas underlying traditional understandings of migration and accompanying processes. . . [58]

Regarding the Irish diaspora in Scotland, evidence demonstrates that Irishness and Irish identity remain relevant in the personal, social and community composition of people born in Scotland whose parents, grandparents or great grandparents migrated from Ireland. The process of interviewing involved in the Irish 2 Project allowed participants to reflect on their own Irish identities. In doing so, a number of interviewees reported a lack of recognition within Scottish society with regards to Irishness. Again this is an important comment on the condition of Irishness in modern Scotland. Importantly, Hickman and Walter also note that:

> . . . well-documented evidence of the racialisation of the Irish in contemporary Britain and of discriminatory practices is consequently ignored.[59]

In relation to notions of identity, exclusion and a lack of recognition, Irish 2 Project interviewee Francis Daly expressed his Irish identity as closely linked to his support for Celtic.

> It was the only place you were allowed to express. . . a sort of an Irish identity. You were allowed to go see Celtic matches and express your Irish identity. . . it's maybe a lot more important, it's not just the football club of course, it's a lot more. Celtic is all about attitude and that as well. You know you can express an Irish identity and there's safety at Celtic Park, whereas you wouldn't be able to express it outside [of the Celtic environment].[60]

Another second generation respondent, Peadar McGrath, opined that:

> I don't watch football, but sometimes I'd turn the radio on and listen to the Celtic game hoping that Celtic would win but I don't go to see them. . . the only way I've got any interest in Celtic at all is. . . I'm not actually

58 B. Walter, Anglia Polytechnic University, unpublished paper, 2003

59 For reference, see M. Hickman 1998

60 Interview ESRC Irish 2 Project

interested in football. . . my interest in Celtic is I see them as the Irish team in Glasgow. I used to go to see Celtic up till I was about eighteen. I went to see Celtic because I felt everybody standing there in the Jungle was the same as me. But all these guys had the same views, sang the same songs and just thought the same as me. I mean I could be totally wrong, but standing there in that crowd, that was the feeling I got and it was the only time in the whole week I could get that feeling. . . every week you could stand there and sing to your heart's content and it made me feel really Irish, it made me feel this is good, here's other guys who think the same as me.[61]

Although Harry McGuigan emphasised the cultural identity of Celtic, he also referred to the 'unease' that many Celtic people encounter in negotiating their Irish identities in Scottish society. He stated that:

They play a central part, they should do and they should continue to do. When Irish emigrants' children had nothing, the only thing they had to anchor themselves here was Celtic. Why should they apologise for that and why should Celtic? That gave them something to anchor their identity to. 1887/88 all of those years that gave Irish Catholics in this country something to identify with. You can't just turn around and say you can't have that any more.[62]

The implied hostility within Scottish society to Irishness, Catholics and Celtic had numerous facets as argued and revealed by the interviewees. In a situation where one female subject was in a stable relationship with her secular-minded Scottish Protestant boyfriend, and where marriage was in the offing, Rosaleen Connolly offered the view that her Irish Catholic identity continued to provoke tension within this relationship.

I don't just go to Ireland or love Ireland or support Celtic or go to church because I'm meant to do it, because I'm from Coatbridge and everyone else does it, it's because I want to now. . . At first, it bugged him because as I said earlier that I supported Celtic and people from Ireland were all alike, just wee Paddies. Now he knows. He can understand how important it is to me, the culture and all the rest. What he doesn't like is when I say I'm Irish. It

61 Ibid
62 Ibid

drives him round the bend. In fact we had this conversation again the other day. It's just something that is mentioned all the time. When we went to Barcelona this year, I had my Irish passport and he said he couldn't believe that it was an Irish passport. It bugs him a bit.[63]

Cultural activities around sport, particularly soccer, Irish music, dance, political activities relating to Northern Ireland and the apparent growth in the use of Irish fore-names for children are only a few examples that show that Irishness remains a significant factor in west-central Scottish life. Further, and more significantly, the comparative strength of the Catholic Church and Catholic education in Scottish life are considerable manifestations of the impact made by Irish immigrants in society.

DISCOURSES OF IRISHNESS AND CELTIC FC

Dominant discourses and narratives can involve ideas, statements or knowledge that are predominant or central to a relevant society or culture. These often provide a way of seeing other individuals or the social environment and world generally. Issues of power, influence, shaping opinion, attitudes and actions, as well as 'identities' are all relevant for issues relating dominant discourses. Discourse involves all means of communication. It can also include ways of seeing, categorising and reacting to the social world in everyday practices. Underlying meanings are crucial to our understanding of discourse analysis. Hidden texts are equally important. Language, (or other means of communication) is not neutral. Language does not describe or discuss something objectively. It is a tool that can mean different things to different people.

The importance of narratives and discourses is inferred by for example Hoberman, who states that 'sport has no intrinsic value structure, but it is a ready and flexible vehicle through which ideological associations can be reinforced'.[64] Likewise by Hobsbawm who believes that 'the identity of a nation of millions seems more real as a team of eleven named people'.[65] Similarly, Blain and Boyle state

63 Ibid

64 Hoberman, in Sugden and Bairner 1993, p.10

65 1990, p.4

that 'the complex nature of collective identity formations associated with Scottish sport parallels the complexity of Scotland as a political [and cultural] entity'.[66] All of these authors demonstrate their awareness of the importance of visual and textual discourses as well as how sporting mediums acquire their meaningfulness.

With regards Celtic, what is clear in such observations, and indeed from those of the Irish 2 Project interviewees, is that sport, particularly football, has the capacity to embody, actualise and express a multiplicity of identities; national, cultural, ethnic, religious, social, political, economic and community, in a way few other social manifestations can. It is for these reasons that the institution of Celtic Football Club demonstrates the fallacy in the argument that the Irish in Scotland have 'ceased to exist'. Further, as will be demonstrated, the existence of Scottish-born Irish in Scotland and such denials of their existence and relevance represents a crucial aspect of the experience of that community. This is an indication of the exclusion and marginalisation of important aspects of that community's experience over a century and a half.

In terms of wealth, the winning of competitions, media focus and size of support, Glasgow Rangers FC has historically been the largest club in Scottish football. Celtic is the second biggest football institution but, since the mid-1960s, has possibly become Scotland's greatest football success story, winning numerous leagues and cups and appearing in at least the quarter-finals of European competitions ten times in seventeen seasons in the period from 1964 until 1980. This includes becoming the first northern European side to win the European Champions Cup in 1967 and appearing again in the final in 1970. This successful period went unrepeated until May 2003 with Celtic's UEFA Cup Final appearance in Seville, Spain.

Despite the traditional popularity of football in Scotland, the only clubs to win European trophies have been Celtic, Rangers and Aberdeen, while Dundee United were losing finalists in the UEFA Cup Final of 1987. Such

66 1994, pp.125-141

Celtic FC 1958

a gap in relative European success meant that the media coverage of the match in Seville in 2003 against Portugese club Porto was both extensive and intense.

As is often the case in other countries when club sides play in international competitions, not everyone in Scotland was behind Celtic winning this trophy. Such fragmented patronage from non-Celtic supporting parts of society is typical of other football societies where club rivalries can be paramount. Few countries are united in a way that all of the people all of the time will support sometimes perceived 'national' representatives beyond national borders. The club rivalries of Catalan Barcelona and historically perceived royalist and centralist Real Madrid, and the rivalry in northern England between Liverpool and Manchester United, are only two of the many examples where it is unlikely that opposing fans will suspend their club rivalries (and identities) and support the 'other' in European competitions.

However, the UEFA Final in Seville in 2003 can be

viewed as important for reasons beyond football rivalries and winning prestigious trophies. Media discourses surrounding the match offer an opportunity to acquire a sense of the historical Irish presence in Scotland. After all, if the Irish in Scotland remain part of the worldwide Irish diaspora, and if this is a tangible identity in modern Scotland, one might expect that some evidence for this would manifest itself at such a public occasion through a club founded and sustained by that community in Scotland. It might also be expected that this would reflect in the discourses surrounding the high profile event.

Celtic's involvement in the Final provoked numerous letters and comment in the print media in Scotland. Almost all press commentary on Celtic and its fans' journey and presence in Seville were favourable but, characteristically, reference to a context of Celtic being the club of the Irish in Scotland and of the Irish diaspora beyond, was virtually excluded from almost all communications.In communicative discourses, omission can be as important as inclusion.

Part of the reasoning behind this omission relates to commonsense understandings and constructions of sectarianism in Scotland. It has been customary for journalists and feature writers with Scottish daily and weekly newspapers to 'sectarianise' Celtic and its supporters' Irishness. For example, in response to Celtic fans not supporting rivals Glasgow Rangers against an Italian club in a European match in 1998, a feature writer with a Scottish broadsheet stated:

> The Italian team had just scored an equaliser against Rangers, a Scottish club. Three people had a semblance of an excuse for this display. . . all of the others were exercising that bigotry which poisons Glasgow life. Those thumping the atmosphere were Scots, Scottish born, educated here, with all the advantages of a welfare state unknown to Italians or their own Irish grandparents. . . Three generations and a welfare state on, we should surely expect a man. . . to follow his country's team: his country is Britain. . . a little pub where people punch their own noses because of their notions of identity. . . the apologists for football sectarianism.[67]

67 J. McLean, Scotland on Sunday, Sport, 13/12/98

Another journalist expressed a similar opinion in 1994 believing that with regards Rangers playing in Europe, everyone in Scotland should support the club and set aside their 'trivial little loyalties' while 'only the most bigoted' would not allow themselves to do this.[68]

Such positions reflect a number of important notions in terms of ethnic, religious and national identities in Scotland (and Britain). For these journalists at least, the prism of 'sectarianism' is a commonsense one, as well as being an undefined concept. Nonetheless, an understanding of football identity and rivalry eludes their writing and questions are raised regarding the acceptance of people in Scotland who wish to maintain the heritage and identities arising from their non-Scottish places of origin. In addition, both writers quoted here reflect the central role of sports journalism in the general process of identity construction and maintenance.

These discourses can be considered dominant because they are pre-eminent, all-encompassing, recurrent and exclude alternative accounts that may be viewed as challenging such commonsense and ideological based arguments that pass for objective, neutral and qualified commentary. The dominant discourses that prevail in relation to Celtic and its support are frequent features of the Scottish print media. This is also reflected in a quote from a letter to a Scottish broadsheet:

> . . . Celtic are a Scottish club playing in Scotland and whilst their heritage should be acknowledged, this over emphasis on Irishness is at best an embarrassment and at worst an excuse for bigotry and violence.[69]

During the period surrounding the match in Seville, this was also demonstrated by a popular football commentator in Scotland's best selling tabloid newspaper, the Daily Record. On the eve of Celtic's match in Spain the columnist wrote:

> Celtic, a Scottish team whether some of their fans are willing to admit it or not. . . Celtic ARE Scottish so they belong to more than the supporters who follow them

68 J. Traynor, The Herald, Sport, 22/8/94

69 Scotland on Sunday, Sport, letters, 2/8/98

week in, week out. . . This is Scotland against Portugal. . . right now Celtic, albeit unwittingly, are flying our flag. . .[70]

Amongst other things, this columnist and others deny Celtic and its fans' desire to be seen as Irish, to esteem their Irishness or to publicly display Irish symbolism. He refuses to acknowledge the Irish diaspora in Scotland and its right to consider itself in some way, Irish not Scottish, as he says, 'whether they are willing to admit it or not'. In this light, such discourses can be viewed as part of an assimilationist (as opposed to integrationist) approach to those who have different identities and cultural expressions in Scotland, particularly second, third and fourth generation Irish. Through such discourses, the club and its support is constantly being divorced from and denied the relevance of its Irish roots, origins, heritage and identity. The club and its supporters' Irishness is constantly being rendered irrelevant and invisible, unless viewed historically. In a further context, the most central and significant identities of the support and the club are also being rendered 'sectarian'. Finally, there are few in significant or powerful enough public positions to refute (or who are willing to refute) the dominance of such arguments and thus to counter the diminution of Irishness in Scotland. In turn, this assists in the continued sectarian-isation of Scottish society.

However, this account cannot be seen in isolation and is part of a dominant stream of discourses used to discuss affairs Irish and Catholic in Scottish society. Around the time of the UEFA final, various newspapers carried letters that demonstrated the contentiousness of Celtic and its supports' Irishness in Scotland. The journalists' view was a popular one and some letter writers reflected this:

I was absolutely appalled and disgusted when watching the UEFA Cup Final. I am sure I am not the only non-Celtic supporter who was urged to 'get behind' the Scottish team. How many Scottish flags were in the stadium? I counted one but maybe I couldn't see the others due to the sea of Irish Republican flags on display.

70 J. Traynor, Daily Record, 19/5/03

Isn't it about time that people like this decided which nationality they are?[71]

I could have sworn the UEFA Cup Final in Seville was between teams from Scotland and Portugal, but judging by the flags in the stadium I think it was actually Ireland against Portugal; there were more American, Canadian, or Australian flags than Scottish. How do you expect neutral football fans to support their Scottish team when the fans make it very clear that they have no loyalty to Scotland and where their true allegiance lies? I can't imagine what the rest of the world thought as they watched this disgraceful sight which was attended by some of our politicians who supposedly abhor this type of behaviour. This was not a good reflection on our culture and a bad night for Scottish sport.[72]

Although this correspondent was criticised by several letters in subsequent editions of The Herald, it is remarkable to note the linking of Celtic fans' flying of the Irish flag with symbols not to do with Scotland, reviving again the arguments and accusations of the SFA against Celtic in 1952.

The idea of football fans or any other section of society being neutral is also notable. It is a term frequently used when matters religious and cultural, especially in relation to football, are discussed publicly in Scotland. However, as an aspect of commonsense everyday language and in relation to ideology, the concept of 'neutrality' is nonsensical. For people who live in Scotland, the debate concerning sectarianism has already been shaped by centuries of religious cleavage and decades of the term's usage in media reporting on a range of relevant matters from religion to culture and social affairs. In reality, objectivity in this matter can only be acquired through knowledge acquisition, the basis of which does not exist in Scotland. For issues concerning 'sectarianism' in Scottish society, generalising, stereotyping and labelling 'feeds on ignorance, taps into prejudice and, most importantly, undermines the pursuit of real knowledge'.[73]

71 Daily Star, letters, 26/5/03

72 The Herald, letters, 23/5/03

73 Y. Suleiman, Sunday Herald, Seven Days, 18/1/04

In this light, media commentators can be blinded by the myth of objectivity thus reducing their role to transmitting what are in fact ideological perspectives. These are partly based on the assumption that there is a consensus within society, while they also objectify what are often in themselves 'sectarian', racist and xenophobic narratives, that invent and sustain the hegemonic discourses. Most of this comment constitutes a sharing of the same story while other accounts and narratives are marginalised and 'sectarianised'. In Scotland this adds to and sustains the objective sectarianism that permeates different levels of society.

Therefore, many opinions in relation to non-Scottish identities in Scotland, sectarianism, or a range of other related matters are ideologically linked and are constructed in opposition to other ideological perspectives. The head of the Dundee United Supporter's Association said with regards Celtic:

> They need Scotland. I just wish you'd see a few more Saltires amongst their support, rather than tricolours.[74]

Another supporter's letter to a Sunday broadsheet denied Celtic's Irishness stressing that the club should end such manifestations.

> Celtic should remind their fans that they are a Scottish club. They should stop flying the tricolour on their stand and consider restoring it only when their fans waving the Scottish Saltire outnumber those waving the tricolour.[75]

A different Sunday broadsheet added to the ideology that viewed Celtic supporters' Irishness with hostility, complaining that Celtic's identity 'still contains a large Irish component'.[76] Another Scottish broadsheet sports journalist offered a similar view. Decrying the renditions of Celtic and Irish folk songs being played live before some matches over the course of a season, he believes the fans should be left to their own devices:

> . . . especially coming from the musical equivalent of

74 S. Fisher, Sunday Herald, Sport, 18/5/03

75 Scotland on Sunday, Sport, letters, 24/3/02

76 A. Massie, Scotland on Sunday, Week in Review, 29/7/01

Darby McGill [O'Gill?] and the Little People with their 'Have A Potato' style of hokey Irishness.[77]

Another journalist also criticised Celtic and its fans' Irishness, demonstrating both the widespread nature of this criticism and how it is embedded in Scottish culture. This journalist referred to the diaspora in Scotland as the 'pseudo-Irish' who support Celtic as well as their penchant for 'diddly-dee music'.[78] As an aspect of Scottish culture, the widespread nature of this hostility is further demonstrated in a News of the World newspaper column that again reflected on Celtic and its fans' ethnic identity. For this sports columnist, Celtic Park was full of:

Plastic Irishmen and women who drink in plastic Irish pubs and don't know their Athenry from their Antrim when it comes to Irish history or politics. . . Celtic must stop. . . flashing their Irishness. . . if Celtic are so keen to flaunt their Irishness perhaps they could do us all a favour and relocate to Dublin.[79]

Similar outlooks are frequently demonstrated in other areas of life in Scotland and are not restricted to the football arena or in relation to Celtic. A letter printed in the Daily Record stereotyped Catholics of Irish descent by offering the view:

I don't believe the latest proposal to pay mothers to stop working after having a baby. Can you imagine it – all the Catholic mothers not only doing what the priest tells them but getting paid for it as well.[80]

The subtle, popular and visceral nature of this kind of prejudice was reflected in the story of another interviewee who told how her Ayrshire-based company personnel representative, making his way through student applications for a post, made the comment, 'another one from a tattie howker' (ie, someone from an Irish background denoted by their Catholic forename and Irish surname).[81]

The contentiousness of public displays of Catholicism and Irishness in Scotland was also demonstrated prior to

77 E. Grahame, The Herald, Sport, 8/4/02

78 B. Leckie, The Sun, 8/4/02.

79 G. McNee, News of the World, 6/5/01 and 7/10/01

80 Daily Record, letters, 3/2/01

81 Information from an employee of an Ayrshire based company processing job application forms with a colleague, 1/8/03

the UEFA Cup Final and for several weeks in early 2003, debate ensued regarding the organisation of a St Patrick's Day Festival in the Lanarkshire town of Coatbridge. This dominated letters to the local newspaper and although some letter writers defended the celebration, reflecting one aspect of the contested nature of Irish identity in Scotland, much of the hostile comment reflected a belief that despite Coatbridge being uniquely populated largely by people of Irish descent, such a celebration should not take place. Analogous to comment on Celtic's appearance in Seville, correspondents to the newspaper emphasised the primacy of Scottishness over Irishness. Frequently positioned within a 'sectarian' discourse were references to the Irish nature of the celebration.

> I read with some disappointment the article in last week's Advertiser regarding the proposed St Patrick's Day celebrations in Coatbridge. While I realise the vast population of the area we live in comes from Irish descent, I would think by now we would class ourselves as Scottish.[82]

> I personally feel that this planned festival is more linked to the Catholicism of the area and not of any great heartfelt link to the Irish. This is one of the many factors which results in the cancer of sectarianism, which still blights our society.[83]

> I am writing to express my utter disbelief at the shocking event held in Coatbridge. . . Why wasn't there anything similar to celebrate the Queen's Golden Jubilee?. . .[84]

> I was dismayed to see the announcement of plans to hold a St Patrick's Day Festival in Coatbridge. . . How can this be organised when no corresponding celebration is ever planned for St Andrew's Day – you know the patron saint of the country we actually live in. . . Also, the majority of families with Irish heritage can only trace their links back to great-grandparents/grandparents etc.[85]

In 2001, the erection at Carfin in Lanarkshire of a national monument to the victims and refugees to Scotland of the Great Famine in Ireland of the mid-nineteenth century, caused a furore. The unveiling of the monument by the

82 Airdrie and Coatbridge Advertiser, letters, 12/3/03

83 Ibid

84 Ibid, 19/3/03

85 Ibid

Irish premier, 'an Taoiseach' Bertie Ahern, was originally cancelled because of fears of a sectarian reaction. The Scottish media reflected Scotland's embarrassment as an aspect of the country's sectarianism was made visible for people throughout Britain, Ireland as well as internationally.[86] Most of the subsequent media comment stated that this should not have happened and that Ahern should have been made welcome. Nonetheless, the incident provoked comment hostile to the Irish and Catholic nature of the proposed event. This comment was similar to that referring to the Saint Patrick's Day Festival in Coatbridge as well as that in relation to the identity of Celtic's supporters at Seville.

> How kind of the Scottish people to erect a memorial to remind us of the Irish potato famine. I'm assuming this has been done because Ireland has erected memorials for Bannockburn, Culloden and the Highland Clearances. Quite what the Irish potato famine has to do with Scotland (apart from the Irish coming over here) is beyond me. I can only think that part of Lanarkshire is full of Irish-Scots who want to re-create Ireland in Scotland. I am not bigoted in any way – I am from the Highlands— and think that Irish history should be remembered there, just as Scottish history should be remembered here.[87]

Such correspondence frequently appears in the popular Scottish media and various ethnic and religious institutions and events can prompt similar responses on a routine basis. Matters Irish and Catholic in Scotland are often a focus for critical comment.

> The problem with the west of Scotland is the RC Irish descendants still hang on to their Irish roots – flying a tricolour at Celtic Park is like a red rag to a bull where Scots are concerned. . . If I love my native land more than the one that gave me a living, I would move back to that country. . . Before you write me off as a bluenose, I have a daughter married to a Catholic, and when we lived in the Canadian Arctic I played the organ in the RC mission in the morning and the organ in the Anglican mission in the afternoon.[88]

86 See for example, articles in The Scotsman 10/2/01 and The Herald 9/2/01

87 Evening Times, letters, 16/2/01

88 Sunday Mail, letters, 27/4/03

This particular writer 'establishes' his own self-defined 'neutral' and 'non-sectarian' credentials before demonstrating a hostility that in fact might militate against 'evidence' of such credentials. The writer also suggests that affinity for Ireland on the part of the Irish diaspora in Scotland should mean a kind of repatriation back to Ireland. Again there is a claim to 'neutrality' in this matter, while in fact this writer contributes to and sustains a recurrent and widespread ideological polemic against public manifestations of Irishness and Catholicism in Scotland.

The existence of Catholic schools holds a particular focus of hostility for many such people.

> The answer is simple. The Roman Catholic Church should be given two options: their schools remain within the State system and appointments are made by the education authority; or Roman Catholic schools opt out of the system and are funded by the Church. . . The situation as it stands is unacceptable.[89]

> . . . Scotland's very own 'apartheid' – separate schools with children divided by religion. . . In an increasingly secular society, why should religion, any form of religion, be taught in state schools? Religion is divisive.[90]

> . . . referring to the last Old Firm match at Ibrox, and the continuation of segregated schools. . . If we are serious about eradicating the hatred which is vented in the name of sport, let's not try to ease our conscience by arresting a few overpaid footballers. The only solution is for a full integration of our schools.[91]

> Surely it is time for the Scottish people to become free thinkers and make morals the subject of our general debate. Let's do our children a favour and consign religious schooling to the dustbin of history.[92]

Similar discourses regarding Catholic schools in Scotland have dominated much of the Scottish media for several decades. Alternative views regarding these schools and other aspects of Catholic and Irish heritage, culture and practice exist in Scotland but are usually subsumed within a context of other more dominating discourses.[93]

89 The Herald, 5/11/90

90 Ibid, 14/9/90

91 Ibid, 18/11/87

92 Ibid, 10/12/02

93 On several occasions during interviews people have relayed how their letters were not published in various newspapers (even during a debate on the relevant issues) on matters concerning Celtic, Ireland, Catholic schools and Catholic social and moral issues in particular. Amongst these people have been a university lecturer and a retired secondary school teacher. The author has documented some copies of these letters.

One letter writer to a Sunday broadsheet offers an alternative view regarding the issue of distinctive Catholic schools in Scottish society:

> The letters. . . attacking denominational schools fly in the face of evidence. Denominational schools are more prevalent in England than in Scotland, whereas religious antagonism is far less so. There are denominational schools all over Europe. . . on this evidence, bigotry has more to do with attitudes in Scotland than with religious schools. . . Your correspondents combine hostility to allowing a multitude of cultures to express themselves, while playing a full part in society as a whole, with an unthinking support for bland, centrally controlled state education.[94]

Outside of the spiritual and Christ-centred rationale for the existence of Catholic schools, Maley also offers a varying account to those that dominate:

> [The issue] remains above all a cultural and political one. It affects all aspects of national identity. Anti-Irish racism and anti-Catholicism are inseparable in a Scottish context.[95]

In relation to references to Irishness in Scotland, analogous discourses are characteristic of the Scottish popular media diet. In one sense they may be considered in the context of a wider and broader contest where the dominant narratives and representations pursue cultural homogenisation in Scottish society, driving the seemingly centrifugal tendencies of Scottishness and its primacy at the expense of other cultures and identities. In this context, the essentially minority Irish identity is either omitted or misrepresented while Scottishness becomes the 'natural' and 'commonsense' identity. Professor Maley adds that the Scottish media have persisted in their refusal to stand up to the realities of anti-Irish racism.

> Scotland is a country which does not respect cultural difference. Only the cloistered academics and other privileged professionals, cushioned from the vicissitudes of economic deprivation could fail to see that sectarianism rather than religious bigotry is the product of national and social discrimination.[96]

94 Scotland on Sunday, letters, 4/1/04

95 W. Maley, Glasgow Herald, Weekender, 29/6/91

96 Ibid

The fact that such references are frequent in relation to Celtic and its supporters' Irishness also shows the contested nature of this natural, commonsense and assumed 'Scottish identity'. As suggested by Maley, the hegemony of Scottishness over Irishness is also evident. This has developed from struggle and the substance of the letters and journalistic comment referred to further demonstrate that this cultural contestation within Scottish society is one of power relations and is ongoing. Whether in relation to Celtic or other cultural and ethnic issues that have a Catholic or Irish dimension, such discourses reflect that football in Scotland is penetrated by cultural and political ideologies. The notion of how sport is 'enmeshed in the media's reproduction and transmission of ideological themes and values which are dominant in society' is reflected in such print media comment.[97]

Likewise, Blain and Boyle report on the capacity of the Scottish print media to construct national character-istics through reporting on Scottish football, emphasising the hegemonic capacity of popular sources of information, values and cultural practices.[98] Again the comments of O'Hagan and Devine link with this encounter in terms of the struggle of Irishness to be recognised in Scottish society. Such dominance is widespread, frequent and characterises numerous elements of the Scottish media. Talking about Celtic's supporters, a former 'Young Scottish Journalist of the Year' criticised them for seeing:

> No inconsistency in packing their ground to wave the flag of another country. They flap the Irish tricolour and sing sad Irish songs and roar of the Irish struggle. There's a country called Ireland for goodness sake, why don't they go and live there?[99]

Such privileged narratives have served to undermine and marginalise Irishness and the second, third and fourth generation Irish in Scotland who constitute part of the Irish diaspora. They have assisted in distorting and shaping public perceptions of Irishness while offering little opportunity for Scotland to build a society equal in its

97 J. Hargreaves & I. McDonald, 2000

98 N. Blain and R. Boyle, 1994

99 J. MacLeod, The Herald, 18/2/02

respect and recognition for the numerous peoples that constitute Scottish society in the early twenty first century.

Celtic FC in 1967

INTEGRATION OR ASSIMILATION

National cultures and identities can be interpreted as the privileged discourses of the dominant social groups (often political, economic, cultural and religious) that manufacture identities through symbols, stories and meanings. Such identities are continuously communicated through popular culture and in the dominant means of transmission, usually television and newsprint media. In this sense the imagined community manifests as 'reality'.[100] Sport is a cultural process and in Scotland football is a significant contributor to the formation, constitution and sustenance of national and other identities. In this context, Irish identity is viewed as oppositional instead of being one of the many identities that makes Scotland multicultural and plural.

Omission or misrepresentation of Irishness in popular and public outlets is an important consideration in relation to the condition and outward appearances of Irish identity in modern Scotland as well as the social, cultural and

100 See B. Anderson 'The Imagined Communities' 1991

59

political context that Celtic and its supporters occupy. It constitutes a social milieu where being a member of the Irish diaspora in Scotland and esteeming this as fundamental to one's social and cultural identity is laborious, strenuous and constantly contested. The choice to avoid being Irish is constructed as a pragmatic one via the harsh reality of striving to be Irish in Scotland. Simply put, it is far easier to be Scottish than to be Irish in Scotland. This may also have had some consequence for the Catholicism of many Irish immigrants and their offspring. During 2003, interviews of Catholics from Irish descent in the thirty–forty age range demonstrated numerous instances of perceived ridicule as a result of public displays of Catholic piety or practice. For example, the annual public display of 'Ashes' on Ash Wednesday invited ridicule from work colleagues for one Catholic female interviewee. After hearing her plight, the woman's parish priest advised her to 'keep it quiet when in the workplace'.[101]

In 1997, a Scottish Sunday broadsheet journalist inadvertently raised questions about the capacity of Scottish society to be inclusive, multicultural or, as plural as it may aspire or imagine itself to be. With reference to the Irishness of the Celtic fanbase and his perceptions of what Scotland should represent to them, the journalist expressed the view that:

> . . . there is a section of the Celtic support, in particular, who turn my stomach with their allegiance to the Republic of Ireland in preference to the nation of their birth.[102]

The ideological dimensions to this journalist's discourse seem clearer when read in conjunction with other pieces. A few years later the same journalist wrote an article purporting to reflect on a television programme about sports people's interaction with God and some aspects of religion in football. However, on discussing a section of the programme that looked at the Celtic–Rangers rivalry in stereotypically 'sectarian' terms, once again a penchant emerged for making political and cultural comment regarding Celtic, Catholics or Irishness in Scot-

101 Interview with Maureen O'Neil, October 2003

102 R. Travers, Scotland on Sunday, Sport, 9/11/97

land. The journalist talked of a 'sectarian' mindset and accused both Celtic and Rangers for attracting 'bigoted' boneheads before adding:

> One day, Scotland will benefit from the abolition of denominational schools, so called religious education will be restricted to church and home and Old Firm accountants will finally realise that purging their supporters of sectarian scum will not necessarily have adverse commercial implications.[103]

Attitudes that aspire to elevate Scottishness to become the primary identity of Celtic and its support, while simultaneously marginalising Irishness, also permeate some elements of the Celtic support, partly reflecting the resultant consequences of over a century of hostility towards Irish identity in Scotland.

> I'm off to Seville tomorrow and I'll be taking my Saltire with me. The Celtic fans who carry the Irish tricolour everywhere would do well to realise we are a Scottish club representing our country in Europe.[104]

This hostility and intolerance even extended to one reporter with an in-house Celtic publication when he cynically referred to most Celtic fans' Irish heritage as the 'ancestral homeland beloved of many of the Parkhead faithful'. Holidays abroad were also referred to as being places where:

> These quasi-Irish spend every night in Paddy's Oirish Bar (proprietor one Miguel del Santos) where they can while away their holiday proving their love for Ireland by singing teary-eyed laments about how much they miss the Ould country. . . The truth, for most fans of our indisputably Scottish club. . . [105]

As the references to St Patrick's Day in Coatbridge reveal, contention surrounding the Irishness of a section of the population in Scotland has not been limited to Celtic Football Club and its support. Celtic FC and its fanbase seem only to be the most notable and popular manifest-

103 R. Travers, Scotland on Sunday, Sport, 30/11/03

104 Daily Record, letters, 20/5/03

105 Celtic match programme V Rosenborg in Champions League, 10/10/01

ations of an embedded anti-Catholicism and anti-Irishness in Scottish society. This is also reflected in the few references noted by some of the main Christian churches in Scotland as well as the Orange Institution. These examples demonstrate that Catholic attitudes and practices as well as Irishness have a capacity to stir heated debate in various areas of life in Scottish society.

Celtic FC in the centenary year 1988

Hegemony through discourse

Gramsci's concept of hegemony refers to the capacity of dominant groups to not only impose their ideas on subordinate social groups, but also to create the active consent of these groups in contributing to and even maintaining their subordinate status.[106] This may help explain the letter from the Irish-named Celtic supporter heading for Seville carrying a Scottish flag and advocating others to do likewise, a letter sent to and published in at least two media outlets. The important point for sport and Irishness in Scotland is that this hegemony creates limits to what is perceived as acceptable and possible. This reinforces the dominant group's agenda and place in the social hierarchy under the guise of freedom, choice and often of 'neutrality'. In terms of sport, limitations are imposed by way of these dominant values, norms, regulations and attitudes. Nevertheless, as the historical example of Celtic and its supporters demonstrate, these can also be challenged, at least within the confines of sport.

Despite the capacity of many Celtic supporters to be Irish, or celebrate their Irishness in Scotland, it might be argued that over many decades one of the results of hostility shown towards this in Scotland is the diminution of Irishness as a viable esteemed identity. If, in relation to Irishness, people, communities and organisations of the Irish diaspora in Scotland perceive an unremitting atmosphere of coercion, anxiety and contestation in public spaces and outlets, if there are few positive public references to this identity, if there is perceived omission in symbolic terms and through public representations and presentations (and these perceptions are evidenced in the

106 See Gramsci, 1999

63

Irish 2 Project and other research), it seems inevitable that at least two responses may occur.

The first is the minimising and privatising of Irishness through a process of social negotiation. The second response is less obvious and relates to Gramsci's concept of hegemony. This is less a matter of choice and more one of socialisation, where Scottishness becomes the primary identity because it is advocated as the evident and approved one. It is the one taught, reproduced and promoted through the everyday channels that endorse identity in every society – television, education, war, news reporting, national sports competitions and form completion to name a few. In essence, these are the channels that frequently dominate in relation to the formation and construction of views, attitudes and identities. (Britishness is also a factor and Scottishness and Britishness are of course often in competition with each other.)

In both instances, the effects of 'sectarianising' Irishness is a significant factor in its diminishing in Scotland and reducing it to a few stereotypical or learned social negatives as demonstrated by The Herald sports journalist. The agents for such change in the Irishness of the Irish diaspora in Scotland are many and varied. If Irishness is absent or poorly reflected and represented publicly in song, popular culture, the media, literature, academic analysis etc, then the agents and mechanisms for the sustenance, maintenance and promotion of Irishness amongst the diaspora in Scottish society become limited and negligible. Further, linked by the same sources to sectarianism and atavistic identities, these dominant narratives become powerful agents in constructing and sustaining Irishness as a contradictory and contrary identity in Scottish society. Indeed, in this light it becomes more legitimate, acceptable and as a matter of commonsense, to be hostile to anything that isn't sufficiently Scottish in Scottish society. In this way it becomes accepted without question. In the light of its contestation with Irishness, Scottishness becomes ideologically hegemonic, a commonsense identity and perspective, the one that is 'natural' and self-evident. The singing by supporters of Aberdeen FC in the early 2000s that Celtic supporters are 'in the wrong country' encapsulates this popular attitude.[107]

In relation to such singing and the comments of Devine and O'Hagan concerning the marginalisation and absence of academic and popular works on Irish Catholics in Scotland, and by implication on 'sectarianism' in Scottish society, Miles and Muirhead note the lack of academic work carried out on the issue of racism in Scotland and how this:

> . . . allows the widespread commonsense view that Scotland has good race relations because there is no racism here to go unquestioned.[108]

In this sense racism against non-white peoples in Scotland has received little serious attention, allowing people frequently to believe that 'racism' is a problem in England but not in Scotland. The commonsense view that sectarianism is only a problem involving 'the Old Firm' provides a similar smoke screen that covers up the origins, history and manifestations of sectarianism in Scottish society.[109]

A common experience for many second and third generation Irish involved with the Irish 2 Project as well as others interviewed elsewhere is the belief that in Scottish society it is difficult to raise the subject of Irishness or claim Irish identity. Often people hostile to the concept of being Scottish-born Irish resort to a discourse of sectarianism, negative comment regarding the Northern Ireland conflict or the accusation that they are 'Scottish, not Irish and that if they liked Ireland so much why don't they go back and live there?' (as repeated and relayed in several of the press commentaries noted). The consequences of such polemics over many decades and generations are virtually incalculable but they invariably contribute to the socialisation of many Irish towards Scottishness, a less contested choice of identity. In the words of a second generation Glasgow Irishman, Peadar McGrath, Irishness

107 Celtic v Aberdeen, 25/10/03

108 See R. Miles and L. Muirhead 1986

109 See Bruce 1992

has been 'sectarianised' by those averse to it in Scottish society:

> . . . I find that whenever if you're talking to people and you say that you're Irish, they don't actually hear the word 'Irish', they hear you saying 'bigot'. . . I don't know how many debates I've had with people actually. . . even Catholic teachers in the school, when you start talking about it, they start talking about bigotry. I'm saying, I'm not talking about that, I'm talking about me being Irish and about a culture. But they can't see the culture, they just keep relating it back to bigotry.[110]

A number of the letters quoted are thematically similar in that they emphasise the primacy of Scottishness above Irishness. Historically with regards the Irish in Scotland, this reflects little understanding of the notion of diaspora or of the Irish and Catholic experience in Scotland. It elevates country of birth above country of origin as well as above the notion of ethnicity and it lays a disabling significance on the factor of time in the mistaken belief that time is neutral and in itself changes people's identities. In this context, time is relevant only when qualified by consideration of the socialisation processes important in the shaping and constituting of identity.

In themselves, the letters and the reporting by the Daily Record journalist can be viewed as constituting important aspects of socialisation and culturalising in Scottish society. Like other sources of knowledge and discourse, they help shape views, opinions, attitudes and identity. In this sense they also represent the dominant views, discourses and narratives, with regards Irish identity in Scottish society: the consequences of which appears to be a factor evident to the Irish 2 interviewee in his attempt to be 'Scottish-born Irish in Scotland'.

The emphatic statement of the Daily Record journalist that Celtic and its supporters were Scottish and of the other correspondents that the Celtic supporters were not sufficiently prioritising Scottishness over Irishness can be aligned with the sentiments of former British Government

110 Irish 2 Project, interview, P. McGrath

Minister Norman Tebbit who demonstrated a comparable perspective during the 1980s. He suggested a novel type of cricket test (or loyalty test). Asian immigrants' integration could be tested by asking which cricket team they supported: England or Pakistan/India. He went on to suggest:

> . . . that those who continue to cheer for India and Pakistan are wanting in Britishness. . . that the only satisfactory way to be an Asian in Britain was to cease being Asian.[111]

This probation, in its form as a 'football test', has also been applied regularly by the Scottish/British press since the 1980s as it became common for British-born second and third generation Irish to represent and support the Republic of Ireland in international football. Critical comment, mainly regarding the immigrant identity of many members of the team, has been a significant aspect of the discourse discussing the merits of the team.[112] Nevertheless, some of the logic underpinning such an argument was exposed by a respected British journalist:

> . . . the assertion that we are one people has always been a lie used to justify the unjust dominance of one group (whites, Protestants or Anglo-Saxons, for example) over the society as a whole.[113]

Along with the other print media comment such narrative reflects a widely held broad ideological and attitudinal position and constitutes a dominant discourse. A similar narrative is also exposed with regards Celtic and Catholics in Scotland on the part of a number of the letter writers and journalists referred to. These narratives serve to construct a 'Scottish test', one akin to Norman Tebbit's British 'cricket test' where affinity towards Ireland is viewed with hostility. In this light, some commentators even suggest a return to Ireland if such cultural allegiances exist.

Exclusion of the Irish diasporic and Catholic context with regard to Celtic's achievement in reaching Seville

111 The Observer, 16/9/90

112 See The Sun, 27/6/90, Evening Times, 10/6/94, Daily Record, 16/6/94, Irish Post, 12/12/92

113 A. Lively, The Observer, 22/7/90

also characterised the best wishes of Scotland's First Minister as Celtic departed for the match.

> Celtic's involvement in the UEFA Cup Final is a great occasion for Scotland. . . we want Celtic to do the country proud. . . This is a big week for them [the players] and Wednesday is a very big night for Celtic and Scotland. . . It is very important that every fan who goes to Seville is a good ambassador for Scotland as well as the club. . .[114]

In his statement, Jack McConnell expressed a logical sentiment in that Celtic would partly reflect something positive about Scotland, since the 1980s a country that has dramatically declined on the stage of European and international football. However, the established prism of interpretation with regards to the politics of identity and sectarianism in Scotland meant McConnell conformed to conventional discourses by continually mentioning Scotland and excluding mention of Celtic's heritage and connection with the Irish diaspora and what the appearance in Seville might have represented and meant for the Irish diaspora in Scotland: ie, many Celtic supporters themselves. In the light of the reported letter writers and journalistic comment it may not have been politically advantageous to refer to the core identity of Celtic and its support if such comment would have instigated negative political observation. If so, this is but one small example of the silencing of alternative narratives in relation to identity in Scotland.

One can only guess as to the extent of fragmentation and the demise of Irishness in Scotland as a result of over a century or more of such discourses. Linking with Finn's arguments concerning the recycling of racism from former stereotypes to a format less obvious but nonetheless embedded in popular attitudes and beliefs, a similar process can be evidenced in the newspaper reports of the nineteenth century to those references regarding Irishness in contemporary Scotland.

114 P. Jardine, Daily Mail, 19/5/03

As Celtic supporters repeatedly demonstrate, Irishness

is not completely obscured in Scottish life but the evidence suggests that it is frequently marginalised, rendered atavistic and sectarianised by such labelling and represent-ations. Further, such labelling and representations are social, cultural and political and assist in the exclusion and misrepresentation of the Irish in Scotland while obscuring a range of factors that have shaped social relations in Scottish society. In addition, with regards references to Irishness in Scottish society, dominant forms of discourse ignore the:

> . . . deep consensus on the construction of a category or any other knowledge [that] often results in a form of collective unawareness or amnesia of its construction. Because the consensus is deep, that which is made is mistaken for that which is found.[115]

In addition, the ideas and language that dominate in the construction of Irishness in Scotland, as something deeply associated with sectarianism, means that the roots and causes of sectarianism in Scottish society remain relatively unexplored. An example of the omission referred to here (ie, the 'unawareness' and 'amnesia') is found in the frequency of letters and articles in popular newspapers that blame Catholic schools for sectarianism in Scotland when in fact, sectarianism existed in Scotland before the existence of Catholic schools. As this work suggests, sectarianism has other roots and origins.[116] Another common example arises in the discourses over Celtic supporters' flying of the Irish flag. As a basic level such 'analysis' is excessively simple and general though its use is not unsophisticated. In these contexts, the use of the term 'sectarian' is not neutral and is in fact an ideological construct.

115 D.J. Gallagher 2001

116 Examination of Scotland's post-Reformation anti-Catholic character and its significance is but one avenue requiring further exploration

AGAINST PREJUDICE

In the period surrounding Celtic's journey to Seville, only a few sportswriters reflected on the Irish nature of the Celtic support. Award winning sports journalist Hugh McIlvanney stated that:

> Observers unfamiliar with the breathtaking phenomenon of the most remarkable support in the whole of football were struck by the overwhelming ratio of Irish tricolours to Scottish flags.[117]

McIlvanney's reference is akin to the suggestion that despite some public references to matters representing Native Americans or Indians in the USA, in these depictions, relevant reporters 'appear averse to acknowledging Native Americans as real people'.[118] They are used in the imagery concerned but this is achieved without context thus partly avoiding uneasy questions about both the dominant social cultures and identities in society and those which represent other groupings. In a Scottish context, this is similar to many existing references to the Irish, Scotland's largest immigrant community.

Herald journalist Hugh MacDonald, offers the view that the BBC could have created some interesting 'reality' television around the Seville event by examining:

> The way Celtic became a rallying point for the Irish diaspora throughout the world.[119]

Glasgow-based academic, Willie Maley, stressed the core identity of Celtic Football Club and its support. He believed Celtic Park to be:

> . . . one of Glasgow's most impressive structures, and a tremendous monument to the Irish in

117 H. McIlvaney, Sunday Times, Sport, 25/5/03

118 C.R. King, E.J. Staurowsky, L.R. Davis, C. Pewewardy 2002

119 H. MacDonald, The Herald, 20/5/03

Scotland, marking the significant contribution of the country's largest immigrant community to the rich and vibrant culture of the West of Scotland.[120]

Likewise, Graham Spiers has been one of the few journalists to treat the subject of Celtic and its supporters' Irishness and Catholic identities as a matter of fact and of interest rather than as something to be omitted from relevant texts or, to be treated as sectarian.

> Whoever heard of any organisation or any institution not being allowed proudly to proclaim their roots? Celtic were a club founded by Catholics, yet the very mention of this evolved into something that was almost to be detested. . . a loss of a sense of history seemed tantamount to a loss of collective identity. . . because of the evil of bigotry, of course, the notion of identity is compromised.[121]

Such references to Celtic's inherent Catholic identity plays a strikingly minor role in relevant narrations though they are features essential to understanding Celtic, its support and their place in Scottish society. In the case of Seville, this is implied by McIlvanney as most people reporting on the match with an interest in football might have been expected to know already about Celtic and its supports' Irishness, unless this has been concealed or misrepresented in previous discourses. Such expected knowledge might be seen to parallel the way that many people know about the Catalan identity of Barcelona FC, Glasgow Rangers' British-Scottish identity, the Scottish identity of world champion boxer Scott Harrison or the Irish identity of Boston's Fighting Irish basketball team. A lack of acknowledgement of characteristics relating to one's heritage and culture changes the core and traditional image by manufacturing something else. This is accomplished by excluding the past and memory to the point these become vague, distant and difficult to manage in relation to assuming contemporary relevance. They become points of contention and conflict rather than something to be proud of or something recognised as

120 W. Maley, Celtic View, 29/5/02

121 G. Spiers, The Herald

facilitating the constitution of self, family and community. They are unwritten and unremarked upon except in negative terms.

Those discourses that emerge in relation to the Irishness of the club broadly recognise Celtic as being founded in the context of Irish Catholic circumstances in Scotland, but this is a recognition usually devoid of the social, cultural and political context without which the traditions, history and identity of Celtic and its support cannot be fully understood. Thus the language used to discuss the Irish in Scotland is directly related to the language used to construct knowledge about sectarianism and dominant ideas about the Irish. Ultimately, this also engenders and gives succour to 'sectarianism' in Scottish life.

THE WIDER CONTEXT

In its historical context the marginalisation of Irish identity has been a long historical process linked with the British colonisation of Ireland. This is partly evidenced in a quote from Sir William Parsons about the Irish in 1625, a statement with connotations of current arguments about Irishness in Scotland. For Parsons, only the depreciation and destruction of Ireland's cultural traits and identities could result in the Irish being absorbed into the Crown's realm:

> We must change their course of government, apparel, manner of holding land, their language and habit of life. [122]

Simply put, manifestations of Irishness were unacceptable in British-conquered Ireland. A perception on the part of British colonists was that the Irish were required to change if Ireland and its people were to be shaped in the interests of the British Crown. For contemporary Irishness in Scotland, the process encouraged by Ireland's colonial administrator Parsons seems to be ongoing in a different time, space and place, thus constituting a metaphorical, though no less real, colonisation.

In a similar vein, for 'white' groups raised and educated in Britain whose language patterns have become almost indistinguishable from the 'white' majority, cultural and ethnic differences are largely unrecognised. 'Whiteness' frequently signifies sameness with the 'indigenous' mainstream. In the case of the Irish in Scotland, a concept of 'whiteness' is partly used to assert and justify assimilation. It might be argued that the Irish diaspora has traditionally formed the great 'other' in Scottish society.

122 Irish Post, 8/12/90

The arguments at the 1997 University of Stirling conference (and arguably reiterated through a range and variety of examples reflected here) that the Irish do not exist in Scotland can be viewed within the context of the dominant discourses that prevail. Such arguments may also be viewed as minimalist, constrained and ethnocentric. In this sense these discourses become ideological. Social, cultural and political exclusion is related to this. Generally the Irishness of the Irish in Scotland is denied or sectarianised. That these polemics have been used frequently in relation to the Irish diaspora in Scotland is evident. Conroy suggests that such commentators as those at Stirling probably misinterpret Catholics in Scotland, 'for whom keeping one's head down and appearing "normal" may actually be quite important'.[123]

The idea of keeping one's head down was indirectly referred to by a Glasgow-born second generation Irishman, Johnny Kiernan, an interviewee on the Irish 2 Project when he spoke of the experience of his parents not buying him a Celtic replica top as a youngster, lest he be identified and attract hostility. Kiernan's awareness of sectarianism was also provoked at school when his headmaster advised job seekers not to enter St Patrick's High School on their application forms but instead write Dumbarton High on the basis that not to identify themselves as Catholic might help them gain employment.[124] Another interviewee explained how a friend changed their Irish Catholic name to a more Scottish or neutral-sounding one in an effort to acquire suitable employment.[125]

In similar fashion, a newspaper obituary in 2000 told how a Glasgow-born Irishman was called Sean but changed his 'public' name to John when he entered the labour market, realising that his name denoted his Catholic background and this might create difficulty for him in seeking employment.[126] A woman respondent, who offered the view that 'we know we're Irish but we should keep it in our hearts', seemed to recognise that the privatisation of Irish identity was the best way to negotiate social progress and a peaceful social existence in Scotland.[127]

123 J. Conroy 2003

124 Interview, Johnny Kiernan, Irish 2 Project, ESRC

125 Interview, focus group, Irish 2 Project, ESRC

126 The Herald, Obituary for Sean Tierney, 22/4/00

127 Contribution made by parishioner to discussion on location and erection of the Irish National Famine Monument in Scotland, 11/11/99

Somewhat related to this Murray notes that during the finals of the Scottish Schools Cup played at Ibrox in 1996, a seven-a-side competition in front of 50,000 people was held at the half-time period of the crucial Rangers versus Aberdeen 'league decider'.

> The winning team was Christ the King Primary School from Holytown, but they did not play under their own name, being called 'the red team' instead. . . the decision to label the teams by colour rather than by their real names was taken when the finalist became known: in addition to the winning team, the losing semi-finalists were St Bridget's of Baillieston and St Flannan's of Kirkintilloch. In explanation, it was pointed out that the organisers wanted the boys to enjoy themselves without a section of the crowd turning against them.[128]

This reflection on the hiding of Catholic identity in a specifically perceived hostile environment can be seen to go beyond such obviously hostile confines on consideration of Johnny Kiernan's story. Likewise, numerous people in Lanarkshire are aware that when St Mary's High School, Coatbridge was replaced with 'Columba' High School in the early 1970s, a choice was made not to call the school 'Saint Columba' in case it might prejudice people into not offering its pupils positions in the employment market. It has also been suggested that new schools in Lanarkshire such as Taylor High and Cardinal Newman have emerged as a result of a similar mindset, one that desires to disguise the true faith-based nature of the schools, lest its pupils are the victims of prejudice.[129] That this is an ongoing process in the new millennium was suggested by one member of the teaching staff at Columba High, a school facing merger with St Patrick's Coatbridge around 2005.[130] Although both saints have particular relevance in an area primarily inhabited by thousands of members of the Irish diaspora, the teacher said that the renaming of the new school would follow a similar 'name check process'. Possibly in relation to such a mindset, by the end of the 1990s, it has been suggested that North Lanarkshire seemed to have removed the letters RC (Roman Catholic) from many of the nameplates on the

128 B. Murray 2003

129 These insinuations and narratives have been familiar to a number of people in Lanarkshire since the 1970s

130 Discussion with teacher at Columba High, 15/12/03

outside of numerous Catholic schools in its region thus downplaying their specific Catholic identity.

In the 1962 Hollywood version of the story of Indian Chief Geronimo, the white cavalry officer tells the rebellious Indian:

> . . . now you behave yourself Geronimo, that's all you have to do. You'll get along fine. Otherwise, I'll lock you in a cage where you belong.

When Geronimo enquired to his friend why he was complying with the White Man's reshaping of the Indian social world, his friend replied, 'They don't understand us. So we do the best we can. At least we stay alive.' Notwithstanding standard Hollywood historical inaccuracies or sensationalist film making, the colonisation of Native American Indians and the imperialist expansion of white Europeans is an historical fact. What is less appreciated is how the Indian way of life was changed, not always by force and by killing millions of Indians, but also by stealth and, as suggested in the film's discourse, Indians keeping their heads down to simply survive, 'Indian or not'. In this light it is unsurprising that Native Americans are virtually invisible throughout modern public and representative US society.

Throughout the Irish 2 Project and in terms of a variety of interviews, for many members of the Irish diaspora in Scotland such experiences are illustrative of how numerous strands – social, religious, sporting and general life chances – conflate to contribute to a more complete impression of a generally unreported and only partly visible aspect of life in Scotland. The consequences that such experiences have had over the course of a century and a half for Catholic religious practice and Irish identity are incalculable. However, this evidence and the continued pressure on the Irish in Scotland to change, as demonstrated through the prism of the Celtic football experience, has contributed to a process whereby many Irish become Scots and many others negotiate their Catholic and Irish identities by 'keeping their heads down'.

Conroy suggests that in human relations social progress may indeed be best bought by 'keeping one's head down'.[131] Horgan posits the enquiry in another way. He asks the question, where were the Irish so defeated and crushed that to survive, 'they had to, in effect, cease to be'?[132] He asks, if, like Native Americans and Australian Aborigines, the Irish have been told to 'stop being who they are or were and become somebody else'?[133]

Although the resultant invisibility becomes transformed to one of visibility in the social and cultural environment that constitutes Celtic Football Club and its supporter culture, this work illustrates the contestation that confronts members of the Irish diaspora in Scotland who exhibit and celebrate their Irishness. Indeed, as this book evidences, discourses on the part of many Celtic supporters reflect a feeling of powerlessness regarding this confrontation, despite celebration of their Irishness in a Celtic context. Further, this also demonstrates that this cultural visibility and invisibility are social constructions.

Taken as research instead of polemic and received as knowledge rather than as part of a well-established line of enquiry and reporting on the Irish in Scotland, the 'Stirling argument' can be viewed as the production and dissemination of accounts of the Irish that are partial, inaccurate and devoid of context. However, as reflected throughout this book, such an argument does not stand in isolation. For example, Bruce argues that Catholics in Scotland have been 'successfully' assimilated and that the Irish in Scotland 'desired to be integrated'.[134] McCrone and Rosie believe that Catholics of Irish descent in Scotland have been assimilated and have become accultured.

> Scottish Catholics at the start of the new millennium are not the people they were. Their past is indeed history.[135]

A contrary and more analytical view is articulated by Buckley who in turn notes the importance and role these dominant accounts play in impressions of Irishness in Britain.

131 J. Conroy 2003
132 Irish Post, 5/11/03
133 Ibid, 10/1/04
134 S. Bruce, 2000
135 M. Rosie & D. McCrone, 2000

> Another difference between Irish ethnicity in Britain and in other countries is the assimilationist approach in Britain towards all expressions of Irishness, whether immigrant or not. . . [and that] identity and cultural practices which refer to the country of origin may be maintained and shielded from the alien environment of the street.[136]

Significantly in relation to post-colonial theory and the effects of colonialism, on not only those people who continued to live in Ireland, but on those who emigrated and who along with their offspring have become a part of the worldwide Irish diaspora (arguably as a result of this colonialism), O Ruairc has an incisive insight. Ireland under British colonialism has:

> . . . not only been a geographical entity dominated by the British state, but also a history, geography, culture and population written and represented by what the British said about them.[137]

In this light it is less difficult to understand and contextualise the arguments, polemics, prejudice, stereotypes, misinformation, racism and 'sectarianism' that may arise from the dominant discourses evidenced here. In these terms, the process of the colonisation of the identities and mindsets of second, third and fourth generation Irish people in Scotland becomes more discernible. Indeed, this process is partly reflected in the quote by Parsons, the British colonial administrator of seventeenth century Ireland, and might be witnessed where any country or people wishes to dominate another by marginalising and negatively labelling its constitution to suit its own intentions. Whether it is by labelling as 'savages', 'uncivilised' or by 'sectarianising', the results have a similar outcome. In this context, the importance of Celtic for the Irish diaspora in Scotland also becomes clear.

Assimilationist, marginalising and sectarian accounts directly contribute to the invisibility of the Irish in Scotland. For Hickman, this is also about 'forced inclusion' and the

136 M. Buckley 1997

137 L. O Ruairc, Fortnight, October 2003

'myth of homogeneity'.[138] In addition, being frequently confronted with representations of your community, heritage, origins and identity, that are offensive and filled with ridicule while simultaneously making Scottishness appear suitable and even normal, and thus negatively hegemonic, assists in the creation and sustaining of an Irish identity typified by negative imagery. 'Keeping one's head down' may more often than not lead to assimilation and even invisibility as opposed to integration. Negative labelling, silence and an ideological process of sectarian-ising Irishness has a depressing and diminishing effect on the identities of individuals, families and communities who choose to esteem their Irishness.

This silence was unintentionally emphasised to the author when discussing a project on Celtic with possible backing from the club. After expressing his delight and support for the research a former Celtic Chief Executive abruptly requested the author not to 'play up the Irish bit too much'. The Chief Executive seemed to be saying, 'let's keep the heads down, don't antagonise, keep it quiet, to a minimum, keep it private'. He may even have been saying, 'let's create another more acceptable image'? As further evidence of this minimalist and hesitant approach occurring from within the club, this was repeated more strongly with a subsequent Chief Executive employee in conversation with the author and also via the Club's official publication, the Celtic View.[139] The evidence of several generations suggests that these views are an integral part of the Irish Catholic mindset, partly created in response to perceptions of anti-Catholicism and anti-Irishness in Scotland.

It is crucial also to recognise the aspect of hegemony in much of the discourse about the Irish diaspora in Scotland. The letters may fit into a broader context where histories and perspectives of this diaspora are silenced, often unarticulated, undermined and are powerful tools in preventing this community from learning about and understanding itself and its past. They are also concerned

138 M. Hickman 1998

139 Interviews with former Chief Executives Alan MacDonald 29/1/2000 and Ian McLeod 28/2/02. MacDonald was acutely aware of discrimination against Catholics in the workplace and had experienced such an environment in previous employments. This aspect of his socialisation may have influenced his perception when adopting an attitude of requiring to 'keep quiet' or 'not playing up the Irish side of the club', lest hostile elements in society were further antagonised. The perceptions of McLeod (who was not from a Catholic or Irish background) were different although his alluding to 'obscuring' the Irishness or Irish dimension of the fans and the club was strikingly similar to the attitude of MacDonald. Similarly, he believed Celtic and its supporters attracted hostility because of Irishness and the club's and its fans' Catholic identities. However, notably, his attitude was akin to other fans in Scottish football that demonstrate hostility to many Celtic supporters for their absence or lack of affinity for the Scotland national team (see Bradley, 2001 & 2003). Indeed, during his two-year tenure at Celtic Park he actively attempted to change this and align Celtic supporters

with ideas relating to control and consent in an atmosphere in which the dominant identities are viewed as the only ones publicly acceptable. Reflecting Conroy's suggestion of Catholics of Irish extraction in Scotland learning to 'keep their heads down', many second, third and fourth generation Irish in Scotland may have chosen to keep their heads down by becoming Scottish. That many have not become Scottish and remain Irish is also true, as is most publicly evident through Celtic Football Club fandom and culture.

Related to this and although based more on perception and emotion than on social scientific research and analysis, journalist Joe Horgan's point is valid. It reflects the feelings, emotions, perceptions, and the imaginations that help define all people in seeing themselves as being a part of something: in this context, of those born in Britain who see themselves as part of the Irish diaspora. His view resonates with many interviewees who participated in the Irish 2 Project and also with many Celtic supporters. Horgan reasons that:

> We are Irish nonetheless and always will be. That does not change. Anything else would merely be a case of telling lies about ourselves.[140]

with the Scotland national side through a 're-education' or 'socialisation' strategy and process. Part of this was demonstrated via an in-house published Celtic View supplement, 'No Frontiers: Only Goals', in January 2002. Some Celtic fans believed this supplement to be 'a piece of propaganda that extolled the virtues of being Scottish at the expense of being Irish'. This in fact reflected much of the pressure that Celtic and its support had perceived themselves as being under for many decades from those hostile to the nature and identities of the club and its support. Essentially for McLeod, Celtic was to be shorn of its Irish Catholic distinctiveness and character in favour of a Scottish secularist identity. Indeed, an identity where Irishness was relevant only as an historical fact, one that could be used for merchandising, one comparable to that proposed by many other elements in Scottish society and therefore one seemingly more widely desired and acceptable.

140 Irish Post, 18/10/03

CELTIC FANDOM

It would be misleading to believe that the Irish Catholic and Celtic experience in Scotland has been shaped solely by anti-Catholicism and anti-Irishness: by hostility and marginality and matters racist, sectarian and prejudicial. However, these are aspects crucial, common and familiar, and indeed, although largely repressed and not articulated publicly, they are central to the experience of that community.

Likewise, there is no straightforward and simple dichotomy of identity among people in contemporary Scotland. Like any other society Scotland has a number of regional, class and racial features which affect wider issues of identity in different ways. In terms of the cultural, social and political dimensions of Scottish/British Protestantism and Irish Catholicism, people can have one-dimensional affinities, they can inhabit a multi-layered set of identities or they can lie at any point in between. Irish identity and Irishness as well as Scottish identity and Scottishness are not unchanging. Communities do not exist as hermetically sealed eternal entities. Even beyond Celtic's traditional Irish Catholic fan base the contemporary active Celtic support contains around ten per cent of fans not from a Catholic or Irish background and others from a mixed Irish Scottish ethnic-religious background or with little affinity for Irish culture and identity.[141]

Nonetheless, within the context of the growing literature on hybridity, situational ethnicity and the unfixed nature of contemporary identity,[142] and in realisation of the sometimes fluid nature of identity, as was noted by McIlvanney, the overwhelming identity of Celtic Football Club and its supporters since its foundation has been

141 A survey carried out in 1990 showed ninety-three per cent of Celtic supporters as Catholic and four per cent of the Protestant faith. Three per cent claimed no religion. See Bradley, 1995, p.61. In a more wide-ranging and extensive survey carried out in 2000/01 these figures were largely upheld with ten per cent of supporters being non-Catholic. See Bradley, forthcoming.

142 See M.J. Hickman, B. Walters, S. Morgan, J.M. Bradley, A. Brah

characterised by matters 'Irish'. The vast majority of Catholics in Scotland originate from Ireland and Celtic's social, cultural and political meaningfulness in Scotland can only be considered significant within the context of the Irish diaspora. Celtic Football Club is an institution conceived and constructed from within, and sustained by, the immigrant Irish and their offspring in Scotland.

Celtic is of foremost cultural importance for vast numbers of Catholics of Irish decent in Scotland. The club functions as a socialising agent into a unique form of Irish cultural activity and it exists as a public space where many of the Irish in Scotland demonstrate and celebrate their identity. Celtic's Irish identity and the offspring of the Irish immigrant community that founded and sustained it make it a unique representation of Irishness amongst the Irish diaspora. In Scotland, football is bound up and inherently linked with the process of community construction. The existence of Celtic and its community of supporters also demonstrates notions of the imagined community and of diaspora: Irish and Irishness are not limited by place of birth or the geographical landscape of the island of Ireland.

For those people who are descended from Ireland and are born and live in Scotland and who view Celtic as intrinsic to their Irishness, the club remains a public site for the preservation of their cultural traditions, customs, political preferences and in the socialisation and sustenance of Irish identity in Scotland. It exists as a site for a sense of community born from the majority of these supporters sharing familial and kinship origins in Ireland. Celtic constitutes a setting for friendship and association with people often inter-married, having experienced the same denominational school format, sharing similar geographical spaces in Scotland (frequently in the Glasgow and Lanarkshire areas and within a thirty mile radius of Celtic Park in Glasgow), having forenames and surnames that denote Catholic and Irish origins, lineage and heritage, and with a sense of belonging to Ireland, Catholicism, Irish history and Irish culture. Celtic is a site for the mobilisation and expression of Irishness in Scotland. Celtic is often a social marker of ethnic and religious distinction in Scottish society. For many Celtic supporters who care passionately about the their own and their club's Irish origins, history, traditions and identity, their ritual is one of crying out to be heard and be visibly accepted in Scottish society. It is a society perceived as ignoring and marginalising them, one that is hostile to their Irishness and refusing esteem to their ethnic and religious identities.

For them, Celtic is evidence and a reminder to themselves as well as others in Scottish society that the Irish remain in Scotland. Those who esteem their own Irishness, their community's Irishness as well as that of Celtic's, are the supporters who make Celtic Football Club culturally, socially and politically significant. It is these supporters, as well as those who identify with the club and its supporters' core identities, that make Celtic unique in the sporting world.

Blain and Boyle believe that 'collective identity is not only centrally important in human experience but also rendered visible in particularly revealing ways by the discourses of the mediation of sports events'.[143] Through sport, we can find notions of the individual and of the individual's links with other people becoming manifest through community. Football in Scotland allows the Irish in Scotland to become publicly manifest and identifiable, to themselves as well as those outside that community. Celtic and its supporters' Irishness challenges notions of assimilation amongst the children, grandchildren and great grandchildren of Irish migrants in Scotland. This points to the need for more nuanced understandings of 'white' diasporic identities, as well as Scottishness and Britishness. Without the Irish diasporic community's sense of Irishness in Scotland, Celtic would not exist, have become established or have gained widespread recognition as one of the most significant institutions in world football. For the Irish in Scotland, Celtic Football Club has emerged as a definition of Irishness itself.

143 N. Blain and R. Boyle, 1994

ROOTS

'The Odessa' — on board an Irish famine ship
detail from a painting by the marine artist Rodney Charman

Commemorating the Great Famine in song and deed

Edward O'Neil

Not a devil or witch had a hand in this deed
Of this I assure you now
But the cuckoo of men, this crippling foe
Though its little that you might have
He's exploited the work, of the labouring man
And while his belly expands
A great hunger came o'er the land.[1]

Many of the songs of the Celtic support are imbued with a strong sense of history: a strong sense of memory, of experience and story. The act of remembering, as a song like 'Hail, Hail' points out, is important:

> Sure it's a grand old team to play for
> Sure it's a grand old team to see
> And if you know the history
> It's enough to make your heart go. . .

Critics of some of the songs of the Celtic support have long found their content distasteful or even irrelevant in a 'modern Scotland', whatever that is? However, intolerance towards Irish Catholic immigrants to Scotland and a desire for social, ethnic and political conformity might be the key to understanding such criticism. There often seems a strange confusion with many of the Celtic support's antagonists: 'You're Scots, you're not Irish' or equally, 'you're not welcome here, go back to Ireland'. In

Notes

1 From 'The Great Hunger'
  Brian Warfield

these discourses we get some idea of the experiences of refugees in modern Scotland. And yet often, unprompted and beyond the control of the disapproving voices, a song such as 'The Fields of Athenry' will emerge from the Celtic support, the chorus a clear signal, if ever there was one, that the past the song evokes continues to be relevant to Celtic fans today. The events of the Great Famine that devastated Ireland and its people in the years 1845-1851 have been etched into folk memory. It is a song of the Irish diaspora and most Celtic supporters are part of that diaspora.

Just as the songs prove controversial, so have official attempts to commemorate the Famine – at least in Scotland. In February 2001, MP Frank Roy raised fears about public safety when the Carfin Irish Famine monument was due to be unveiled by the Irish Premier, an Taoiseach, Bertie Ahern. In June of the same year, the Taoiseach finally arrived and the unveiling of the monument, attended by amongst others, the former Church of Scotland Moderator Andrew MacLellan, and numerous Scottish and British political figures, passed without incident.

There are Famine monuments throughout the world, wherever the Irish settled during and after the years of the Famine. There are monuments in England, Wales, Australia, Canada and several in the USA. The monuments are positioned sometimes prominently in city centres. Boston's Irish Famine memorial is located in a busy section of the city, its creators additionally conscious that the conditions that contributed to the Famine in Ireland have not disappeared: hunger and starvation continue to plague much of the world. In December 2000, Bertie Ahern unveiled a sculpture of a Famine ship in the United Nations Plaza in New York. The centrality of these monuments and sculptures is recognition of the scale of the human suffering endured and the plight of all emigrants who flee from adversity. They also recognise that Famine is a scourge in a world of plenty and a greater and fairer distribution of the world's resources would almost certainly help end this continuing obscene travesty.

The events of the years 1845-1851 have been variously described – 'The Great Starvation', 'The Great Calamity' but perhaps the Irish term 'An Gorta Mor' (the Great Hunger) is the most widely used. In 1904, Michael Davitt, member of the Fenians, politician and Land Leaguer, and an important figure in the founding years of Celtic, referred to the events of those years as the 'holocaust of humanity'.[2] This phrase is nowadays more widely associated with the extermination of the Jews in World War II but it nevertheless has a brutal resonance that may help us gauge the enormity of the events of those years. But however these events are described they do not tell the whole story and in one crucial sense may actually be misleading.

'Just as the songs prove controversial, so have official attempts to commemorate the Famine – at least in Scotland'

Christine Kinealy in her book, 'A Death-Dealing Famine, The Great Hunger in Ireland', writes that: 'Much of this suffering resulted from ideological, political and commercial constraints, rather than the simple fact of a potato blight in Ireland'.[3] There was total destruction of the crops in the years 1846 and 1848 but that alone should not have precipitated such widespread hunger and starvation. Ireland, at that time, was known as the 'granary of Europe' so plentiful was corn. Nevertheless, as a subject nation, Ireland was part of the British Empire (some would argue its first colony). The commander-in-chief of Famine relief, Sir Charles Trevelyan, had called the Irish 'an indolent and unself-reliant people'.[4] The British Government's policy of non-intervention showed an adherence to economic concerns rather than to humanitarian ones. For many, their actions, or rather their lack of action, is enough to signal culpability. Ireland's Famine had its roots in the colonisation of the country and the actions of its dominating colonising neighbour during the 'the great hunger' were hardly those one might expect of a Christian nation.

All in all, it is estimated that one million died and a further one million emigrated in a handful of years. Many

2 Christine Kinealy 'A Death-Dealing Famine, The Great Hunger in Ireland' Pluto Press 1997, p.2

3 Ibid, p15

4 Ibid, p.4

of those came to Scotland: some 100,000, a significant number from a rapidly declining population of around eight million. Many survivors of the Famine subsequently suffered ill-health because of the deprivation of those years; many more would die premature deaths. The descendants of the survivors would also find the legacy of the Famine difficult with an increased likelihood of them suffering, amongst other problems, mental illness. The psychological scars would take many years to heal. Indeed, it might be argued that many Irish Catholics who live in the most deprived areas of the West of Scotland still bear those scars and many have not in fact 'healed'. So crushed were the Irish, those who stayed and those who journeyed elsewhere, that it would take many years before those events would weave their ways into song.

It is understandable perhaps that a strong sense of resentment of the governing power of the time, the Crown, and of Trevelyan's comments, should remain. After all, it is a resentment with relevance today. It certainly helps many Celtic supporters know who they are and from where they have come. What are we without such memories? Another question might be, who would wish us to forget our community and people, our own recent past history?

The Famine destruction was widespread, affecting not only individuals but also whole communities. One observer noted how,

> 'the years of the Famine, of the bad life and of the hunger, arrived and broke the spirit and the strength of the community. Recreation and leisure ceased. Poetry and music and dancing died'.[5]

Beyond that, those who emigrated surely would have been conscious of several things: in particular the devastation they had left behind and the opportunity of a new life they might be afforded in other countries. Their dispiritedness and the memories they carried would make life elsewhere a difficult prospect.

5 From 'The Field Day Anthology of Irish Writing, Recollections of Maire Ni Grianna' cited in 'A Death Dealing Famine, The Great Hunger in Ireland' p.155

From Famine times, transport this community four or five generations onwards, adding along the way other more recent migrants who decided to leave Ireland due to economic, political and cultural factors, and we find the institution of Celtic FC and its supporting community in Glasgow and the west of Scotland. It is in the context of the great Irish Famine and Irish immigration to Scotland that Celtic Football Club was founded, built and sustained. It is only in the experience of Irish migration to the West of Scotland that Celtic can be understood. It is this Irishness that makes Celtic a unique club.

Amidst the deprivation, suffering, discrimination and despondency, it is remarkable to think that Celtic arose from this community of Irish Catholics in Glasgow's east end. Brother Walfrid, as the Headmaster of the local Sacred Heart School, would have been aware of the needs of the poor in his parish community. His 'Poor Children's Dinner Table' was organised to provide food for those unable to feed themselves. For the Irish in Scotland, the Famine in Ireland continued to stalk them in another environment.

Who can say what motivated Walfrid? Where would we be if people like Mother Theresa of Calcutta or Frederick Oznam (founder of the St Vincent de Paul Society) had decided not to 'intervene' and create good from evil. What memories did Walfrid carry of those turbulent years of the Famine and what must he have thought when he observed his own in Glasgow, still hungry? His involvement in football was an attempt to provide sustenance of another kind, an attempt to instill pride in a community that was often despised by native Scots. Walfrid's was a positive conception from something that was inhuman and unchristian.

These facts and their significance may be denied (and indeed they are by many) in a multitude of ways. They might be re-packaged to sound ancient and therefore deemed irrelevant. They may be ignored and their importance gradually erased from popular memory. Modernity develops a convenient amnesia. Such accounts are often slated by people who do not and will not recognise how evil is created and perpetuated. Such memories and their contemporary relevance may even be termed 'sectarian' by people whose colonising forefathers actually invented sectarianism and imposed it upon Ireland and its people, in Ireland and beyond.

Celtic's story is an astounding one. Many of those who fled Ireland did not prosper much better on foreign shores than they had on their native ones. The true plight of the emigrant was bleaker than people care to imagine. Hunger remained and many in Glasgow and in other countries were unable to escape it. But the establishment of Celtic FC, its history on the field of play, its support, is indeed a triumph over adversity.

Although the Famine monument at Carfin and the establishment of a specific Irish memorial site in 2001 was long overdue, the physical and spiritual monument that is constituted through Celtic Football Club has been a symbol of both the survival and presence of the Irish in modern Scotland. To recall the Famine in song or deed is a simple way of illuminating this important truth about the club and its supporting community. The singing of such songs at Celtic Park has a multi-fold purpose: it signals a concern for the past, it informs us of significant events, it passes a sense of history to the next generation, it provokes a political and social consciousness often dulled through other experiences, and it strikes a chord of opposition and rebelliousness against the pressures to conform and lose personal, family and community identity. Stone memorials and other sites of memory have a similar function as one writer observed: 'to remember is to affirm community, to assert its moral character, and to exclude from it those values, groups, or individuals that placed it under threat'.[6] In Celtic FC, the Irish in Scotland have established a means to express themselves and to acquire identification where such recognition is frequently obscured and denied.

6 From Jay Winter 'Sites of Memory, Sites of Mourning: The Great War in European Cultural Memory' (Cambridge University Press, 1995) cited in Margaret Kelleher 'Hunger and History: Monuments to the Great Irish Famine' Textual Practice 16(2), 2002, pp.249-276

Celtic and charity

FRANK O'HAGAN

Low lie the Fields of Athenry
Where once we watched the small free birds fly
Our love was on a wing
We had dreams and songs to sing
Now it's lonely round the fields of Athenry.[1]

From Old French 'charite', from Latin 'caritas' meaning affection or love, charity is the giving of help, money or food to those in need. A charity is an institution or organisation set up to provide help, money or food to those in need. The roots and original rationale, mission and raison d'etre of Celtic Football Club are inextricably linked to the concept of charity. Famously, the club was founded by Brother Walfrid, a Marist Brother.

The Society of Mary, known as 'the Marists' came to Glasgow in 1858 and made a formidable contribution to the education of poor Irish Catholic children in the East End of the city.[2] Their religious dynamism allowed the Marist Brothers to dedicate much of their lives to the community they helped to build and subsequently serve. They attracted adult learners to night classes and lending libraries were organised under the Parish Young Men's Society, supplemented by brass band groups and drama societies. For such work much help was given, both practical and financial, from the philanthropic bodies, notably the Association of St Margaret, established in 1848

Notes

1 From 'The Fields of Athenry' Pete St John

2 See J E Handley 'History of St Mungo's Academy' John Aitken & Sons, Paisley, 1958 pp.80-83

93

Taking Celtic to Zambia.
Celtic supporters from Belfast
working with orphans and victims of
famine

to raise and distribute funds to poor parishes, to pay for seminary education and schools and unite the various classes in one cohesive Catholic body.[3] This highlights the importance of the role of the Marists in combating secularisation and developing a sense of community and achievement in Glasgow. It also demonstrates and exemplifies not a withdrawal and a siege mentality but rather a genuine attempt to equip Catholics to go out and succeed in the world. The Marists sought the amelioration of society through participation. Their approach was essentially pragmatic.

The Night Schools served not only educational purposes. They were also social centres for immigrant Irish groups in the city. Clearly, the mission of the Marist Brothers in Glasgow had a much wider impact than merely on education. However, in the post-1872 era, when education had become compulsory for five to thirteen year olds, grants alone could not keep Catholic schools functioning and the Marist brothers continued to exploit various fundraising ideas. Indicative of a commitment which went beyond the specifically educational area, creating Celtic Football Club demonstrates the concern the Marists showed for the welfare of their pupils and is also a prime example of the Victorian self-help activities of the period.

The inspiration of forming a football team for charitable purposes was in keeping with the ethos of the Marists and would appear to contrast markedly with the contemporaneous self-help philosophy typified by Samuel Smiles and its distorted Christian ethic. The Victorian philanthropy of Smiles referred to concepts of deserving and undeserving poor.[4] The Marist interpretation of Christian welfare was that they would never give up on anyone and this would be characterised by a belief in the dignity of all human beings and the rejection of the concept of an undeserving poor. It was also strongly based on community effort as opposed to being individualistic. The Marists were concerned not only with the preservation of

> The Marist interpretation of Christian welfare was that they would never give up on anyone and this would be characterised by a belief in the dignity of all human beings

3 See B Aspinwall 'The Scottish Dimension: Robert Monteith and the Origins of Modern Catholic Social Thought' Downside Review, 97, 1979, pp.46-48; and David Urquhart 'Robert Monteith and the Catholic Church: A Search for Justice and Peace' Innes Review, 31, 1980 pp.57-70

4 See Jarvis, Adrian 'Samuel Smiles and the construction of Victorian values' Sutton, 1997

the Catholic faith but also with providing children with the motivation to go out into the world and succeed, not to withdraw from it.

Money was needed to achieve their objectives and the Marists charged reasonable fees for those whose parents could afford them. However, the amount realised by the fees was too small to pay for the running costs of the schools and sources of finance were expanded by fundraising events such as concerts, exhibitions, trips, prizegiving nights and later, of course, football matches. A fundraising idea which met with considerable success and was a very obvious indicator of commitment to the poor was the 'Penny Dinner' scheme started in 1885 by Brother Dorotheus, the Marist headmaster of St Mary's, Abercromby Street.[5] Brother Dorotheus had referred to money received from a friendly football match organised by Brother Walfrid in 1886 between the Edinburgh Hibernians and St Peter's, Partick, and another one in the Spring of 1887 between Hibernians and Clyde which raised £50 for the scheme.[6]

Born in 1840 in the village of Ballymote, in County Sligo Ireland, Andrew Kerins took the religious name Brother Walfrid when he joined the Marist order in 1864. He spent a long useful life working in more than one part of the British Province of the Marist Brothers, but he was chiefly associated with the East End of Glasgow, where for a quarter of a century he was an outstanding figure. He taught in St Mary's, Abercromby Street, and later became headmaster of the newly opened Sacred Heart school in 1874 when the new parish of Sacred Heart was carved out of St Mary's. In his own sphere of action he gave much assistance to Father Noonan whose task it was to build the new parish.

During the 1870s and 1880s, the working people of Scotland had become so fascinated by the new spectacular phenomenon of soccer that they were prepared to pay for the excitement of watching exponents of the sport at play.[7] This coincided with the fact that working men in

5 The penny was the obligatory charge for the meal for those children whose parents were reluctant to accept charity. Premises near the school were hired as a kitchen and then were moved to a blacksmith's shop in the school yard where soon it was providing a thousand dinners per week. See Handley, 1968 'A History of the Province of the British Isles' Unpublished Manuscript p.43

6 Handley J E, 1968 'A History of the Province of the British Isles' Unpublished Manuscript p.43

7 Handley J.E, 1960 'The Celtic Story: A history of the Celtic Football Club' p.13

Scotland had newly-acquired leisure time. Whereas in the 1850s, most employees worked over sixty hours a week, by the early 1870s this had been reduced to a standard fifty-four hour week, with a Saturday afternoon off.[8]

Brother Walfrid was obviously aware of the enthusiasm for football among the working-class. He noted the success of the Edinburgh Irish Catholic club, Hibernian, in winning the Scottish Cup in 1887, and so decided it was time Glasgow had its own club with a similar identity. Since Glasgow had a larger Irish community than Edinburgh at the time, a similar club in Glasgow could surely raise considerable sums of money for charity? He was helped in his campaign by a coterie of hardworking Irish and Catholic businessmen who had emerged as leaders of their community.[9]

He had the enthusiastic support of the builder, John Glass, and with other Catholics they got together on 6th November 1887 to propose the formation of the Celtic Football and Athletic Club. In January 1888 they issued a circular calling for support for the newly founded club and over the next few months a horde of volunteers worked tirelessly to create a football ground and rudimentary spectator accommodation.[10]

The subscription list was headed by Archbishop Charles Eyre, the first Archbishop of Glasgow after the Restoration of the Hierarchy in 1878. Eyre, an Englishman, knew nothing about football but was always prepared to support any scheme that had for its object the welfare of the Catholic poor. The subscription list was a lengthy one, representative of Irish Catholic life in Glasgow at the time.[11] The establishment of Celtic Football Club provided an environment where many of the Irish and their offspring congregated and where there was a sense of security and expectation that was difficult to come by in other areas of life.[12] There was very obvious evidence of community building in the east end of Glasgow when Irish Catholics realised that an established football team in their community would be an excellent financial source

8 See Murray, B, 2000 'The Old Firm' p.31

9 Campbell, T. and Woods P, 1998 'Celtic Football Club 1887-1967' p.7

10 Murray, B, 2000 'The Old Firm' pp.12-13

11 Handley, J.E, 1960 'The Celtic Story: A history of the Celtic Football Club' p.15

12 Bradley J.M. 1995, p49

of free meals for poor school children. The objective behind the club's formation was explained by Brother Walfrid and a committee of fellow Catholics in the circular issued in January 1888:

> The main object of the club is to supply the East End conferences of the St Vincent de Paul Society with the funds for the maintenance of the 'dinner tables' of our needy children in the missions of St Mary's, Sacred Heart and St Michael's. Many cases of sheer poverty are left unaided through lack of means. It is therefore with this object that we have set afloat the 'Celtic'. [13]

Within a short period of the founding of the club considerable sums of money were being raised. The club provided the local branches of the St Vincent de Paul Society with tickets to sell for the various matches. Since the branches retained the money, an incentive was provided for the promoters and all concerned to sell as many tickets as possible. The result was that in the first full year of its existence, 1888, the club gave over £400 in charity as well as playing matches for charitable events in various parts of the country, the income for which was estimated at £150. [14] Its regular contribution was £20 a month to each of the children's 'dinner tables' of the three East End parishes. This finished, however, in 1893, when the coming of professionalism to football put an end to the service of charity and a company was formed to run the club and share the profits.

In 1892 Brother Walfrid was transferred to St Anne's, Spitalfields in the east end of London, Celtic Football Club was turned into a business by its directors and its original function lapsed. The penny dinner fund collapsed after 1892 but not without having helped the Catholic poor in the parishes of the East End for several years. [15] For a considerable period of time, the original charitable mission of the club was neglected insofar as the charitable work that was done was not officially publicised. Throughout the twentieth and into the twenty-first century Celtic has developed into a thriving professional football club and international business with a reputation and heritage

13 Maley, W. 1939 'The Story of the Celtic' p.14-15

14 Glasgow Observer 2/6/1888

15 Brother Walfrid continued his school charities in St Anne's, London, and in the spiritual interests of the parish he maintained a Boy's Club and a Young Men's Club. He retired from active work in 1906, died in Dumfries, 75 years of age on 17th April, 1915, and is interred in the Brothers' graveyard at Mount St Michael, Dumfries. See 'The Marist Family' Spring 1978 p.27

known throughout the world. During this period Celtic supporters have enthusiastically maintained the charitable ethos of Walfrid and Celtic's other founders. In the 1990s, however, the Club's management, whilst seeking to maximise Celtic's potential as a football club and business, re-emphasised Celtic's social dimension with a return to supporting charitable causes in line with the founding principles of the Club. In 1995, the 'Celtic Charity Fund' was formed with the aim of revitalising Celtic's charitable traditions. The stated aims of the Celtic Charity Fund are;

1. to raise funds and support specific areas of charity work selected each year by Celtic Football Club

2. to uphold and promote the charitable principles and heritage of Celtic Football Club [16]

Some of the principal areas that Celtic Charity Fund has identified to support are charities in support of children's needs and community action on drugs projects that develop and promote religious and ethnic harmony. Charities which have been supported by the Celtic Charity Fund since the mid-1990s include: Yorkhill Hospital, Northern Ireland Children's Events, Northern Ireland Children's Holiday Scheme, Scottish Asian Sports Association, Loaves & Fishes, Glasgow Simon Community, Parkhead Youth Project, Fairbridge in Scotland, and Glasgow Taxis Outing Fund for Sick Children. In this way, Celtic Football Club, at the beginning of the twenty-first century is true to its founder's vision and clearly recognises that it has a wider role in its responsibility of being a major social institution promoting health, well-being and social integration.

[16] The three subsidiary areas that Celtic Charity Fund has identified to support are: Supporting the homeless, helping the unemployed, supporting and research for projects aiding the afflictions of illness, famine and innocent families within the areas of war. See Celtic Charity Fund Information Pack for more information.

The Case for Brother Walfrid

MARK BURKE

We're carving out a monument for thousands forced to flee
From Famine and old Erin grá mo chroí
And down through all the years
We won't forget the tears
Of the hungry children forced to cross the sea.[1]

CARVING OUT A MONUMENT

Brother Walfrid

In January 2003, the Celtic Supporters Association in conjunction with the Affiliation of Registered Celtic Supporters Clubs, the Association of Irish Celtic Supporters Clubs, the North American Federation of Celtic Supporters Clubs and the Celtic Trust launched a venture to erect a monument in front of the main stand at Celtic Park. A monument funded entirely by contributions from ordinary Celtic supporters: a people's monument. A legacy to future generations reminding them (and us) who we are and where we have come from. A memorial in bronze, the story of Celtic encapsulated.

But what would constitute this monument? Who could be a Celtic icon, a model of something positive as well as something we could not only relate to, but something that represents a positive aspiration? Of whom could we erect a monument around which the support would rally unanimously? Whose image would most likely tell the story of Celtic? Whose image would make the milling thousands

Notes

1 From 'The Field of Dreams'
   Charlie Fealy

on future match days stop and ponder, would, in a moment of reflection, confirm our most innate feelings that this is a club apart, special, distinctive?

Jock Stein? The greatest Celtic manager ever. Billy McNeill? Celtic legend, captain of the Lisbon Lions, the first Celtic (and northern European) player to lift the European Cup. Willie Maley? Servant to Celtic as a player and manager for fifty-two years. John Thomson? The prince of goalkeepers who died tragically in his prime tending goal for Celtic. Jimmy McGrory? Charlie Tully? Robert Kelly? Celtic legends all. All worthy. Who would it be?

The decision once arrived at was obvious and in deference to the esteemed assemblage mentioned, the choice of the combined supporters groups would have no footballing pedigree as such. Indeed, he most likely had no cognisance of the nuances of Association Football, no appreciation of the 4-4-2 or 3-5-2, no understanding of tactics or total football. He saw football as more than mere sport. Football was a vehicle for something else, something special.

The person whom supporters would identify as the definitive icon of Celtic, the person whose image would be cast in bronze for eternity at the gates of Paradise would be Andrew Kerins. Obscure when referred to by his birth name, but eminent to Celtic supporters under his vocational title, Brother Walfrid.

IRISH & CATHOLIC

Amongst the abundant works that have been published on the history and origins of Celtic Football Club, it is a curious yet consistent trait that apart from the opening chapters the dominant characters are generally recorded as being notable by their contribution to the sporting aspect of Celtic FC. In this sense, one history of Celtic Football Club has been fashioned by the exploits of its players, its managers and to a lesser extent, its directors.

However, that history of Celtic FC does not capture the essence of Celtic FC. The essence of Celtic, the quint-essential spirit fashioned at its inception, was forged by motives that were cultural, political and religious.

Celtic FC was established in circumstances that have a less obvious sporting context. The principal figures in the formation of the club were clergy, joiners, tailors, publicans, grocers and restaurateurs. Their context was political and religious. All were Irish. All were Catholic. All were agitators for independence in their homeland through participation in the Young Ireland Society, the Irish National League and the United Irish League, and defenders of their faith by way of the League of the Cross and the Total Abstinence Society.

TAKING THE SOUP

Life in the heavily industrialised British cities of the late nineteenth century was grim for working people. It was grimmer for the poor and unemployed and infinitely worse for the poor and unemployed Catholic Irish in Protestant Scotland. The Great Famine of 1845-51 and the decade afterwards banished over half of Ireland's eight million inhabitants to death or exile. The poorest of the exiles, natives of counties like Mayo, Sligo, Leitrim, counties in the Irish midlands and, in particular from those of the province of Ulster, fled to Scotland. However, there was to be no refuge in Scotland for these Catholic migrants. Subsequent to the Reformation, Scotland had been ferociously extricated of all vestiges of 'Popery' and was firmly established as the citadel of fundamentalist Protestant doctrine. The characteristic of anti-Catholicism seemed to dominate in the land of John Knox. It was into this hostile, intolerant, indeed sectarian environment, that Andrew Kerins, a native of Ballymote, Co. Sligo, was commissioned by the Marist Order to take charge in the role of headmaster of the Sacred Heart School in the Calton district in the east end quarter of Glasgow in 1874.

Walfrid despaired at the utter poverty of his flock.

Indeed, it must have reminded him of Famine times in Ireland. His flock hardly seemed to have improved on those dreadful conditions. The flood of immigrants continued unabated until the first decades of the twentieth century and the growing population of impoverished Irish exhausted the Poor Children's Dinner Table and the soup kitchens Walfrid oversaw with the help of the St Vincent de Paul Society.

Some amongst the Protestant establishment who perceived an opportunity to thwart the spread of the Catholic threat opened soup kitchens to the swelling throng of starving Irish. A hot meal would be provided upon the simple act of renouncing their faith. Desperate and famished, many felt they were left with little choice but to 'take the soup'.

> Celtic FC was established in circumstances that have a less obvious sporting context. All principal figures in the formation of the club were Irish. All were Catholic. All were agitators for independence in their homeland

To alleviate the poverty in his parish and to ensure his flock remained within the embrace of the Catholic faith, Walfrid sought increased funding for his kitchens. A born organiser, he had energetically formed athletic clubs for young Catholic men as a means to provide recreation through sport. Providence moved in his favour with the emergence of football as the favoured sport of working class men in the late nineteenth century. As both a participant and spectator sport, football was thriving. Football clubs were springing to life all over Britain with rules being drawn up and leagues formed.

In February 1887, the Edinburgh Hibernians travelled to Glasgow to play Dumbarton for the Scottish Cup. Hibernian, one of a number of Irish Catholic football teams in Scotland, drew strong support from the Irish community in Glasgow. The victorious Hibernian team and officials were waylaid from their return to Edinburgh by way of a celebration reception in St Mary's Hall in Calton. The Hibernian secretary John McFadden intoxicated with generous refreshments provided by his hosts and the success of his team gave a rousing toast to the assembled throng extolling them to follow the example of Hibernian by forming a similar club for 'Irishmen' in Glasgow.

Listening attentively amongst the gathering was Brother Walfrid. The words resonated with purpose in his mind, giving him the vision of a solution to his dilemma. A football club to further his objectives to provide athletic activity for Catholic youth, a focus through which the Irish community would rally. The receipts from games would fund his soup kitchens.

In the moment that the challenge of John McFadden touched Walfrid, Celtic was born. In that moment an institution was born: an institution that would eventually touch the Irish diaspora all over the world, far beyond the vision of Walfrid. In that moment, Walfrid stamped his mark on the destiny of Celtic Football Club: on its name, its ethos, its identity and its heritage. On Sunday 6th November 1887, at a meeting convened in St Mary's Hall, the new club, Celtic, was formally constituted. The Celtic Football & Athletic Club, forged from famine, founded in charity and shaped by Irish and Catholic identities.

And what of the Charity?

The incorporation of the Celtic Football and Athletic Club as a limited company in 1892 was preceded by the transfer of Walfrid to London. Without his guiding influence, the charitable origins of the club were gradually discarded by the directors. In time, the club's Irish identity would too be downplayed by club officials possibly as a reaction to the perceived sectarian environment that the club found itself operating within. However, to the supporters, Irish identity and the cause of charity have remained primary tenets, principles that set them apart as a club and a people. Amongst the support, Walfrid's and his fellow Irish Catholic's legacy lives on.

Over a century after Walfrid purposefully founded our institution, monumental social, political and economic changes have ensured that he would find his parish unrecognisable today. The appalling poverty and hardship of his times have been greatly alleviated (though not eradicated). Undoubtedly his impression of twenty-first century Glasgow would leave him disorientated, but he would find something familiar and recognisable. What is certainly true is that Brother Walfrid could relate to the supporters and the supporters could relate to him.

Despite the colossal transformation very little of the essence of the football club he gave birth to has changed for the people who continue to support it. The Glasgow Irish football club Walfrid brought to life in 1887/88 lives on amongst its supporters. The visual image, the paraphernalia that constitutes the favoured colours, symbols, icons and music of the modern Celtic support, despite many attempts to change them, remains Irish. The colours and symbols are distinctly Irish. The songs are unmistakeably Irish. The gathering of the Celtic support today is an outpouring of pride and joy; a leitmotif of who we are and where we have come from; a tribute to the generations who came before us; a tribute to the vision of the man who created Celtic. A football club, an identity, a people, unique, inimitable. An identity as relevant today and in the future, as it was in the past.

Over one hundred years after the founding of our great club and since he departed Glasgow and Celtic, the spirit of Walfrid has been maintained at the Club by the supporters. The presence of his statue at Celtic Park confirms to future generations of Celtic supporters, the essence of the club. From whence and whom emanated the Club's Irish and Catholic essence and, the cause of charity. These are matters relevant, important and without which our club would just be like any other club. They constitute the explanation, the reasons for our faithful support. The gentle old Irish cleric, standing at the gates of Paradise, behoving of all who pass his monument to consider, his rationale, his meaning and his legacy.

DIASPORA

Not a fan. I don't go.
I don't like football.
But!

DES DILLON

My heart is in Ireland, that's where I long to be
Her hills and her valleys are calling out to me
Though born here in this land
My heart is in Ireland
The land of the old folk is calling out to me.[1]

When I was young I wasn't a football fan. And I wasn't Irish. First thing I remember about Celtic was the song my auntie Sadie used to sing to us: 'Celtic for ever Rangers in the river.' Celtic was us. Rangers was them. Whoever they were.

Next memory was Celtic winning the European Cup. I remember walking through Coatbridge as fat women on doorsteps listened to radios and relayed the score to the streets.

Or do I?

Because my mother says I'm havering. That we all watched it on telly. That we were dancing and singing. That I was over the moon. I don't remember. And I don't know where the fat women and radios comes from. One thing I can deduce is this: I remember many things from

Notes

1 From 'My Heart is in Ireland' Brian Warfield

childhood. Vividly. But I can't remember Celtic winning the European Cup. Football had little effect on me.

Next Celtic memory (and I do remember this) was getting a lift on one of the double-decker busses that used to leave Phil Cole's. Me and my cousins, Jim and Boone, who were fervent Celtic fans. They knew all the songs. All the players' names. They were good at football. Me? Always last off the wall. My name was – Okay, we'll take him then. A right duffer. I hated football. I can't tell you who Celtic played that day or what the score was. But I can tell you how terrified I was of the dookits lined along the disused railway at Stamford Street. Black and sinister. The squads of men marching towards Parkhead like people streaming into Mass. We passed gang names daubed on walls with gloss paint. Spur. Torch. Shamrock. What reverberates most was how the Glasgow accents terrified me. Why should pronunciation scare me?

Much later in life I realised that the language in Coatbridge is Irish English spoken with a Scottish accent. When they came from Ireland, the immigrants couldn't speak their Irish English. They wouldn't be understood. They couldn't speak Scottish English because – well – they couldn't, they weren't. So they had to speak a polite English. Plain English words embedded in Irish rhythms. Tug boats on turning streams. I had said to me once by a Glaswegian:

Aw aye, Coatbrig? That's a where they talk half n haulf an drink thon funny wine int it?

Yes. I mean Aye. Sure. Ye're right so ye are.

A small sample; quick example: In Easterhouse they say – doon the shoaps. In Coatbridge they say down the shops. Cross the border into Airdrie and it's doon the shoaps again. There, they even say stair when Coatbridge folk say ster, they say hair and in Coatbridge they say herr. Instead of film we say filim when we're talking about the movies.

Shoap – shop
Bowl – Bowel
Old – Oul (or El)
Cauld – Cowel
Soul – Sowel.

Add to this the ubiquitous end of sentence emphatic phrases: So I will. So I am. So it is. So it did. Etc.

These language differences allowed me to tell if the speaker was one of us. Or one of them.

Round about that time Feyenoord beat Celtic in, I think, the European Cup final. The ball went over the line and the Feyenoord keeper dragged it back. Everybody was ranting about it. Except me. I don't remember the score.

About that time, in my head, there were schisms popping up all over the place. I realised that along with praising Jesus, Our Lady, and the Chapel, you had to hold Ireland, or Erin, Or Erie, Or Home, Or Donny Gol, in high esteem. Those vague feelings of perplexity I can now describe with the clarity of adulthood. (I have in fact explored these in great depth in my novel The Big Q. It's not a plug by the way since it's out of print.)

St James' Primary School. 1971. Anyone in their early forties might remember Singing Together. A posh BBC accent welcomed us to Singing Together over the school tannoy.

Today children, we are going to sing Rule Britannia.

I wonder if our teachers are aware now that their job then was to wash that Irishness right out of our skin? To homogenise the children of the children of immigrants? Do they feel guilty? Or were they driven by utilitarian motives similar to this: instead of calling me Patrick Dillon, (my father's name) my mother and father, to shield me from discrimination, called me Derrick.

Anyway, we were singing Rule Britannia and I was a true patriot. We'd never be slaves. Never! Ever! Ever! The

> I wonder if our teachers are aware now that their job then was to wash that Irishness right out of our skin? To homogenise the children of the children of immigrants?

whole class was singing. It was good to be British. Ruling the waves. At playtime a group of boys were saying that we were Scottish. We should be singing Scotland the Brave, not Rule Britannia. We all sang Scotland the Brave in the playground. It was good to be Scottish. Who wants to rule the waves and never be slaves when you can be land of the purple heather?

I was British in the morning, Scottish all afternoon. But on Sunday I was at mass.

> Hail glorious Saint Patrick
> Dear saint of our isle
> On us thy dear children
> Bestow a great smile
> On Erin's green valleys
> On Erin's green valleys. . .

We were asking St Patrick to shine his big smile on us. His children. On our isle. And where are we? On Erin's green valleys. That thought troubled me. The thin end of a wedge which would be driven home in my early twenties with an almighty crack. One minute I'd be Scottish; next I'd be Born Again Irish.

The next time Celtic came into my life I was a teenager and drinking that funny wine behind the Woodside Bar. Everybody was singing Celtic and Rebel songs. I wouldn't join in so this fat drunk tried to force me. I said I wasn't a football fan and anyway I was Scottish. So he can get his self tae f...

One black eye, two cops and a night in the cells later I was more Scottish than ever. Lifted because some madman thinks he's Irish.

I've been called Irish twice in my life. The first time I was sixteen. I had got a job, ironically, in Bridgeton Cross. Working for a company that fixed fruit machines, jukeboxes and pool tables. My mother, thinking she was protecting me from the arrow that flies by day, pinned a wee Scared Heart lapel badge on my jacket. I was sent for the rolls at dinner time. On Landressy Street a massive guy picked me up off the ground, held me against the wall with one hand and plucked the Sacred Heart out like a weed. He flicked it away.

Ye're lucky ye're so young or ye'd be dead ya fuckin Mick.

Wh. . . what's a Mick?

His mates laughed.

An Irish bastard, he said.

He let me fall to the ground. I got the rolls and went back to work crying. From then on, when I went for the rolls, I carried a hammer in my jacket.

When I was twenty-three I went to the Rapid Vienna game in Manchester. Celtic had beaten Rapid Vienna but one of their players had been struck by a coin. . . supposedly. . . not! A replay was ordered. The whole of Coatbridge was going (like it did for Seville in 2003). It was a bit like Dunkirk. Anybody with a car was drafted in to ferry supporters. I had Sholts, Bonzo, Kesh, our Stevie and two guys from Carfin in my fruit machine van. And a massive carry out. I was driving so I decided not to open my Buckfast until Carlisle. But they were drunk by Lesmahagow, singing and kicking the sides of the van by way of percussion. By Carlisle I was drunk too. But here's the thing: I couldn't join in. The songs were daft. I felt self conscious and childish. Especially:

'C-E-L-T-I-C Celtic I-C Celtic on the ball'.

Inside Old Trafford, of the sixty thousand supporters there, I was the one not singing. There must have been an atmosphere but it didn't affect me. I couldn't wait to get home. Celtic got beat one nil. That's the last time I was at a game.

In the early eighties I found myself at uni studying English. I didn't identify with any of the Scottish Literature. Less so with English. I felt alienated and incapable. I was telling this to someone who must've been a linguistic psychotherapist (if there is such a thing). They prescribed me 'Juno and the Paycock' by the Dublin playwright Sean O' Casey.

I had a literary awakening. There on the pages was the language we spoke in our Coatbridge living rooms. Words and phrases that tripped daily off our tongue had made it into the world of literature. Maybe I had protested too much about not being Irish. Maybe I had repressed it? Maybe if I had been called Patrick discrimination would've forced me to wake up earlier. But in an almighty flash I realised just how Irish my upbringing was. The meandering crack of the characters, the bawdy retorts of the women, the devil-may-care attitude to life and death. To the BIG THINGS. The ordinary chat about extraordinary political events and the extraordinariness of everyday events. The use of simple words to convey complex and profound philosophical thoughts.

What are the stars?

I was trying to be a writer knocking at the doors of Scottish Literature. I now knew where my literary path lay. I was chapping on the wrong door. In the wrong streets. I had to represent that different language, value system and thought structure of the immigrant Irish. I had a culture of my own. It was a great day! I don't know what Celtic were doing at the time. Nor since. But my mother tells me there's a guy called Larsson who's been playing for them in recent years. And she loves the way he sticks his tongue out and runs when he scores. Me? I couldn't give two. . . I'm still not a football fan.

But I think I might be Irish.

The Scottish-born Irish and Celtic

Joseph McAleer & Brendan Sweeney

In the city of Chicago
As the evening shadow falls
There are people dreaming
Of the hills of Donegal.[1]

Our stories are common to many Celtic supporters. Despite this common element, ironically, in that context, they find uniqueness. They help explain the phenomenon that is Celtic Football Club. Our stories have become unique in a Scottish context because they have given rise to the existence and success of the one football club in Scotland and Britain that can be considered Irish. Our stories are rarely accounted for, rarely listened to and rarely comprehended. If Scotland is to be a truly appreciative multicultural country then our side of the story requires to be told. Our difference with the majority of people in Scotland should not be a matter for conflict. We have no animosity against indigenous Scots because we hold a range of different identities. We loathe and abhor 'sectarianism', a scourge in Scottish society. We equally detest racism – as Irish, we have been the victims of it for so long. We are Catholic and practice it to the best of our abilities. We are Scots-born Irishmen. We are of the working class. We are Celtic supporters. We support the Republic of Ireland in international football. This is a small part of our story.

Notes

1 From 'The City of Chicago' written by Barry Moore (aka Luka Bloom) and made famous by his brother Christy Moore

Jimmy Delaney

JOSEPH

I was born in Scotland in the city of Glasgow on the 8th day of March 1963. Life has had its ups and downs but I have been lucky enough to be happy most of the time, thank God. I was born in the house where I lived most of my young life (up to the age of twenty-four) at 80 Royston Road. I am the middle brother of three. Patrick is the older by two years whereas Martin is three years younger than me. My father, Peter, was also born in Glasgow. My mother, Winifred, hails from Donegal. Although four of the five of our immediate family were born in Scotland, for my family and me, birthplace is where our Scottishness began and ended.

My father's father also Joseph, was a native of County Tyrone in what we have always considered to be the British occupied part of Ireland. My grandmother Bridget, came from County Derry, also in Ulster, and, with my mother's side from Donegal, we most definitely have our roots as Ulstermen, something we were brought up to be proud of.

Though born in Glasgow, like many Irish families we settled in the Garngad area in the east of the city, just a few miles from Celtic Park. When asked about Irish areas in the city and beyond most people would think of the Gorbals or Govanhill or Coatbridge on the outskirts of Glasgow. For me there was nowhere like the Garngad. Most people in Garngad are of Irish descent and the vast majority have been Roman Catholic. Garngad has long had various nicknames, 'The Garden Of God' which many people on 'The Road' would say was a direct Irish translation of Garngad. The '33rd County of Ireland' was a common shout in the pubs in the Garngad every weekend (although I know that in some other areas like Coatbridge this term is not uncommon either). 'Little Ireland' and 'the good and the bad'. The latter being a reference to the fact that a lot of people frowned on the mention of Garngad, as we were not just Irish we were the 'fightin Irish'. Importantly too, we were amongst the poorest sections of Scottish society. Deprived of many things material but never of the love, emotion and friendship that comes from close families, a strong community and a heritage in Ireland. Finally, we had and indeed, we still have, Celtic Football Club. All of the things to do with family, community, my faith, being the offspring of Irish immigrants and Ireland itself – for me, they come together in Celtic. That's what makes Celtic what it is: special and unique.

> Deprived of many things material but never of the love, emotion and friendship that comes from close families, a strong community and a heritage in Ireland.

BRENDAN

Derry docks in 1945 was no place for a nine year old in charge of his younger brother. World War II had just finished and Europe was in turmoil. Nonetheless, for the young Donegal boys, Tommy and John Sweeney, there were more pressing thoughts on their minds like getting a roof over their heads as they were put aboard the Derry-Glasgow slow boat destined for a strange land and a very uncertain future. Since their mother died they had spent the last few years in an orphanage in Derry as their father struggled to bring up the family of nine on his own. A new life beckoned in Scotland and as they clambered onboard the cattle ship, little did they know it would be many a year before they set foot in their homeland again.

It's a very familiar tale and one that can be recounted over and over in many homes amongst Irish diaspora worldwide. Emigration is a word synonymous with the Irish and therefore it is no surprise that those claiming to come from an Irish background in many parts of America alone number more than the population of the homeland itself. Emigration is part of our psyche. It's a part of our identity.

For Tommy and John there was a welcome at the Broomielaw Docks Glasgow, as their new stepmum embraced them like her own and gave them a good home in Clydebank, or 'Claybanks' as they told everyone on the boat in their childish exuberance. The connection between Clydebank and Donegal was well established over previous decades and the young brothers soon settled amongst their own.

Ironically, if Tommy and John had travelled west instead of east they would have become part of the massive Irish contingent in cities like New York or Boston. They would grow up to become proud Irish Americans and they would be able to celebrate their Irishness every year in the Saint Patrick's Day Parades which is one of the biggest days in the American calendar. Unfortunately as they soon discovered, the west of Scotland was not the land of the free and it was more advisable for the minority Irish to keep their heads down rather than wear their hearts on their sleeve. Irish Scots, Clydebank Irish, Glasgow Irish, Port Glasgow Irish, Dumbarton Irish, Coatbridge Irish, Carfin Irish, Glenboig Irish? Despite the massive influx over the years, curiously these terms don't even seem to exist except in the very private spaces within our hearts. Might this say something about the environment experienced by the Irish in Scotland?

Over the years Tommy integrated well and married a Donegal lass who had taken the same route as himself and, together, they brought up four children, never to forget where they came from. Every year they would look forward to the highlight of the year, the summer holidays spent back home in Donegal, which would play a major part in instilling that special feeling in many of us, that special pride in our Irish roots.

Closer to home in our adopted land, Celtic Football Club is and has been since 1887/88 the main focus for those of an Irish background in the west of Scotland. A Club formed to feed hungry Irish Catholics in the east end of Glasgow is one we could relate to and is a story of humble beginnings and of overcoming the odds to strive for the best. It's our story. The inextricable link between Celtic and Ireland was born, a link that can never be broken. Celtic FC to many of us is the embodiment of the story of the Irish in Scotland, a link between our past and our present.

Therefore a question often thrown at us by other club's supporters in Scotland and in the media is 'why do many Celtic fans support the Irish national football team?' Maybe the question should really be why shouldn't many Celtic fans support the Irish national football team? In the sporting arena quite simply many of us support 'The Bhoys in Green' because we consider ourselves Irish, or at the very least, Irish-Scots. Over the years first, second and third generation Irish have become a valuable and integral part of Scottish life whilst at the same time retaining a strong affinity with our land of origin. It's this most natural of feelings which cannot be accepted by some who see any outpouring whatsoever of Irishness as unacceptable. For me, this is the institutionalised bigotry in Scotland in its worse form. To many, the Irish are an easy and acceptable target and in such eyes proclaiming our Irishness makes us the bigots. Few would dare to have a go at the Indian population in Glasgow for supporting their homeland's cricket team because that would be seen as racist. In a related sense the celebrations and occasional cavalcades of cars around George Square in Glasgow city centre when Italy's teams met with successes in the World Cup in the 1990s did not seem to attract any opprobrium.

As Irish-Scots our identity is unique. We aren't Irish Americans or Irish Australians or even the Irish in Ireland. We're part of the Irish diaspora. We're Irish, Scots-born Irish: the Irish of Chapelhall, Govanhill, Clelland and beyond. To many, supporting Celtic is an expression of our identity and this is the reason why we express it so passionately. Supporting the Irish national side can also be a reflection of this identity, culture and heritage. We seem conditioned in this country to feel guilty about our feelings for 'the oul country' but why should this be? We are non-sectarian but we are fiercely proud of our Irish roots. These two things DO NOT go together despite some of the best efforts of our antagonists, particularly in the Scottish media, to equate one with the other and to label us so. Does anyone ever question the next generation of immigrant Scots in places like America, Canada and Australia or, why they retain affection to the Scotland football, rugby or shinty teams?

Perhaps the question should not be why do many Celtic fans support the Irish national side but why in this land should anyone have a problem with such an affinity and expression?

Scottish-born, living in Canada and being Irish

James Rooney

Will you stand in the band like a true Irishman
And go to fight the forces of the crown?
Will you march with O'Neill to an Irish battlefield?
For tonight we're going to free old Wexford town.[1]

My wife thinks I'm crazy, my children are starting to live it and one of the main influences in my life as to why I am 'Celtic Minded', my father, also thinks I am a little off the wall. Why can't I be just like him, someone who imagines he is a Canadian, doesn't even look for 'the' results anymore and now follows 'baseball'?

Me? Wee 'Bhoy' from Clydebank who would have thought? I live in Canada with my Dublin-born wife and three children, James, Ailish and Iain. I wonder if you can guess my heritage. I have been in Canada since the early 1980s and still as ever football daft and, to use the phrase that isn't politically correct, 'Celtic Minded'. You can take a Bhoy away from Celtic but you can't take Celtic away from the Bhoy.

One of my earliest memories in life is from my two great uncles dressing me up as a soldier and marching me around the couch singing 'We're off to Dublin in the Green'. Me of course, thinking nothing of it but then being told I couldn't sing that very same song when I was with

Notes

1 From 'Irish Soldier Laddie' by Paddy McGuigan, a song about the rising in County Wexford during the 1798 Rebellion against British rule in Ireland. This song has been sung by Celtic supporters since at least the 1970s while other songs about this period in Irish history have been sung for generations by the Irish diasporic community in Scotland.

certain other family members. So began the 'separation', the feeling of not belonging, the belief that somehow, 'we' were wrong, 'they' were right. A mentality that is forced upon us by being part of what's called west of Scotland society.

There was tension in my family right from the start of course. You see, I come from a 'mixed marriage'. But even though my father converted to Catholicism, the reason was love of my mother and not faith. I grew up in an atmosphere where arguing over religion was common-place. Although many of these marriages probably work well – whatever that may mean – I know of other 'mixed' marriages that have been the same as my own experience and where eventually ethnic and religious distinctiveness became a problem.

Being 'Celtic Minded' elicits many thoughts and many different feelings. A good way for me to describe it in this part of the world (North America) would be to put 'us' in the category of 'Irish', or 'Irish-Scots' as some might say. Just as there are Italian-Canadians or Portuguese-Canadians, the only difference is they are not required to lose their identity or culture in foreign parts, something I believe is forced upon the Irish in Scotland.

Irishness is not a disease or a passing fad. It's not something to be packaged up and sold back to us as something from our weird and wonderful past. For many, it is a way of life. It reaches into the deepest part of our soul. It makes us who we are. It plays a big part in the way we think and the way we act. It allows us to be the people we want to be.

My Irish-born wife winds me up. She calls me a 'wanna be' because of my knowledge of Ireland and the music with which I associate my heritage, a heritage I try and to some extent she tries, to instill in our children. Of course, for some people in Ireland that might make me a 'Plastic Paddy'. I often wonder if James Connolly, Tom Clarke and James Larkin might be considered 'Plastic Paddys?: all

British-born but Irishmen nonetheless. Their status as leaders of the 1916 Easter Uprising and as great socialist thinkers and leaders of their time hardly makes them 'Scots' or 'British'. What about Ray Houghton and his goals against England in 1988 and Italy in 1990? Glasgow-born but Irish surely? Ireland claims them as its own. We also claim them as Irish. Neither Scotland nor Britain has much of a shout there. They are of course members of the Irish diaspora, just like me.

In Canada we can wear the colours we want to wear and we can sing the songs we want to sing. Here, we do not have people labelling or condemning us because of our history, our political views, our faith, our culture or our identity. For that I am grateful to Canada. Here, it is called a multicultural society – not a melting pot, that has different connotations. We have Italian communities, Greek communities, Portuguese communities and Chinese communities. And of course, our Irish and Irish-Scottish communities.

> Irishness is not a disease or a passing fad. It's not something to be packaged up and sold back to us. It reaches into the deepest part of our soul. It makes us who we are.

Generally speaking, in Canada you can openly celebrate your ethnicity and do so in many walks of life – something I believe we, as Irish immigrants, are not allowed to do in our country of birth. You know the language. We are called bigots and sectarian. We are labelled Papists and Fenians. We are supporters of terrorists. How wrong people can be? We are judged through ignorance and I believe part of it is our own fault. Maybe one of the things that can change Scotland for the better is for the rest of the world to realise how backward a country Scotland can be. Maybe the furore over James MacMillan's 1999 Edinburgh speech and that of the erection of the Carfin Famine monument in 2001 are two recent examples of some of Scotland's shame being flushed out? It's about time, thank God.

What is this thing they call 'Celtic Minded'. Are you born with it or can you be brought into its fold first as an outsider and then become a full member. Living in this part of the world I will tell you it's both. On the political side of things, in the Celtic family we are not all nationalists or republicans and we are not all taken by our Irish history. Many are republican though and many are versed in Irish history, some of the things that give us our heritage and identity in this era of globalisation. However, what can for sure be taken for granted, is that we all love the club of the Irish in Scotland – Celtic F.C.

When I came to Canada in the early 1980s the first thing I looked for was a football team where I could play or as most people would say, 'try to play'. I knew that I would find Scots, Irish and English people who were drawn to a similar social life as I had. My mission was complete sooner rather than later and before long I had found a Celtic Club to be part of: the now disbanded Toronto West Celtic Supporters Club. We used to meet every Saturday afternoon, watch tapes of Celtic matches, have a few beers and socialise, having the odd party night with a variety of entertainment.

Subsequently, I started to develop stronger relationships with fellow Tims and found myself a part of the greatest Celtic Supporters Club this side of the Mississippi, to steal a phrase. The 'Bramalea Celtic Supporters Club', founded in 1984. By the early years of the new century, it contained a three hundred plus strong membership. This twenty-years or so is the period of time when I have seen the Celtic family grow in North America.

Me, wee 'Bhoy' from Clydebank. Who would have thought? The reason for me bringing this up again is you have to picture this. In 2000 I am in the middle of a desert in Las Vegas. It's 100 degrees outside where there is cornered off, table settings for fifteen hundred people. All around me is green and white, ties, shirts, trousers, skirts, dresses, suits and shorts. The sun is setting and the 'Fields Of Athenry' is blaring from a sound system that can be heard for miles. I am standing in line with my wife. Who do I find myself having a conversation with? Bertie Auld, the famous Lisbon Lion. Who have I been mingling with and who calls me 'wee man'? The Lisbon

Lions and various other Celtic greats of course.

A year later, in my own CSC social club in Bramalea, hosts of the 2002 'North American Federation of Celtic Supporters Clubs' annual general meeting, on stage there is Fallon, Auld, Chalmers, Lennox, McBride, and McCluskey. Also, included is Mr Las Vegas himself Hugo Straney. From his sound system he is blasting 'You'll Never Walk Alone'. I am holding Pat McCluskey's hand as the club and its membership are linked together singing 'Walk On'. By then, the tears were pouring from my eyes.

Paul McStay

That day will be forever etched in my mind. During that fantastic week I was also playing golf with Pat, Joe and Bertie (see — now on a first name basis). I left our 'Convention Night Gala' and a number of these players shared my car. It was then that I thought to myself, 'wee Bhoy from Clydebank'? Who would have thought? Celtic players and the wee bhoy from Clydebank, 'together'? That's one of the things that makes us so special.

Would I have been able to do this in Scotland? Maybe? At the end of the day though, it is not the doing, it is the experience along with the feeling of belonging to something that is so powerful. That is most important for me. Academics can talk about displacement, hybridity and dislocation. This was it in action for me. This was my reality. A Scots-born Irishman being with his community's living legends. All because I follow a team and because of that team I have a family with members in all parts of the world. It is a family whose foundation is built on poverty and justice for all. Mainly Catholic and Irish, but, if they want to be 'Celtic minded' then, be they Protestant and Scottish or any other background, who cares? To celebrate, to feel part of this great experience to join us 'hand in hand'.

Yet still till this day in Scotland there are people who keep telling us we can't or we should not celebrate. Although Celtic and the Irish diaspora is part of Irish history, it is also a part of Scottish history. The way that Celtic has given our Irish Catholic immigrant community in Scotland pride and self-esteem in the late nineteenth and through the years of the twentieth century, Celtic has also helped me on yet another foreign shore. What a great institution Brother Walfrid founded.

At the Bramalea club, a young Canadian who has no Irish ties, except he married into a family with strong Celtic connections, said it best when he called it, 'a family with character and history'. He said he was made to feel welcome from his very first visit to the club and now considers himself to be 'Celtic Minded'. He is welcome. 'Cead Mile Failte'. Another member said it is like the Hollywood baseball movie called 'Field of Dreams'. In that film the subjects tried to recreate something of their past and heritage by building a playing field while saying 'build it and they will come'. The idea of old players coming back to play one last game is like an analogy of the Bramalea Club. One difference though, we have built it and they still come week-in and week-out to watch their beloved Celtic. James Rooney thanks Celtic for being Celtic and the support for being Celtic also. Other things are more important in life. However, Celtic is also important and I am unashamed in my identity in being 'Celtic Minded'.

FANDOM

Jimmy Johnstone

Living the dream

EDDIE TONER

> For some it's the horses I've no doubt,
> with others it's the whisky or the stout
> for some it's every pretty girl they see
> but it's always been the Celtic for me.[1]

This is part of a song sung by the Blarney Pilgrims. Now I am sure we all have our own particular vices when it comes to seeking enjoyment but that is a chorus with which I can quite easily identify because it really has always been the Celtic for me. So where did it all begin? Why Celtic?

I don't have to look that hard to find the answers. You see, like countless thousands of others, I was born into what can only be described as a Celtic family. I was born, bred and have lived all my life in Glasgow's east end, my great grandparents having settled there from Ireland at the turn of the nineteenth century. From a very early age Celtic was to play a big part in my life. In retrospect, the connections are easily identified. My family is part of the Irish community in Glasgow and we were all brought up in the Catholic faith. Supporting Celtic was an extension of being part of that community and seemed natural for us.

Celtic provided the focus for my family's weekend enjoyment but the allegiance to this great institution goes much deeper. As a very young child I can fondly recall the

Notes

1 From 'It's always been Celtic with me' Charlie Fealy

Saturday morning chaos in my Granny's house. My Gran and Grandad lived in Helenvale Street, about two hundred yards from Celtic Park. Due to its close proximity to the Stadium before every home game the house became a gathering point for what seemed like the entire family. My mother and father, brother and sisters, aunts, uncles, cousins and family friends, would all visit at various times. The topic of conversation was always that day's match and how well the team would play. My poor Granny worked tirelessly providing tea, soup, sandwiches and other refreshments for all.

My grandfather, who was the groundsman at Celtic Park, would have been down at the Park from early that morning but always returned home for his lunch before returning to finish his preparations and make sure the pitch was ready for the big game. I remember waiting eagerly for him to come home for his dinner as he could provide us with the most up-to-date news. Who was likely to play that day? Who was injured? Were there any new players? My granda was always first with the news and in the days before blanket television or radio coverage we felt privileged to be among the first to hear the news.

I also recall that on match days a large number of my relatives had worked at the Park in some capacity. Whether it was serving pies and Bovril from the stalls, working on the turnstiles, being a ballboy or sweeping the terraces after the game, we all had a role to play. I was always proud of the fact that my family were contributing to and playing a part in the ongoing success of Celtic. For many these may seem like trivial meaningless roles but for me, it gave me an insight into how the club operated and sowed the seed for what has become a lifetime association with Celtic. It also cemented the belief that Celtic was a club where we all had a role to play and that every role no matter how small was important. It was a family club with family values and most importantly, it was my family, my club.

Celtic was always the topic of conversation at the

family social gatherings. Whether it was a wedding, birthday, New Year or some other special occasion, there would always be the good old fashioned sing song to round it off. We all had our own songs to sing but 'The Celtic Song' along with great Irish favourites like 'Sean South of Garryowen' and 'Irish Soldier Laddie' seem to be sung with the most vigour, and it wasn't long until we as kids were well versed in the repertoire.

I was lucky that I was born at a time when the Bhoys were about to embark on the greatest period in the club's history. At that time I was a frequent visitor to the Park and used to love having the opportunity to take my pals down for an unofficial guided tour. We were able to get our hands on the Scottish Cup, the League winners trophy and others like the Coronation Cup. You could almost cut the feeling of pride with a knife. During these visits it was not uncommon to bump into the great Jock Stein, Billy McNeill or Jimmy Johnstone and others. There we were, a bunch of young tearaways who had cycled down from our home in Easterhouse, rubbing shoulders with the guys who helped make Celtic the greatest club in Europe. However, what struck me most about these great men was the fact that there was never any aloofness or self-importance about them. They never looked down on you and you were always treated with courtesy and made to feel every bit as important as them. You always felt a sense of togetherness and had a feeling that we were all part of one big family. I cannot help but feel that, in these days of mega rich superstars and multi-million pound contracts, this quality has been lost to the game and I often wonder if it will ever return. However, I digress!

It was during those golden days of the late sixties and early seventies that my love for Celtic took root. I often dreamed about having the opportunity to play in the green and white hoops, just once, and score the winner in a European Cup final! Therefore you can imagine my delight when I was given the opportunity to become a ball boy on match days. My father had told me that Jimmy

> There we were, a bunch of young tearaways who had cycled down from our home in Easterhouse, rubbing shoulders with the guys who helped make Celtic the greatest club in Europe.

Johnstone had started off as a ball boy so it was with great pride and anticipation that I ran out of he tunnel for the first time bedecked in my Celtic tracksuit dreaming of the days to come. Sadly for me, but perhaps fortunately for Celtic, any similarities between my own and Jinky's career path were to end there! Maybe it was because I was never really much of a player but it didn't stop me dreaming. However, I can always say that I led the team out onto the park in a Celtic versus Rangers game!

Although my career as an employee of Celtic came to an abrupt end I never stopped supporting the team and as soon as the opportunity presented itself I joined my first supporter's club and became a regular attendee at the home and away games. I have remained a supporter's club member to this day and probably always will be. It was while travelling to the many away games on the bus that I realised the importance of the fans to the club.

My travels have taken me all over Britain and Europe. The most alarming thing to strike me during these journeys was the contrast in the reception we received when travelling abroad to that which greeted us in Scotland. In Europe our fans are universally well received, we mix well with the locals who in turn seem happy to party with us. Football becomes the great celebration and spectacle it should be. Sadly, for me the same cannot be said closer to home when the reception more often than not is hostile. What is it with Celtic that the fans of other teams in Scotland find difficult to accept? Sure we are vociferous in our support for the Bhoys. We are also proud of our history and origins. We love to celebrate our culture, wave our flags and banners and sing our songs. But why should that be seen as a threat to anyone? It is not our intention to threaten, but merely to celebrate and rejoice in what we are and what we hold as valuable.

If a lifetime of supporting Celtic has taught me anything it would be the importance of being part of a family. Celtic has given me a sense of belonging, a sense of community. It has strengthened the bond in my own extended family and fostered a great sense of togetherness but on a larger scale it has made me feel part of something special, a feeling that I will never need to walk alone. This is a feeling that gives me an enormous sense of pride. One of the underpinning values I learned is that although we can be proud of who we are and where we come from, we should always show respect for others no matter their race, creed or colour. Is it too much to ask that that same respect be afforded to us? The Celtic family have undoubtedly enriched the world and I for one am proud to be part of it.

The Celtic phenomenon

Tom Grant

On alien soil like yourself I am here;
 I'll take root and flourish of that never fear,
And though I'll be crossed sore and oft by the foes
You'll find me as hardy as Thistle or Rose.
If model is needed on your pitch you will have it,
Let your play honour me and my friend Michael Davitt.[1]

The young Celtic supporter standing next to us on the platform at Brussels Midi station, looked like most other Celtic fans following their team: he was decked out in the club's colours, hoops and all. It wasn't until I asked him if he, like us, was heading for Zeebrugge for the ferry home that I noticed there was something a little different. This was Philippe, he was Belgian from Ghent, and was travelling on the same train as us, only as far as that. To me, the question was obvious, why Celtic?

Philippe explained that he had first really become aware of Celtic when the club played the local team in his hometown some years previous. He befriended some Celtic fans and now frequently met up with them to follow Celtic, even occasionally travelling to Dublin to meet up with his buddies. He went on to explain, that he didn't watch football in Belgium, he simply enjoyed being part of what, he described as, 'the Celtic phenomenon'. When Philippe left the train, my mate Mick, said to me very simply, 'That was brilliant, it's great being a Tim, isn't it?'

Notes

1 Anonymous poem in an Irish Catholic newspaper to welcome the laying of a sod of Shamrock by Irish patriot Michael Davitt at the new Celtic Park on 20th March 1892.

Celtic's first Board of Directors 1897

Although I agreed, Philippe's comments made me think about the nature of my own support for the club. I have supported Celtic since I was 10 years old, having previously been a Motherwell fan. I still have my scarf to remind me how uneducated you can be as a child. Why Motherwell?

I lived in Cardowan near Stepps just outside of Glasgow. My father was in the Merchant Navy. I was football daft and wanted to go to see football matches, but he was at sea for months on end. He had an uncle who watched Motherwell, so my mother would take me by bus, via Tollcross, to his house in Bothwell and, he would take me to Fir Park. All was well, until one day, Celtic came visiting.

I was in the queue for my usual pie and Bovril. 'Well scarf and all,' the man behind me asked, 'where do you come from son?' I replied that I came from Cardowan. He then asked, rather sardonically, 'what are doing supporting that team for then?' I responded, telling him that I had always supported Motherwell. But, his comment had provoked me to think deeper about this support. In retrospect and with some reflection, maybe the thinking part is one of the things that distinguishes Celtic FC? Celtic's history is so rich and awe-inspiring, going beyond the straightforward ninety minutes on the football pitch, it does make you think. I have long viewed the Celtic support as a socially conscious and politically aware group of people. Maybe this consciousness and awareness is one of the reasons why many people from this community got involved in politics (especially labour and socialist ones) wherever the Irish diaspora has settled, including Scotland?

When I returned home, my grandmother (my mother's mother) asked how the game had gone. I relayed the story to her. My grandmother, one Mary MacNamara, replied, stating that the man, 'God bless him', was dead right. Well, like all good grandmother's, Gran MacNamara had given me lots of advice and had guided me in other facets of life. From that day on, Celtic captured me. Various other uncles and family friends were given the task of educating me in the ways of Celtic. Future trips to Fir Park were subsequently made in the emerald and white of Celtic.

At that time I had no idea that my family had been associated with the Club almost since its foundation, certainly since it became a limited company. So, I discovered it had been my destiny to follow Celtic – actually a bit like most of those of Irish Catholic decent in the west of Scotland. My great-grandfather, James Grant, had been one of the club's first directors[2] and had built the Grant Stand in 1898, a double-decked timber structure, originally with windows that misted up with condensation. For all its faults it was a formidable structure for its day. My grandfather, who I am named after, was involved in the Irish War of Independence and spent the latter part of his life in Toronto, Canada, where he died and is buried. He never had the privilege of watching Celtic and I know very little about him, unfortunately. My own father was a

2 The first directors of the new company were; Michael Dunbar, John Glass, James Grant, James Kelly, John McKillop, John H McLaughlin and John O'Hara.

Chief Engineer with Cunard and could only attend games when on leave, if that coincided with the football season.

I started travelling to games with the Cardowan CSC in the 1960s with men such as Danny Brady, Hughie O'Neill and Danny Foran. The sixties and seventies were as good as it gets for Celtic people. Championships every year, Scottish Cup Finals as an annual day out, fourteen League Cup Finals in a row and winners, finalists and regular semi-finalists and quarter-finalists in the European Cup over such a long period of time. I wasn't allowed to go to Lisbon, I was too young I was told, but I did make it to Milan for the Final against Feyenoord, almost missing one of my Higher exams in the process.

> Celtic's history is so rich and awe-inspiring, going beyond the straightforward ninety minutes on the football pitch, it does make you think.

They were great times, enlightening times, it seemed that every season was a record breaker. History was being made in front of our eyes as each victory was won, each point gained. It was a lot to take in. I had never been abroad before that trip to Milan. I thought the world started and finished in Ireland and could only be reached by boat from the Broomielaw in Glasgow.

As a youngster, the seven weeks of my school holidays were always spent in Ireland. Although born in Scotland, my grandparents on my mother's side came from Westmeath and Dublin. My father was born in Toome-bridge, Co. Antrim. My mother's father, Timothy MacNamara, a steelworker, spent his evenings with an ear glued to Radio Athlone. Our whole life seemed to revolve around our trips 'back home' to see the family. There always seemed to be a bus strike in Dublin during the summer months. To this day I could lead a walking tour of Dublin, because my mother walked the legs off me visiting one cousin or another in that city. My constant visits to Ireland certainly made me aware and appreciative of the place that shaped my family and my community's history.

In a sense, Celtic extended our Irishness from beyond the island of Ireland to our adopted home in Glasgow.

When we came back to Scotland, it was back to see the Celtic for me, back to St Joseph's Chapel Social Club for my ma, the radio for my granda and back to being told by my gran that I really should have seen Charlie Tully. Well, I would have, wouldn't I, if my dad hadn't gone to sea.

As I got older, I became aware of a certain old aunt of my dad's. She lived in Toomebridge, Co. Antrim, where my dad was born. She had inherited shares in Celtic through the family and, amidst the Celtic fraternity, was often referred to as 'the old lady in Ireland who owned Celtic'. My dad took me to his hometown of Toomebridge on the banks of Lough Neagh. The house was at the end of a long tree-lined driveway and the Lough lapped gently right up to the back garden. When I met her, it was like taking a step back in time, she smoked almost non-stop and talked with a gentle lilt. Above the fireplace was a photograph of her favourite Celt, John Thompson. We just talked, got to know each other while we had 'a cup of tay in the hand', as you do in Ireland.

Some years later, when aunt Felicia died, she left half of the family shares to my dad and the other half to several of her nephews and nieces. I remember Bob Kelly, the Celtic chairman, at the time, actually tried to stop the share transfer. She had a lot of shares and he wanted them. Thankfully for me, he failed. When my father died in 1979 the shares passed to me, this time unchallenged. Almost immediately, Desmond White, a man I had a lot of respect for, knowing that I attended games home and away, asked if I would start coming to the boardroom on match days. I accepted and even started travelling on the team bus to away games.

It was dream and a privilege for a young Celtic supporter to actually be so close to the core of the club. Billy McNeill was manager and players like Danny McGrain and Roy Aitken graced the Hoops. One player, John Doyle, became a close friend: we both lived for Celtic and enjoyed being part of the Club. John was of course tragically killed in an electrical accident in early 1982 as he worked on his loft extension at his home in Kilmarnock. When, later that season, we won the league and the fans in the Jungle began to spontaneously sing 'we won the league for Doyle', that really pulled on the heart strings.

Before long, I realised that I had to do more at Celtic than just travel with the team. Having a fairly substantial shareholding meant that I had more shares than most of the Board members at the time. I felt that I could offer something new and pushed Desmond White to accept me as a club director. Eventually, he relented and, I joined the Board of Directors. Even had I known then what was to unfold for me personally, I would not change a thing.

Being a director was a special privilege, I have always realised that. I met some good people: Celtic fans, sponsors, directors of other clubs, Celtic staff, stewards, and all sorts of folk, many of whom remain friends. Ironically, despite future events, at that time the directors actually trusted each other to do what was best for Celtic. When other people later joined the Board, amongst other things, it was lack of trust that almost brought the Club to its knees just a few years later. That period in the Club's history is well documented.[3] Celtic seemed to go from one crisis meeting to the next, without interval. Phone conversations with Fergus McCann in Arizona, meetings with Dominic Keane and Jack Flanagan, and spending so much time at Celtic Park. I don't know how my wife Angela, put up with it? Well I do, really. She feels the same as I do about Celtic.

After the revolution, life at Celtic Park was never really the same again. As Stadium Director, I assisted the Project Management Team in the rebuilding of Celtic Park. We played at Hampden Park for a season whilst the old Paradise was dismantled to make way for the new. As each of the new Stands were erected, it was almost as if the Club took a new breath of air: although the Jungle was gone, so too was the old Board. Surely it could only get better? Thankfully, it did.

3 For example, see A Caldwell 'Sack The Board! Celtic the end of a dynasty' Mainstream Publishing, Edinburgh, 1994 and A Caldwell, 'The McCann Years: The Inside Story of Celtic's Revolution' Mainstream Publishing, Edinburgh, 1999

When we opened the new Celtic Park, it was the sign that our Club was back, strong and proud once again. I could imagine the pride those first committeemen and directors must have felt. All the fathers and mothers, uncles and aunts, all the grannies and grandfathers that brought all of us to see 'the Celtic'. All the players, throughout the seasons: Willie Maley, Jimmy Quinn, Patsy Gallacher, Johnny Thomson, Jimmy McGrory, Charlie Tully, Billy McNeill, Jimmy Johnstone and, Henrik Larsson.

Each and every one of the Celtic community carries the responsibility of preserving Celtic. The founding ideals, aspirations and identities of our club's first and subsequent generations of officials, players and supporters, are what make us special. Even though Irish and Catholic are the core identities of our club and its support, we are open to all who wish to enjoy and celebrate our successes, to work for us, to play for us as well as support us. What our club represents means so much. It's what makes us what we are. To be created to assist the poor of the city's east-end and become a unique symbol of our heritage and identity. As the Irish were scattered to the wind in Famine times and in the years thereafter, there was a blessing in disguise for those who came to Glasgow and the west of Scotland. Those Irishmen, who founded our Club, who played and supported it, did not realise they were also creating a symbol for the worldwide Irish diaspora. Today, people as far apart as New Jersey, New York, London, Birmingham, Sydney, Melbourne and Toronto join together, sometimes at the stadium, sometimes spiritually with people like Philippe in Belgium, all celebrating the Celtic phenomenon.

Why Celtic?

HEIKO SCHLESSELMANN

> Viva La Quince Brigada!
> 'No Paseran' the pledge that made them fight
> 'Adelante' was the cry around the hillside
> Let us all remember them tonight.[1]

Many friends, many other supporters of FC St Pauli Hamburg or, other German football clubs, have often asked why we, St Pauli's Celtic fans, have a strong affinity to Celtic Football Club and its supporters. Even Celtic supporters themselves have asked us why we, as non-Catholic-Germans, support Celtic? On the one hand the answer is easy but on the other, maybe not?

For us, Celtic supporters are special. They are unique in their good behaviour, in their general views, their political opinions and they appeal to us because they are tolerant towards other religions and lifestyles. They are proud of their Irish roots, their founding by Brother Walfrid, but also, they are not hostile to people who don't share their background. To explain what makes Celtic supporters so special to us at St Pauli, I have to consider our history of following Celtic as supporters from the German city of Hamburg.

By the end of the 1980s just over three thousand people were regularly attending St Pauli matches in the German first division. However, beyond football during

Notes

1 From 'Viva La Quince Brigada' Christy Moore

this period, housing was becoming a serious problem for many people in Hamburg. The poorer sections of society were being marginalised and exploited by local authorities and large companies. For the poor in Hamburg, their housing was amongst the worst in Germany. Conditions were archaic and poverty often characterised the area of St Pauli. Gradually, many of the people who inhabited these houses or who moved into them became more politicised. The left-wing tradition of the area seemed to become even more pronounced during this time. Although the roots of modern St Pauli are fairly recent, on the issues of poverty, the development of socialist ideas and opposing the establishment, through our experience we see ourselves linking with the roots and heritage of Celtic and its support.

In a football sense many clubs in Germany were followed by neo-fascists and this included Hamburg FC, the main local club. Neo-Nazis and fascists formed the core of the Hamburg support. Because of this, people with alternative views were being excluded from football as well as other areas of life. Gradually, people began to look to and collect around St Pauli and it was the fans themselves who created this alternative culture: one that opposed the fascism and racism of many other clubs in Germany and around Europe. Over the course of a few years, St Pauli began to attract crowds of 20,000 supporters to league games. We became a club of social and political resistance. We were in the German top division and people were coming to see St Pauli for the first time in large numbers. We had a degree of success and we had a political view and culture that opposed the hatred of fascism. We were alternative, left-wing and we brought our radical and challenging political views to the terraces.

The first non-hooligan/non-rightwing football fanzine (Millerntor Roar) was started by St Pauli fans: the struggle against the dominating influence of racism and fascism in football proceeded to make us known in other parts of Europe. Our football fans became so well-known in their opposition to racism and fascism that the St Pauli Fans against Rechts sticker sold more than two million times, thus demonstrating the degree of support our club has gained because of the stance of its fans. This has allowed us to link to Celtic fans. Gradually our stance and our beliefs clearly appealed to many Celtic supporters. A new fraternity was born.

In the early 1990s an invitation was received from London requesting one of our supporters speak to other football supporters in Britain who held similar views. At this meeting, the first contact was made with Celtic supporters. That first meeting turned out to be a long night and the special link between similar football-loving people was to begin here. Soon more and more St Pauli fans gradually became aware of the Celtic fan culture and they began to look towards Celtic supporters with some admiration. A special relationship began to flower. At games in Bern, Ekeren, Neuchatel, Lisbon, Cologne, Dortmund, Paris, Zurich, Lyon and other places, our fans increasingly mixed with Celtic supporters. This allowed a friendship between both parts of the supporters to develop and grow. But why Celtic? Why do we feel comfortable with Celtic and their supporters?

> On the issues of poverty, the development of socialist ideas and opposing the establishment, through our experience St Pauli fans see ourselves linking with the roots and heritage of Celtic and its support.

Besides being tolerant of other football supporters, the Celtic contribution to left-wing political ideas in football, especially amidst an often neo-conservative and fascist-nationalist football scene, was welcomed by St Pauli fans. We developed a fascination for the Celtic fan scene independent of the club's sporting success. Normally for supporters of a football team, the most important thing in their life is success, being top of the league and aspiring to be the most successful team. Although we all want this, Celtic fans also showed there was more at stake than simply winning. We believed they showed great pride in the very existence and the history of the club. There was something unique going on here. Even beyond our own expectations and natural political affinities.

During the unsuccessful times of the nineties,

including being second behind Rangers almost every season and leaving European competitions at embarrassingly early stages, the supporters always backed their club. They always seemed to remain focused on Celtic unlike many other fans that look only to the opposition to give them motivation. While applauding the hoops and hoping for a win, they still gave credit to better opponents. That impressed us at so many games and it taught us a lot. The positive behaviour of Celtic supporters in the streets, bars and cities of their European hosts was always particularly impressive. In a sense they seem to fight against the bad reputation of many other 'football fans'. Being rewarded as the best football supporters in 2003 for their behaviour in the UEFA-Cup-Final in Seville was no surprise to us, because this is the way they have been behaving for many years and it's one of the things that makes them so special to the fans of St Pauli.

For St Pauli fans, Celtic supporters stand out in their fight against injustice. This is despite what we see as attacks against the club and its support on the part of the Scottish media and other fans in Scotland who show little toleration of the views of Celtic supporters. Celtic's fans are a beacon amid what are often the foetid waters of sectarianism, racism and xenophobic nationalism in European football.

The Celtic fans we have met are frequently interested in other struggles around the globe. They are not selfish and their views often serve as a kind of internationalism, a holistic view that possibly connects with their religious faith. Many Celtic fans often seem well-educated about politics and the freedom and independence movements in Palestine, the Basque Country, Chiapas or South Africa. Celtic fans often seem to support them in a way that reflects their own support for the Irish self-determination struggle. They are knowledgeable football fans.

Another impressive thing is the worldwide fanbase of Celtic supporters. Through their Irish roots and identity there are Celtic supporters and Celtic Supporters Clubs in nearly every corner of the world. On a trip through South America I was in a village in Bolivia with 1500 inhabitants. There was an Irish pub and the owner was a Celtic Supporter. In Seville during the days of the UEFA Cup Final of 2003, we met Celtic supporters with Irish backgrounds from New York, Australia, Argentina and also Antarctica of all places (this particular individual worked there). Through Celtic I first began to make contact with people from Ireland, from Belfast, Dublin or Derry, and they invited me to visit their country. In a warm and friendly atmosphere they taught me more about Irish history and often the history of Celtic, which I now recognise as part of the history of Irish-British relations. I can say that it is unlikely that there exists a more traditional and historical football club than Celtic.

Anywhere in Ireland you can meet Celtic supporters in pubs organising trips to games (which are all away games for the Irish-based fans). The Irish in Ireland have a strong affinity with the club despite being hundreds of miles from Parkhead. Irish people went all over the world in the last hundred years or so but they have taken Ireland with them. Ireland is part of Celtic FC. It is fantastic to meet so many different Celtic supporters from many parts of Europe at games. On one occasion I went to a major Celtic match with a supporters club from Dublin. Being witness to the pilgrimage to Glasgow, the long line of buses and the crowded ferries, was an experience in itself.

When I attended my first Celtic match in the German city of Cologne I was surprised at the friendly and peaceful atmosphere these supporters created. They were always on their best behaviour. It was a mixture of hard drinking, singing, celebrating, behaving like guests in a foreign city and country but, still standing up for their Irish history. I liked them for their anti-racist opinions and their tolerance towards many other peoples.

The Celtic support always makes us feel comfortable and welcome. I have been travelling through European football a lot and at mostly every club in Europe you find aggressive people who are hell-bent on fighting. But the history of Celtic, the Irish roots and maybe the religion of many of their fans make them behave different. In 1996 we organised a double decker bus to Glasgow for a weekend and a home game against Motherwell. It was a magnificent experience. There were Irish bands playing in pubs and we made contact with many Celtic supporters who were social and political thinkers. Their football was more than just a sport. They weren't football's customers. They certainly weren't just consumers of football. There was a spiritual kinship and bond amongst the support. Celtic supporters constitute their club. For St Pauli fans, Celtic supporters are the club.

Celtic's football culture extends into many walks of life. That's why we are attracted to the club and for us, this is what makes the club. Charity, politics, culture and character: these are what make Celtic different. This gives us a reason for supporting this special football club from abroad and being a part of the community around Celtic Park. We are not Irish and we're not Catholic. However, we are part of the Celtic family. We, the fans of St Pauli, are 'Celtic minded'.

Across the Irish Sea

Jim Greenan

> Soldiers are we, whose lives are pledged to Ireland
> Some have come, from a land beyond the sea
> Sworn to be free, no more our ancient sireland
> Shall shelter the despot or the slave
> Tonight we'll man the bearna baoghal
> In Erin's cause, come woe or weal
> Mid cannon's roar and rifle's peal
> We'll chant a soldier's song.[1]

Imagine the scene every other Saturday. Sitting in the luxurious Globetrotter restaurant while onboard the Stena HSS, waiting to depart to Stranraer on our pilgrimage to Paradise. The ship includes three bars, two fast food outlets, one shop and what the staff call, the quiet room! Normally using these facilities is about fourteen hundred Celtic supporters making their way to Glasgow, following the same route some of our kith and kin made on a journey of a different kind back in the late nineteenth and early twentieth centuries.

It's a wonder what it must have been like for the immigrant Irish, boarding the ships in these very same docks, leaving home mainly because there was little food, no work and because the country was living out the experience of British colonialism.

In 1840, the population of Ireland was over eight million. Twenty years later, due to famine, death and mass emigration, only four million survived on the island of

Notes

1 From 'A Soldier's Song', the Irish national anthem written by Peader Kearney, music composed by Paddy Heaney. It was first published in 1912.

Ireland. Of the emigrants, some went to the USA, some to Europe and the rest to Britain. In Britain, some went to Liverpool, others to London and even more to Glasgow. Yes, truly from the 'hills of Kerry to the streets of Free Derry', they left in droves. The Irish who arrived in Britain were probably not as well treated as the cattle they shared the boats with. One thing is for sure, they hadn't a choice of menu the same as the one the fortnightly visitors to Glasgow now have: 'Texas Steak Breakfasts', 'Cod and Chips' and 'sandwiches of your choice'.

Patsy Gallacher

In Glasgow those people who left in hope of better days struggled as the bigotry and sectarianism that had been brought to Ireland by the forces of colonisation also reared its ugly head on the streets of Glasgow. But, as in all trials of adversity, something good always seems to come out of it. A monument was erected to the Irish and their offspring in the west of Scotland, something to be shared with the Irish worldwide. Celtic Football Club was to be the 'monument'. Celtic Park is a monument to famine-ravaged Ireland of the mid-nineteenth century, a monument that Celts all over the world make their way to, to pay homage to the modern day Bhoys.

My trajectory to becoming a Celtic supporter was sparked by my father, as well as his aunts and uncles because they too had to emigrate to find work in Glasgow: Parkhead Cross to be exact. On the wall in a room in my house I have a photo of my grand aunts, Betty and Margaret, alongside the great Charlie Tully. How I used to love listening to them tell tales of the great 'Belfast Bhoy'. They and many others came home religiously every year to different parts of Ireland and no doubt spread the word about this Football Club that resided in the east end of Glasgow. Their stories of the Celtic community made you want to go there and be part of it. Reflecting back, their stories of the club made them feel good about themselves, something that they could look up to and something that made me, someone who was born and reared in the County of Monaghan, want to get a taste of this wonderful phenomenon.

I made my first venture to Celtic Park in August 1980 to see the Celts play – Danny McGrain's testimonial match to be exact. I had already seen the club play in Ireland on several occasions, but seeing them play in Glasgow was the ultimate goal for this teenage 'Tim'. I had travelled with a local haulier who was delivering furniture to Glasgow. Then I made my way over to stay with aunt Betty and her husband Pat in their flat at Parkhead Cross. What a feeling it was to get up every morning that week and, before breakfast, walk down to the park. It was as if I'd died and gone to heaven! Well, over the years travel did become easier: flying was one means of transport, boats was the main way! Getting match tickets for some of the bigger games wasn't easy. But, it was on the boats that the CSCs of Ireland flourished.

> Some went to Liverpool, others to London and even more to Glasgow. Yes, truly from the 'hills of Kerry to the streets of Free Derry'.

In the Northern part of the country especially, it was where the majority travelled on a weekly basis and where Celtic men from all over the country got a chance to meet and forge friendships to last for years. I have often listened to the older generation of Celts from Ireland, including my father and his late brother, speaking of the cattle boats that departed Belfast on a Friday evening and returned on a Sunday. That was before my time 'thank God'. In the late 1980s travel was by two hour sailing from Larne to Cairnryan, on a ship that had only one small bar. It took at least an hour to get a beer but the craic in the queue was great. By the early 1990s, the Celtic support coming from Ireland changed its shipping company and moved to Belfast and, on board the Stena Ferries, three and half hour sailings were the norm. At a time that the Celts on the playing field were in turmoil, the atmosphere on some of those sailings was a mixture of euphoria and deep disappointment. Ironically, it was during these lean times that numerous Celtic supporters clubs all over Ireland began to emerge.

Many's a night we left Monaghan at 11pm on a Friday, arriving in Glasgow around 8am. A pre-arranged breakfast in a Glasgow hotel would have been the norm. Nowadays, a few beers, take in the game and, on some occasions, not getting a return sailing until 10.30pm that night, arriving back home at about four or five o'clock on the Sunday morning. This story is repeated from almost all of Ireland's thirty-two counties as supporters begin their bi-weekly pilgrimage, sometimes travelling straight to a game after a twelve hour journey from places in Galway, Wicklow, Dublin, Donegal, Offaly and Cork.

The way that thousands of Celts from Ireland travel to another country every other week to watch football must be unique for the world of sport. But then again, Celtic Football Club is unique in itself. It isn't just a football club, it's a culture. Celtic Park is a monument to our countrymen and women who made the journey we make with such regularity and that we now take for granted. It is there for all to see and a reminder to those who tried and didn't succeed in putting us down. I'm carrying on what my aunts and uncles passed on to my father. My own children regularly travel with me and I hope they pass on to their kids what I have given them: a love for a club that stands as a monument to an oppressed people, but one that will never be defeated.

Social consciousness, class and political identity

FRANK DEVINE

You'll never beat the Irish
No matter what you do
You can put us down and keep us out
But we'll come back again
You know we are the fighting Irish
And we'll fight until the end
You know you should have known
You'd never beat the Irish.[1]

CELTIC FANDOM

Since 1887/88, Celtic Football Club has been the sporting champions of the Irish Catholic working class community in the west of Scotland. Beyond being a 'typical' or 'standard' football club, Celtic has an intrinsic political character that is evident in the social and cultural basis of its support in its historic heartland – in the greater Glasgow and Lanarkshire areas. By the time of Europe's second biggest football final held in 2003 in the Spanish city of Seville, Celtic's support demonstrated its magnificence in the shape of a reported 80,000 (45,000 without tickets) travelling from all over the globe to Spain, receiving the 'Fair Play' of the year awards from UEFA and FIFA for its outstanding behaviour as well as creating a carnival around the event itself. In the words of FIFA, for 'their exemplary fair and cordial conduct at the UEFA Cup Final in Seville'.[2]

Notes

1 From 'You'll never beat the Irish' Brian Warfield

2 See The Scotsman 'Larsson faces painful past' 29/8/03

'CELTIC CULTURE' AND THE WEST OF SCOTLAND

Celtic has a huge fan base throughout the Irish diaspora. However, the core of the support continues to reside in the west of Scotland, particularly in greater Glasgow and Lanarkshire.[3] This is not surprising in that the club was

St. Mary's brake club, pictured around 1896, travelled to games. They were based in the Calton and were attached to the League of the Cross, a Catholic temperance organisation

founded specifically for this community. Glasgow Hibernian, Duntocher Hibernian, Mossend Celtic, Carfin Shamrock, Garngad Hibernian, Possilpark Celtic, Govan Harp, Whifflet Shamrock, Coatbridge Hibernian, Dumbarton Harp, Blantyre Celtic and other football teams in the west central belt, are likely to have been the original team of choice of many of the forefathers of those who today fill the stands of Celtic Park. By the end of the nineteenth century, these supporters coalesced around 'Glasgow' Celtic, the most sturdy and successful of all the Irish clubs founded during this time.[4]

Although over a hundred years since Celtic was formed, the popular culture surrounding the club remains a primary manifestation of communal solidarity and identity among working class Scottish-born Irish. It is this 'Celtic culture' that makes Celtic unique. It is a particular

3 While there are hundreds of Celtic supporters clubs throughout the Irish diaspora, as well as in Ireland, Bradley (1995, p.44) reports that there are approximately 250 Celtic supporters clubs in greater Glasgow, and another 125 supporters clubs in Lanarkshire, comprised of between 20 and 100 members

4 See Campbell and Woods 1987 and Bradley 1995

manifestation of Irishness amongst the worldwide Irish diaspora. As might be expected from a people deriving its heritage and origins from Irish history, the support is marked by an anti-establishment ethos that is often viewed with hostility in Scotland. Attending a Celtic match, or viewing the match on television in a bar, pub or social club often constitutes an emotional highlight for many. This 'Celtic Culture' provides a context within which attitudes, emotions and feelings that run counter to many of the dominant discourses in Scottish society, can be aired in a more secure and less threatening environment.[5]

The core of the support continues to reside in the west of Scotland, particularly in greater Glasgow and Lanarkshire.

On the morning of 'the game', supporters congregate in thousands of houses throughout greater Glasgow and Lanarkshire. Bank employees, the unemployed, social workers, plumbers, teachers, bricklayers, unskilled production workers and insurance salesmen, as well as a range of other occupations, all come together under the one banner: a community is constituted. The vast majority of Celtic supporters, even those who sit in the expensive seats and the corporate boxes at Celtic Park, are working class or one generation removed from a working class lifestyle.

Before and after matches, many Celtic fans crowd into premises popularly viewed as Catholic, Irish, or Celtic bars – one internet web site lists some 1200 of these bars world wide.[6] In Glasgow, licensed premises such as Bairds Bar, Traders Tavern, Waxys Dargle, Rosie O'Kane's, The Squirrel Bar, The Emerald Isle, The Wee Mans, The Hoops Bar, Lynch's/The Old Barns, The Welcome Inn, Haughian's, The Caltonian, Mulveys and The Tolbooth Bar, most situated in the historic Celtic heartland of 'The Calton' and 'The Gallowgate', are packed with thousands of Celtic supporters. The same is true of pubs in the Gorbals, Govan, Govanhill, Royston, Blackhill and 'the Garngad', as well as other areas such as Clydebank, Paisley, Greenock, Dumbarton and Port Glasgow.

In Lanarkshire, Celtic supporters congregate in the Commercial Bar and Finbarrs, Blantyre; the Clock Bar and

5 Bradley, 1995, p.49

6 These bars are easily recognisable to anyone who walks through the Gallowgate district of Glasgow's east end, as well as other places – some have the Irish tricolour flying from the premises and some are painted in the green of Celtic and Ireland.

The Big Tree, Coatbridge; Franklyns Bar and McCormick's Bar, Bellshill; as well as Tully's Bar and the Railway Tavern, Motherwell. Others will meet up in Kelly's Bar, Cleland; the Big Shop, Glenboig, the Cross Keys, Wishaw, the Era Bar, Craignuek, and Dohertys and The Auld Hoose in Hamilton. Carrigans, The Hibernian Club, Carfin Vaults and McAuleys Bar in the Celtic stronghold of Carfin, as well as dozens of other pubs throughout the Celtic 'heartlands' are packed with supporters. Therefore, this Celtic culture goes beyond the confines of Celtic Park and into the homes and communities of its historic support. One can imagine this community also coming together in bars in Sydney, Hong Kong, New York and Toronto. Celtic lives beyond the 'Fever Pitch' atmosphere of a Saturday afternoon or a Wednesday evening.

Some of the bars frequented by supporters often have a Glasgow/West of Scotland Irish band playing before supporters depart for a game – other bars will have bands booked for after the match. 'The Blarney Pilgrims', 'Foggy Dew', 'Celtic Connection', 'Athenrye', 'The Shamrock Rebels', 'Galtimore', 'Charlie and the Bhoys' and 'Shebeen', as well as solo artists like Patricia Ferns, Gary Og and Paddy Bonnar, are all well-known in the culture that makes Celtic unique in Scottish football. Bands from Ireland, such as the 'Wolfe Tones', the 'Irish Brigade' and 'Tuam', are regular visitors to Glasgow, and their concerts are attended by thousands of Celtic supporters. The Irish bands are hugely popular amongst the support and they are regular fixtures at Celtic supporters' social events.

These bands perform songs that have been sung by Celtic supporters for generations; songs such as 'The Celtic Song', 'The Coronation Cup Song', 'The Ballad of Johnny Thompson' and 'The Willie Maley Song'. They also perform a range of tunes and ballads relating to the political history of Ireland; 'The Boys of the Old Brigade', 'Kevin Barry', 'Let The People Sing', 'The Foggy Dew', 'The Merry Ploughboy' and 'Sean South of Garryowen'. These are all hugely popular ballads that are synonymous with the Celtic support. Songs such as Sean South has been a favourite amongst the Celtic support since the 1960s while the Boys of the Old Brigade has been sung at Celtic Park since the 1970s.

This community singing of Irish songs and ballads has always been a defining characteristic of the Celtic support. 'The Man in the Know', a sympathetic newspaper commentator of the 1920s, records the emotional pull and centrality of these songs to the historical Celtic support:

> They are fond of singing and to this no one can reasonably object. On Saturday the boys sang to their hearts' content. They gave us so many rousing choruses –'Hail Glorious Saint Patrick', 'God Save Ireland', 'Slievenamon', 'The Soldiers Song'.[7]

Before games, much of the support board coaches organised by hundreds of Celtic supporters clubs. Originally known as 'Brake Clubs', they were previously organised throughout the Catholic parishes of the west of Scotland.[8] The Catholic parish has traditionally provided the basis for the evolution of many Celtic Supporter's Clubs in much of the west of Scotland and beyond; the 'Garthamlock Emerald', 'Mossend Emerald', the 'Commercial Bar No 1 Blantyre', 'Claddagh Blantyre', 'Bothwell Emerald', 'Bellshill and District', the 'Starry Plough', 'Sons of Donegal', 'East Kilbride Athenrye', 'Tom Williams Port Glasgow', Linnvale Shamrock', 'Notre Dame Motherwell', 'Che Guevara Kirkmichael', 'Whiflett St Marys', 'Phil Cole Coatbridge' and 'St Mungo's Shamrock' amongst them.[8]

The communal singing and playing of recorded songs that occurs pre-match in licensed premises, the coaches of supporters clubs and in private transport, comes to a crescendo as thousands of supporters from Scotland and, from Ireland, England and beyond, fill the stands at Celtic Park. Supporting Celtic Football Club generates an enormous wave of communal solidarity among the fans. This 'feeling' of community assures Celtic FC of the 'passion of a people'.

7 Campbell and Woods, 1987, p.111

8 See the interior of Bairds Bar in Glasgow's Gallowgate for an original 'Brake Club' banner of Saint Mary's RC Parish in the 'Calton'.

SOCIAL AND POLITICAL CONSCIOUSNESS

Given the cultivated evolution of a social conscience within Catholic education in Scotland, the Irish national origins of most of the Celtic support as well as their history of economic, social, religious and political marginalisation that has characterised much of the experience of the Irish in Scotland,[9] it is unsurprising that Celtic fans have long identified with Irish nationalism as well as working class and radical issues and causes. The Celtic support (as well as many of the club's officials and playing staff) were vocal, not only in their opposition to the detention of Irish political prisoners in the 1890s, but also to Britain's involvement in the Boer War in the early 1900s and the Catholic petition for Catholic schools in the early twentieth century.[10] In 1926 Celtic supporters barracked an opposing player who reputedly 'scabbed' on railway workers during the General Strike.[11] In 1988 tens of thousands of supporters barracked the Tory Prime Minister Margaret Thatcher, a particularly detested figure among Celtic fans (and in Scotland generally) at the Scottish Cup Final of that year.[12] It is consistent with a Catholic and Christian ethos, a view partly shaped by a concern for others, that the flags of the peoples of the Basque country or Palestine (people also perceived as being 'repressed') are occasionally seen being flown by Celtic supporters on match days. The political and social consciousness of this support has been characteristic of the club since its very foundation.

The politics of the Celtic support is one of the things that makes Celtic supporters distinctive in Scotland. In a wide-ranging study into the attitudes of football supporters in Scotland in the early 1990s, one writer records an eighty-five per cent approval rating for the Labour Party among Celtic supporters.[13] In 2001 up to 10,000 people, most if not all of them Celtic supporters, attended a demonstration in Glasgow to commemorate the Irish 'hunger strikes' of 1980-1981.[14] To this day the environs of Celtic Park on match day can be considered a 'no go' area for right-wing, racist and fascist groups.

9 See Gallagher 1987, 1987, Brown 1987, 1993, Bradley 1997, Devine (ed) 1991, 2000, Finn 1994

10 Bradley, 1995, p.35

11 Campbell and Woods, 1987, p.123

12 Sunday Mirror 15/5/88

13 Bradley, 1995, p.69

14 See An Phoblacht/ Republican News, May 2001

Of course, on the negative side, there are likely to be a few Celtic supporters who are 'sectarian', just as there are black people who are 'racist' whether in Africa or the USA. What ethnic or national group in the world does not have its wrongdoers? No group or people has a monopoly on being right or doing good. Just witness those supporters who corrupt the meaning of Celtic and Irish songs by interjecting abusive or swear words or throwing in a rhyming chant that distorts what the song is about. Nonetheless, the vast majority, as well as the core Celtic support, has always rejected such views.

Even apart from their national origins and cultural and religious make-up, it might be proper to conclude that Celtic supporters constitute an ethnic bloc considering their largely similar views on a range of pertinent political, social, cultural and religious issues. This culture of Celtic brings together many different strands of people who share in the Irish and working class nature of the club and its traditions.

CONCLUSION

The core Celtic support has an attachment to the club that has political, cultural, ethnic and religious dimensions. In a popular study of the Irish in Scotland, Burrowes describes what Celtic means to tens of thousands of people and provides a perceptive insight into the culture and ethos of the community that has built and sustained Celtic:

> . . . it is their greatest triumph and [is] about showing what a deprived and impoverished community in a new country could, with determination accomplish.[15]

Celtic is a special football club and their supporters constitute a unique, atypical and relatively cohesive component of west of Scotland society. The club is the sporting champion of the Scottish-born Irish working class. Since its formation in 1887/88, Celtic has functioned as a repository of cultural, political and ethnic identity for the Irish in Scotland.

15 2003, p.292

Playing for Celtic: family and community

Andy Walker

Oh Hampden in the sun,
Celtic 7 Rangers 1,
That was the score when it came time up,
The Timalloys had won the cup. [1]

Why is it that so many people describe Celtic as a family club like no other? What is it about Celtic that makes it so special?

To my mind, as I grew up, the special memories of watching Celtic play centre on my immediate family and what the club meant to us. I was one of eleven children, seven of whom were boys and, like thousands of other Celtic supporters, my dad had a season ticket. However, I'm convinced that unlike other season ticket holders, no one else could possibly have got the same value as we did. We had a special arrangement at 'wee Jimmy's Gate'.

In the days when it was commonplace to get a lift over the turnstiles, 'wee Jimmy' operated the gate to the very left of the main stand. As many as five or six of us would be ushered in by 'wee Jimmy' to watch the game. They were great days. Dad couldn't possibly have imagined what that season ticket meant to his children. Then again, maybe we just didn't think he could imagine?

Notes

1 From 'Hampden in the sun', a song celebrating Celtic's world record national cup final score when they beat their famous rivals Glasgow Rangers, at Hampden Park in the League Cup Final of October 1957

I looked forward to those wonderful family occasions more than most and in my pursuit of a career as a footballer, I could only dream of what it would mean to actually play for the club. Having been born and bred in Glasgow and to then sign for Celtic, the club my family, relations and friends all supported and cared for was, to my mind, a great privilege. I also took it for granted when I was with this 'special club', some extra responsibility to forge links with the fans was an inevitable part of the deal: that's the way it was with families.

I don't know why I thought that. Maybe it was down to the way I imagined the idea of being a footballer as offering the perfect lifestyle and it couldn't possibly get any better than living in Glasgow and enjoying the tag of being a Celtic player, could it? This was a privilege indeed and it was a privilege that I was duty bound to respect. It was partly about self-respect and partly about respect for one's family, some might say 'community'.

I joined Celtic at a significant time in the club's history and will never forget the extra yard I could find when spurred on to greater achievements by the fans. They could literally lift you off your feet

Charlie Tully

with their encouragement and I'm convinced Celtic games have been won in dramatic fashion over the years because of the energy the fans can relay to the players.

The Centenary season of 1987/88 was not only remarkable for the success the club had on the field but also for the amount of events that all the players were expected to attend. I distinctly remember Lisbon Lion and our then Manager Billy McNeill, coming in to the dressing room on a monthly basis with a folder thick with requests for players to go to various dances and functions and he hated anyone showing any sign of reluctance to help out.

In his view – and I agreed wholeheartedly with him – it was part of our job to get to as many local Celtic communities as possible and give the fans some of our time.

Paul McStay, Tommy Burns, Pat Bonner and Roy Aitken, like myself, life-long Celtic supporters, were all at the club then and to their credit, they attended an extra-ordinary amount of functions. If Billy McNeill said it once, he must have said it a thousand times, 'take all the applause that comes your way and enjoy it but give them something back. Let them see that you appreciate their support.' Of course there were some players who loathed the idea of giving up their free time and were unenthus-iastic about it all to say the least. But by and large, they still went along. However grudging they felt, attendance at supporters' functions by players then was pretty high. I would be surprised if it was the same in the early years of the new century and, here's the significant difference, as to why.

When I went to watch Celtic with my dad and my brothers I could easily relate to the players on the field. Tommy Burns came from the Gorbals. My mum was brought up in the same area. I had played against Paul McStay for the school team and if he could make the grade through that system, I sensed I could do the same. Many Celtic players traditionally played with the same boys' clubs, school sides, came from the same towns and villages or had, just like me, wanted to play for Celtic. Indeed, these scenarios could be replicated for many clubs in Scotland in relation to their own traditional supporting communities.

Celtic players have always enjoyed the adulation of the fans but the relationship has become entirely different from that of the past. For a start, nowadays you might be hard pushed to find someone born in Scotland in some of Celtic's starting line-ups. In fairness to the players of today, they come from a very different culture where a supporters' gathering in a hall on a Saturday night in

Govanhill, Carfin, Dundee or Lochgelly means nothing to them. Nonetheless, maybe an aspect of playing for any club should to be something akin to an appreciation of local culture and relevant past histories.

I was used to seeing Celtic players park their car in the school close to the ground and walk through the front door, signing autographs on the way. It was the same after the game; win, lose or draw. Nowadays it seems, players leave by the side entrance and have little or no contact with the fans. They get stewards to bring their cars round to another exit and it looks as though they're sneaking out of the ground. Again, Billy McNeill thought walking through the crowds to get inside the stadium was an education for his players. There was no escape from their thoughts there!

> When I went to watch Celtic with my dad and my brothers I could easily relate to the players on the field.

Increased wages and generally the huge amounts of money invested in the game have also played a part in the breakdown of the relationship between player and fan. Most professionals can handle the huge uplift in their salary and are thankful for it but there's no doubt some have an inflated idea of their own celebrity. Fame and fortune has always been synonymous with footballers in any era (as well as with people in numerous other professions), but the sad truth is that earning huge amounts of money every week can create or bring out a certain arrogance because these players can equate money with power. Little do many of them seem to realise that money and power rarely bring true happiness or wealth.

It seems that many players feel as though they are due an elevated place in society because of the attention football now enjoys. Maybe this helps explain some appalling behaviour in recent years. In these early years of the new century, the alleged assaults, both racial and sexual, by a string of Premiership players, has sadly tainted all footballers, the vast majority of whom are decent, hard-working professionals.

But if criticism is due for the immoral behaviour of

footballers these days, then the same can be said for the clubs themselves. If players are earning too much money, it is hardly their fault. I've never known a player to hold a gun to a managers' head when negotiating a contract. In fact, it is rare for a player to be involved at that level of discussion. Agents and chief executives secure the deal and if agents can command hundreds of thousands of pounds for a few hours work, then the game itself is immoral. In fact, at the top of the profession, it might be argued that much of 'the people's game' has become immoral because of the money involved and all the other temptations and faults that often appear to follow.

To be blunt, clubs should not consider certain players for team selection if their behaviour is offensive. Nonetheless, knowing that everyone has a price and shareholders have to be satisfied, as is the case with so many clubs these days, some strange decisions can be made at board level. Supporters too have a role to play and their voice can be used to create a situation and conditions that engender a sport that we can once again feel confident about in relation to our children.

On a positive note, things can change. Players do not have to behave like this. Indeed, it is evident and worth repeating that many do give their time to the fans and their local community. Many genuinely use their name and club as a lever for good causes and good role modelling. A great strength of football in Scotland and beyond of course is that supporters tend to stick by their club come what may. The moral authority of football clubs lies partly in the identity a club is given by the fans that follow it. Curiously, when I attended supporters' functions as a Celtic player, the welcome and attention given to my wife and I by Celtic fans was, at times, incredible. Incredible, because of the way they spoke about their club. They genuinely loved Celtic. It was their focus and many things in their lives revolved around Celtic.

I must admit to sometimes finding this a bit hard to fathom because it is people I love and care about and not a football club. Of course, I loved going to games when I was younger because it brought me closer to my immediate family. We shared something at an early age though it was difficult to fathom what. Nonetheless, reflection has taught me that in watching and experiencing Celtic we were creating family history and many memories to be told and re-told. I'm sure that like thousands of other households, Celtic games encouraged and engendered a feeling of family. Although Celtic has always been about openness and not discriminating against players of particular creeds, colours or national origins, it has also been true that the very nature and development of Celtic has sprung from and aligned itself with one community in particular in Scotland. That community, the one I spring from, as well as our opened arm approach to other communities, is what makes Celtic different in Scotland.

That's why Celtic will always be special to me.

Celtic 4 Rangers 0 – Scottish Cup Final 1969

'Celtic minded':
a Protestant view

TOMMY GEMMELL

We're on the one road, sharing the one load
We're on the road to God knows where
We're on the one road, it may be the wrong road
But we're together now who cares
North men, South men, comrades all, Dublin, Belfast, Cork and Donegal
We're on the one road, swinging along
Singing a Soldier's Song.[1]

As a Lisbon Lion I have been fortunate to hold a very privileged position in terms of the history of Celtic. All of the Lions recognise this and we have been continually astounded at the generosity and friendliness over the years of the supporters who hold our winning of the European Cup as one of the most special moments in this club's lifetime. Indeed, in their lifetimes and family histories. The Lions (who of course involve all the players who played a part in the European campaign of 1966/67) seem to have a distinctive place within the Celtic family. We have all experienced the generosity, even the love, that emits from this family wherever the Irish and Irish-Scots have settled; Canada, USA, Australia, Singapore, Hong Kong. Of course, it almost goes without saying, from supporters in Ireland and Scotland as well.

Having been born and brought up a Motherwell fan (I was born about 400 yards from Fir Park) and having a dream to play for my local club meant that in some senses

Notes

1 From 'On The One Road'
F O Donovan

165

I was initially a guest of the Celtic family before I became a member. My father (who had played with Bellshill Athletic) was a Motherwell fan and he took me along to Fir Park in my young years. He worked in Dalzell Steelworks all his life and we lived locally. Motherwell was my family's club. Despite our support, I remember him not taking me to the Scottish Cup Final of 1952 when Motherwell beat Dundee. He didn't take me because he anticipated a big crowd. In fact, there were 136,304 fans at the game. Motherwell won and we celebrated in the town's Main Street when the team paraded with the cup in an open-top bus. On match days I still look for the results of Motherwell and, likewise, Dundee and Nottingham Forest who I also played for.

I signed for Celtic as a seventeen year old in 1961, the same night that Jimmy Johnstone also signed. Jimmy McGrory signed us although Bob Kelly was obviously the main power and had all the say. Both our fathers travelled home from Celtic Park on the same bus that evening and Jimmy and I have been close friends ever since those days. I made my first team debut for Celtic away to Aberdeen in 1963 when we beat them 5-0. Jim Kennedy and Willie O'Neill were ahead of me for playing full back at the time but both were injured on that occasion. I became a regular in the second half of 1963 and was well established before we won the Cup against Dunfermline in 1965.

I am neither a Catholic nor from an Irish background and these are two things that help define the distinctiveness of Celtic and its support. When I signed for the club I was aware of its identity but I just wanted to play football and anyway, I knew that Celtic had lots of Protestants play for them long before I signed. Some like John Thomson were regarded as amongst the greatest ever Celts. When I arrived at Celtic I didn't perceive a problem or an issue with regards my religion or background.

Nonetheless, when I signed there were really only two noticeable Protestants around the first team squad, myself and Ian Young. At that time most of the players there were traditional Celtic people. There was a bit of banter and stick on the basis of us being different: not being Celtic people, not being 'Tims' so to speak. There was also a feeling of resentment when Ian Young replaced Dunky McKay and I replaced Jim Kennedy who had been the full back partnership for years. They had been great favourites amongst the players and fans for many years. Not only were they good players but they were the life and soul of the party. However, when it was found out that Ian and I could go out and do a job on the park the banter disappeared. Just before he departed the club manager Jimmy McGrory signed Ronnie Simpson and Bertie Auld, another couple of Protestants. Jock Stein was obviously a Protestant as well and Bob Kelly brought him back to the club as manager to follow Jimmy. Soon after he returned he signed Willie Wallace from Hearts, another player from a non-Catholic and non-Irish background.

> I was living with difference for the first time in my life and I was learning from this experience.

Catholicism has been clearly important at the club. When I played a number of the players used to go to Mass on a regular basis. Chairman Bob Kelly was a daily communicant. I'm also aware that one or two of the current staff at Celtic are daily Mass attenders. However, all this Catholicism never bothered me. It never made me feel excluded as it was part and parcel of that particular environment. I was living with difference for the first time in my life and I was learning from this experience.

Nonetheless, for people beyond the club it did seem to matter and matter in a distasteful fashion. For example, many Celtic people are of the belief that there was a media bias against Celtic in the early 1960s. This was a period when we struggled but we also had a feeling at that time that the bias was because of who we were and what we were seen to represent. This was much harder for the press to do when we became so successful in the late 60s and early 1970s. As is maybe the way in Scotland, with regards referees, we got to know who was a Catholic and who was a Protestant and there weren't many Catholic referees: a couple at most I think.

Numerous referees were either from a Masonic or even Orange background and this probably extended to the SFA as well. We definitely perceived a bias against Celtic on the part of officialdom though one of the most well known referees at the time, Tiny Wharton, seemed also to be one of the fairest. Sometimes the Catholic players in the team were a bit strong on their feelings of bias against them and probably went overboard in their reactions. On other occasions the bias against us was so blatant to be untrue. Jock Stein was well aware of it and Jock of course was from an Orange background. He often took on officialdom in reaction to this bias against us. We even found this prejudice against us in the Scotland international environment as well. Some of our players seemed to be excluded from or restricted in playing for Scotland, even though we were one of Europe's outstanding teams at the time. It was certainly our belief that Rangers players were often favoured and this tied in with the thoughts and feelings of the Scotland crowd that was then Rangers-dominated. Even myself, as a Protestant, I sometimes felt I received abuse when playing for Scotland because I also played with Celtic. Throughout the 60s, 70s, 80s and into the 90s this also happened to Celtic players like Jimmy Johnstone, David Hay, Kenny Dalglish, Brian McClair and Roy Aitken.

I know from experience this existed outside of football as well. I began serving an apprenticeship in Colville's and Son, Ravenscraig in Motherwell, which later became British Steel. You heard it on the grapevine that if a Catholic and a Protestant was going for a job, the Protestant would get it.

On the refereeing front, Willie Syme was actually the official Rangers photographer. He was a referee during my career and his son David later refereed the famous League Cup Final between Rangers and Celtic in 1986. This was the game when manager Davie Hay made his comments about refereeing being so biased against Celtic he wished the club could go and play in England and get away from it all. One of the worst examples of refereeing bias against Celtic has often been assumed to be on the part of Airdrie man Bobby Davidson. Amongst his most notorious of games involving Celtic was the Scottish Cup Final against Aberdeen in 1970. He gave a penalty that everyone knew wasn't. In the 1973 League Cup Final Gordon Wallace of Dundee got the winning goal but, just as a shot from Jimmy Johnstone was sliding towards the net, referee Davidson blew the whistle for time up. Ironically, I was a Dundee player by then and I even lifted the Cup as captain of the club.

When Celtic played a lot of verbal abuse was passed between Celtic players and the opposition. Although this happened when Celtic played Rangers, other clubs were worse, even quite vicious. This was even regarded as part of the game. Though I was a Protestant, I even got called a Fenian bastard at times. Falkirk, Hearts and others, like when Celtic played Airdrie and Kilmarnock, the abuse was worse again. My experience with the club showed me that Celtic faced real bitterness in Scottish football and in Scottish society generally.

I became familiar with the fans because at that time we used to be frequent attenders at their functions. Big Jock used to organise those visits and on many occasions this was decided on the basis of us actually coming from quite near where the fans themselves lived. This was a great way for the fans to see us as people rather than as distant football stars and for us to appreciate them as part of the Celtic family. Sometimes we were like the fans on the team bus before big games. We used to sing a lot as well.

Although I did not come from a family where bigotry played any part, and indeed, a number of my current relatives who are Protestant support Celtic, being part of the Celtic environment has meant that I have learned about Catholics more than I would probably ever have, had I not played with the club. Also, I've learned a bit about Irish history and politics, something I would almost certainly not have done but for my involvement with Celtic. I suppose this started from listening to the fans singing their Irish songs: songs in fact that myself and other non-Catholic Celtic players often join in with at Celtic functions. I began to wonder about some of the periods of history and the events the songs referred to. I've learned a few social and political perspectives through playing for Celtic that I would never had if I'd only have played with Dundee and Nottingham Forest.

Celtic has become a focus and way of life for many Irish Catholics in Scotland. That's where they have found their solace and that's where they have come together and escaped from the bigotry and sectarianism many see themselves as facing in other walks of life. The song 'The Fields of Athenry' has often seemed to me to encapsulate Celtic and its supporters' history and culture. Irish and Catholic are important aspects of Celtic. It might be said that they are fundamental identities to the club and very much a part of the club's history.

Nonetheless, I felt welcome at the club in those early days and, maybe even more importantly, I was made to feel welcome by the supporters. Since first playing and then supporting Celtic, I have very much become a part of this club's history, more so especially as a Lisbon Lion. My recognition as a member of the Celtic family also reflects in there being numerous Celtic supporters calling their supporter's clubs after me, from Dunblane in central Scotland to Craigneuk in Wishaw and the Bogside in Derry. I'm also the honorary president of the Luxembourg CSC. I have long felt part of the Celtic family. I have become a Celt, I am a Celt and, for over forty years, I have been 'Celtic minded'.

FACING PREJUDICE

Let the people sing

Patricia Ferns

> Let the people sing their stories and their songs
> And their music of their native land
> Their lullabies and battle cries, their songs of hope and joy
> Join us hand in hand
> All across this ancient land, throughout the test of time
> It was music that kept the spirits free
> Those songs of yours and of mine.[1]

There's a song called 'Don't be ashamed of the shamrock green'. From time to time, some of the words it contains strike a chord with me, especially the part that says:

> . . . There's no other flower can take its place,
> . . . Though some have despised it in days gone bye.
> Sure I'm proud to be Irish now

It's a song I learned at my gran's knee, and one never more relevant than in recent years, particularly in Celtic circles, where it often seems decidedly unfashionable to be Irish and proud of it. I am aware of and grateful for my heritage, specifically – 'the three fs': faith; family; football. My family history and cultural background is predominately 'Irish'. After the family settled in the Garngad area of Glasgow, it also became very much 'Celtic'. I was encouraged to learn about aspects of our past mostly through song and music. Every Sunday evening we visited gran, and ended up switching off the T.V. and gathering round for a singsong. Everyone had a party piece/favourite song that touched a chord. Although I didn't know it at the time, our history and culture was

Notes

1 From 'Let the People Sing'
Brian Warfield

173

being passed on from generation to generation through story telling, music and song. I feel fortunate to be occasionally employed to pass on something of our culture to current and future generations through music and song.

However, in Scotland it might be argued that the Irish and their offspring are still an unrecognised and unwelcome minority on Scottish shores. Some of my own encounters may reflect aspects of that experience. Through singing about Ireland and Celtic and about the Irish diasporic community in Scotland I have found hostility in the media and in other parts of the Scottish landscape but also, with some 'Celtic minded' individuals. I have often been given the impression that to be Irish, Catholic and Celtic minded, doesn't sit well in Scotland. Many Celts have experienced or are aware of hostility on the part of those who do not share our background. However, when that hostility is replicated from within our own community, one wonders what might be going on.

A lack of knowledge and of course ignorance might contribute to our understanding this, hiding or disguising what we are might be another way to look at it. Ignorance of one's own past, ignorance of its relevance today and the ignorance that allows some people to pronounce my identity, our identities, as something akin to sectarianism and bigotry: 'he who casts the first stone', 'have a look in the mirror'. Once again it is ignorance that has allowed some of Celtic's recent custodians to be content to either apologise for or deny any meaningful Irish association with the Club. Apart from of course when they wish to package it up and sell it as heritage and as something that happened in the long and distant past. Disgraceful hypocrisy?

When one thinks that in 1892, the very blades of grass of the original centre circle turf were placed there in ceremony by Michael Davitt, the renowned Fenian and Land Leaguer from County Mayo. Would Michael Davitt, an Irish hero and a deeply devoted Catholic and humanitarian, be welcome at our stadium today? A political mentor for Irish Catholics in Scotland: a Fenian patriot. What might our critics in the Scottish media say about him, and us for inviting him?

On numerous occasions, I have been invited to sing at supporters' functions held at Celtic Park. On arrival, I have been met at the door by stewards who have proceeded to interrogate me about my selection of songs for that particular evening, being told that 'Celtic songs' (whatever they may be) are acceptable, but not Irish songs, as they may offend the staff. Yes, the staff at Celtic Park. Who you might ask has employed people who do not have Celtic's interest at heart? Who you might ask might be trying to change our great institution? How can people offended by the core identity of the club and its support actually be employed by it – to work in our interest? Should they not be employed at other clubs who have other identities? We don't all require to be Catholic or have an Irish background to be at Celtic but surely the idea of our identity actually offending people who the club employs is an absurd one? What would Brother Walfrid, Michael Davitt, John Glass, Willie Maley and Jimmy McGrory say?

> The very blades of grass of the original centre circle turf were placed there in ceremony by Michael Davitt, the renowned Fenian and Land Leaguer from County Mayo.

The words 'Tiocfaidh ar la' seem often to cause tremors to run through the Parkhead edifice – 'Our day will come'. What is offensive there? Sure it has a political resonance but it seems to me that the phrase also encapsulates something that any football team might aspire to: namely 'success'. Celtic has experienced a number of troughs during its history. This phrase was born amongst the Celtic support (in a football sense) when we were experiencing a downturn in fortunes in the early 1990s. At the time it reflected our hope and anticipation for the future. If it has a further Irish political connotation for our club and supporters then so be it. Maybe it becomes even more appropriate in that context.

At a function held in an Edinburgh hotel, Hibs and Hearts supporters were guests of the Edinburgh Celtic supporters clubs. Requests for Irish songs were coming fast and furious from all the Celtic tables, but were scrupulously checked by the organisers, before permission to sing was granted or withheld. Imagine my surprise when they permitted what would be termed a 'rebel' song to be sung because a Hibs fan had requested it.

Even at our own Celtic Rally (a night supposedly for 'our' supporters), songs are vetted, so as not to offend our own directors and staff, and those guests invited from another Glasgow football club. Or, maybe someone in the media might see or hear? Whoever said the media was prejudice free, objective and 'neutral', whatever that might mean anyway?

Not so long ago, I had the wonderful honour of being invited to sing at Celtic Park before a game. This was a very emotional experience. It brought back memories of family and friends, past and present, the very people who had instilled the love of Celtic in my being. However, even this followed a strict 'vetting' procedure:

> 'No, Willie Maley can't be sung, because some lines of the song rhyme with IRA, and the fans will sing it.'

> 'No, I'm not sure about 'Let the people sing' – that could cause offence too.'

> 'Yes, you can sing 'Something inside so strong', but you can't sing 'Tiocfadh ar la' at the end, because the words 'Our day will come' might offend people.'

But the theme is raised and is addressed in other parts of this book. Perhaps we are right to be on the defensive: we have learned to become like that, victims of 'social conditioning' as sociologists might like to call it.

In the wake of one occasion when I was asked to sing at Celtic Park, sure enough, in a Sunday paper, a columnist criticised Celtic for allowing someone to sing or 'screech' (as he said) 'The Corn Song' or, as we, the Celtic family prefer to know it, 'The Fields of Athenry'.[2] A few months later in condemning some of the club's custodians the same writer spoke of 'people who couldn't lift their gaze from the paddy field'.[3] On reading this a question came to mind. Apart from slandering my family, my community

2 News of the World 25/8/02

3 The Herald 'Champions League special section' 16/9/03

and myself, apart from being disrespectful to the land of our heritage, culture and identity, apart from that, might this constitute a subtle form of racism and bigotry disguised or passed off as 'sports commentary'? There is no such thing as neutrality. Did no one ever tell that to this particular commentator? His kind of bigotry might be of an inverted or uneducated variety but bigotry it is nonetheless.

In turn, this leads me to another song and an article in the club's official newspaper, written tongue in cheek (I think?). 'Henrik Larsson is the King of Kings' goes the song. Those of the Catholic faith will know this song better as one about Jesus Christ being the King of Kings. Blasphemy or what? A dictionary definition of blasphemy (blaspheme), is to speak irreverently of God. In singing about Henrik Larsson, am I comparing Henrik to God? Of course not! In my opinion, he is the King of Kings of football in Scotland, and I reserve the right to continue to sing it, and I can assure you I have no fear for my soul (on that count anyway). What we have then is a series of contested terms. This is usually fine, pretty human really. Except, in many of these cases the contest is often characterised by wholesale ignorance, prejudice and bigotry and it's almost completely one-sided.

So what is 'bigotry'? My dictionary states it as 'intolerant, prejudiced, narrow-minded, biased'. What's that got to do with Celtic you might ask? During the Fergus McCann era, he appeared to come up with a marketing brainwave – the wonder slogan, 'Bhoys against Bigotry'. After all this was Scotland and Scotland many agree has a problem with 'religious' bigotry. This campaign appeared to 'improve' some people's opinion of Celtic, certainly in the eyes of some elements of the media in particular. After all, much of the media have been telling us for years (though only in comparatively recent times has it even brought it up as a subject – previously ignoring a century of the same) that football was at the core of this Scottish disease. But why did Celtic need this? Whilst there are a few mindless supporters attached to Celtic as there is at all football clubs and in all communities, was the institution of Celtic ever a bigoted organisation? Not for us, not for the Celtic support. For us and for many outside of Scotland we have always been known as an inclusive club, and no one has ever been excluded on the basis of race, colour or creed, be it player or fan. Doing that would actually be against our ethos as a club and as supporters. Our Celtic culture might be mainly Irish and mainly Catholic, but not exclusively so. In summary, the fans of Celtic will never allow the club to become prejudiced or to be used in a bigoted way. We don't need a millionaire or an employee working at the club for a handful of years to come and tell us his definition of what he thinks we should do to 'improve' our image.

However, what about the more general and wide-spread Scottish disease of 'sectarianism'? My dictionary defines it as 'devotion to some particular religious denomination; especially, excessive denominational zeal, bigotry'. Well, unsurprisingly, many Celtic people are of the opinion that ignorance on this matter goes beyond football and the media and extends to many parts of the Scottish constabulary as well. At a private function in early 2003, I was singing in a pub at the Clydeside when just before midnight, two police officers arrived and asked the owner of the premises/organiser of the function to, 'step outside'. At the time I was singing 'The Boys of the Old Brigade', a song sung by many Celtic supporters since the 1970s. On completion of that song, I went on to sing 'Hail! Hail!' and the policeman put his head back in the door and indicated for me to stop singing immediately. I stopped at the end of the first verse, and the policeman asked me to 'step outside'. Bear in mind that this was a cold January night, with the temperature 10 degrees below, in the heart of 'demolition Clydeside'.

I was asked for my name and address. I asked why? 'You were singing a sectarian song when we arrived in the pub.' 'No,' I replied, 'I don't sing sectarian songs.'

Obviously this particular policeman had one idea of what constituted sectarianism. It was of course an idea common to many in Scottish society whose people did not come as immigrants to Scottish shores. For many of these people 'Irish songs', particularly nationalist or rebel ones 'are sectarian', simple as that. That these songs represent a national and cultural struggle against a colonial oppressor seems irrelevant to these people. That these songs virtually exclude mention of anyone's religious faith while often commemorating Protestants as well as Catholics and Dissenters like Robert Emmett, Wolfe Tone and numerous other patriots, is simply missed by these people who know nothing of our past except that which they see through bigoted eyes. For many Celtic fans, who are part of that Irish immigrant community in Scotland, these songs help represent part of our history and struggle: they represent and constitute part of what we are. They have been part of the Celtic environment and part of the Irish diaspora since Celtic was founded. These songs tell an important aspect of 'our' story.

Although in the footballing environment idiots have long demeaned some of our songs by introducing abusive words that rhyme or are either meaningless or ignorant, the liberty and freedom to determine our own choice of songs has been a core value of our tradition for hundreds of years: long before even Celtic was born.

This particular policeman refused to give me his name, but did give me his badge number. The following Monday, I checked with his division, and a report had been filed, with regards to one Patricia Rea singing 'sectarian' songs. This report was never followed up, but I was desperate for them to do just that. I firmly believe that until we publicly challenge their ignorance, be it through the court or the media, they will be allowed to perpetuate the myth that Celtic fans that embrace and celebrate their Irishness, even our socio-political songs, are bigoted and sectarian. While these examples demonstrate that much of our identity is denied public space for celebration and our club often finds itself having to apologise for its Irish history and identity, we are expected to live with and accept the intolerance and ignorance of others. Equality, parity? – I don't think so!

'Let the people sing'. I am a Celtic fan with an Irish history and reserve the right to sing our Irish songs. Our Club should be proud to embrace its Irishness as part of the inclusive nature of the Club. Our Irish identity is historical, it's modern and it's relevant. Our Catholic history is important too and should not be denied. Our foundation amidst the Christian principles of charity must be maintained. This is what makes me a Celtic supporter. These are the things that don't make me a Falkirk, a Hearts or an Arsenal fan. Celtic is of me and I of it.

The wearing of the green

STEPHEN FERRIE

St Patrick's Day no more we'll keep
His colours can't be seen
They're hanging men and women
for the wearing of the green.[1]

As we rushed to get ready for what would be his first away match following Celtic, my fourteen-year-old son shouted down to me from his room, 'Dad, do you think I should wear the Hoops to the game?'

It's hard to think of a more innocuous question, but I found myself hesitating in a manner better suited to a challenge about the meaning of life. The obvious response should, of course, have been 'Yes, if you like son'. He doesn't ask me what shirt he should wear when he goes out with his friends, or how he should dress going to school, so why should his choice of clothing going to a football match be any different? The fact that he feels compelled to check – and that I feel a crushing weight of responsibility in formulating a response – begs an important question – why is the displaying of colours and emblems such an emotive issue in Scottish society? Further, what socialisation process has bred this way of thinking?

Issues surrounding the wearing of football colours, particularly those involving basic tribal ramifications, are by no means unique to Scottish society. Nor are they the

Notes

1 From 'The Wearing of the Green', a traditional ballad written about the 1798 Rebellion in Ireland and a song sung by generations of Celtic supporters

sole preserve of the 'Old Firm'. Football, the world over, is an intensely passionate affair and the wearing of your club colours and emblems marks you out as a disciple. The corollary to this, of course, is that you are seen as a rival, an enemy even, in the eyes of your opponents. So, did my hesitancy merely reflect a superficial requirement to weigh up the odds of inadvertently stumbling across a group of opposition fans? A calculation that would be commonplace throughout all leagues across the continents; Lazio fans weighing up the odds of bumping into a bunch of Juventus fans, or Cowdenbeath fans considering the implications of finding themselves at close quarters with a group of Brechin City fans. No. The fixture that day was at East End Park against Dunfermline and might generally have been regarded as a low key affair had it not been for the media hype surrounding Chris Sutton's outburst from the previous season.[2] Whilst there are undoubtedly issues of a merely practical nature to take into account, once I began to analyse my own mind and assess my reaction, I realised that the sensitivity in relation to the displaying of Celtic colours is far more complex.

In order to fully understand this complexity one must scratch the surface a little and get beneath the superficial outer layer, the purely sporting dimension. In medical parlance there is a diagnostic principle that talks about the complaint a patient 'presents' and, the 'real' problem. The two can be very different, and the 'real' problem often turns out to be far more deep-seated and insidious in nature. For example, a patient presents with a problem about weight loss and listlessness. A superficial examination may put this down to any number of trivial reasons, perhaps loss of appetite or lack of sleep. However, more detailed diagnosis may reveal a far deeper malaise, alcoholism or drug dependency perhaps – the 'real' problem. This diagnostic principle works equally well if we apply it to the issue of the wearing of club colours, particularly in relation to the so-called, 'Old Firm', and even more pointedly, in my case, in relation to Celtic Football Club.

2 Celtic striker Chris Sutton made an emotional outburst immediately after the final match of the season suggesting that people knew that Rangers' opposition on the same day (Dunfermline) would lay down to defeat and allow Rangers, instead of Celtic, to win the league on goal difference. Sutton later apologised for this. However, the Scottish football media, players and staff of Dunfermline, maintained an accusatory argument over the course of the summer and, in the build up to the first game of the season which involved both Celtic and Dunfermline (for which Sutton was suspended). Many fans and media commentators called for a lengthy ban and fine to be imposed on Sutton and for the incident to be dealt with with great seriousness. It might be argued that these incidents are elevated to the status of 'news of substance' and 'real issues' because of the small nature of Scottish football. On the other hand, many Celtic supporters also believe that such incidents and their subsequent media treatment, create opportunities for anti-Celtic elements in Scottish society to 'have a go' at the club and its supporters. In this view, this constitutes a subtle form of bigotry and bias disguised as argument for fair play and fairness. See The Herald 31/503 and Daily Mirror 27/5/03 for references.

If we peel back the outer layer that is 'presented': that is, the purely sporting dimension, we are confronted with the reality that most, if not all, football teams represent more than just a club formed for the purpose of participating at a sporting level. Generally, they will be seen to represent the community in which they exist, often a town or city. However, in the case of the 'Old Firm', this community is defined not in geographical terms but in broader, cultural, terms. It is in analysing the tensions and ideological differences between these cultures that we find the key to diagnosing the 'real' problem associated with 'the wearing of the green'.

> It is in analysing the tensions and ideological differences between these cultures that we find the key to diagnosing the 'real' problem associated with 'the wearing of the green'.

Down through the years Rangers have come to be regarded as the establishment club, seen to represent the majority, a cultural norm in Scottish society. Even in the twenty first century, where many would claim we now have a society that is no longer characterised in terms of religion, this secular norm still gravitates towards the Protestant values and traditions of the majority of the population. In his history of modern Scotland,[3] Tom Devine attempts to capture the essence of this prevailing culture by referring to Alan Spence's play, 'The Magic Flute', which encapsulates the Protestant influences that permeate Scottish society. This cultural norm is characterised by 'Sunday School, the Boys' Brigade, Orange marches and Rangers matches at Ibrox to cheer on the 'Protestant' team.'

I experienced this secular 'normalisation' first hand at a meeting in 2003 at which a senior SFA official addressed a group of youth football coaches. He was attempting to illustrate how the new coaching set-up they were pioneering would impact football at all levels. In terms of progressing through the system he was keen to point out that someone could move from coaching youth footballers at amateur level right through to the very highest level. To illustrate what he meant by the 'highest level' he added the words, 'coaching with Rangers'. It was the most imperceptible of statements and certainly

3 T.M. Devine 'The Scottish Nation 1700-2000' p.387

illustrated the point that the system would provide a feed from the lowest to the highest levels. But while I think of Celtic and Rangers as equals, his omission of Celtic in his discourse reveals a significant institutionalised bias in favour of one half of the Old Firm, the half seen as representing the 'norm'. Unlike me, and many people I know of a Celtic persuasion, he did not appear to have any inhibitions about revealing what he was or what he might be labelled as. The question of consequences and life chances also struck me. This was quite a subtle example of a common experience for people in Scotland not of the majority indigenous Protestant community. A bit like the old westerns where the good guys wear white hats, or where the baddies wear feathers instead of hats.

Celtic, on the other hand, is seen to be outside 'the norm': in the language of the sociologist, 'the other'. Embattled by prejudice and discrimination, Celtic has provided the Irish and their offspring in the west of Scotland with a means of association and identity: football serving as a metaphor in a sense, for an existence otherwise denied by society. From the very beginning the culture of the Irish immigrants set them at odds with the indigenous population. By and large they were Catholic, whereas the native majority were Protestant. Not only Protestant, but also, one might argue, fundamentally Protestant, implying, at best, an underlying suspicion of all things Roman or, at worst, undisguised hostility to any manifestation of Catholic ideology or practice.

The Irish cultural and political dimension also brought with it further conflict. The majority of the Irish who formed Celtic's core support were, and generally continue to be, sympathetic to the notion of Irish self-determination. This put them even more at odds with the native community who were generally loyal to the Crown and sought preservation of Union domination in Ireland. In this sense, the Irish came to be regarded not only as being different, but also as representing a very real threat to the prevailing social order. Not surprisingly then, many chose to regard the Irish as 'the enemy within'. This also represents an aspect of the colonial dimension (British-Irish) involved in the football struggle between Celtic and Glasgow Rangers.

Herein lies the underlying tension that marks out the Old Firm rivalry as being 'special', far more intense than other, sporting, rivalries: 'unique' some might say. This intensity has elevated the risks associated with the displaying of colours and emblems to significantly greater levels than might be the case for followers of other football teams. The much-publicised case of Mark Scott, brutally knifed to death in the early 1990s simply for wearing Celtic colours, provides proof, if needed, of the potentially fatal consequences of wearing the wrong colours in the wrong place at the wrong time. On the face of it these risks should apply equally to followers of both Rangers and Celtic, but this is far from the case. Whilst only a fool would assert that Rangers fans are free to display their colours and emblems without fear of hostility, the dice are heavily loaded against those who choose to wear the green. This imbalance is born out of the historical relationship between the communities as outlined. It might also have something to do with religious upbringing and practice. It is also a function of the way in which Scottish society has been inclined to view one tradition as being more intrinisic, more acceptable, more 'normal', than the other.

Jimmy Quinn

However, it's important to point out that not everyone views the wearing of Celtic colours in the same light. Many people accept them at face value seeing them as simply representing a football club. They may also acknowledge, consciously or otherwise, the cultural signals associated with these colours. However, a significant section of the community view Celtic colours in a much more confront-ational manner, seeing instead something abhorrent to what they hold dear, something to be opposed and put in its 'proper' place. The displaying of Celtic colours then in this scenario is seen not so much as being different but as being offensive, provocative even. This tendency to demonise can also be seen in other, non-sporting, expressions of Irishness or Catholicism that have come, simply by their very existence, to be regarded almost as hostile acts. Examples of this include the furore that has often surrounded the flying of the Irish national flag at Celtic Park, or the often automatic equation of Catholic education with sectarianism.

To illustrate this point further the popular ballad, 'The Fields of Athenry', which laments Famine and emigration (fundamental to the very roots and history of Celtic and the majority of its supporting community), was described in one popular newspaper as a 'Republican anthem'. Individually these misrepresentations may be subtle, but with continual reinforcement the cumulative effect is to engender a mindset that sees otherwise legitimate expressions of identity as offensive acts.

It's hardly surprising then that faced with a climate of open hostility many have chosen to be discrete about revealing their allegiances. People learn quickly to keep their heads down. This manifests itself in Celtic followers often choosing not to publicly display their colours. But this caution doesn't confine itself solely to the wearing of Celtic colours. It extends much deeper into the cultural psyche of the Irish-Catholic and Celtic community. Some people have been mindful about the names they have given – or more significantly haven't given – to their children. Others have encouraged their children to be vague about the schools they attended for fear of harming their prospects in the employment market. Some have gone even further and made the conversion from victim to oppressor, a phenomenon that is common in crimes of aggression: rape victims who feel a sense of guilt that they may somehow have contributed to their own fate, assault victims who feel they may have provoked their assailant, or that they should somehow have done more to prevent the attack. In this scenario forces within the community play a role, almost by proxy, in marginalising and denouncing legitimate expressions of identity.

For the Celtic community, the period before and after World War II was a particularly difficult time in terms of overt oppression and spawned, to some extent, an 'Uncle Tim'[4] generation: a generation under pressure to deny its roots and compelled to demonstrate loyalty to the values of the majority. The term 'Parkhead Catholic' is one I became familiar with in my youth as a statement intended to convey that in the eyes of 'real' Catholics, following Celtic was somehow an inferior or unworthy choice. In retrospect, this seems an apposite example of how the immigrant community adapted to pressure by acquiescing in the part destruction of its own Irish and Catholic cultures.

As we have come down the generations some aspects of this oppression have become subtler, reaching the point where they go undetected by many. They are now so 'normal'. Others argue that they have disappeared altogether, swept away by the rising tides of multicultural-ism and assimilation. However, perhaps they have simply found new guises, becoming less visible but remaining equally virulent – to paraphrase the famous film line – 'just because you can't see it, doesn't mean it isn't there'.[5]

So, coming back full circle, how did I reply to my son's question about whether he should wear his Celtic strip to the match? 'Yes, if you like son. But maybe take a jacket with you just in case we need to cover up'.

A new generation learns to keep its head down.

4 In the novel 'Uncle Tom's Cabin' by Harriet Beecher-Stowe, the principal character, the black slave, Uncle Tom, refuses, or feels unable, to speak out against the oppression of his people and comes to be regarded as acquiescing with the white oppressor.

5 In the film 'Small Soldiers', Archer, leader of the Gorgonites, delivers the memorable line 'Just because you can't see something doesn't mean it's not there'.

Jock Stein and Danny McGrain

See no evil, speak no evil, hear no evil

HUGH MACDONALD

> Twenty years have gone by and I've ended me bond
> My comrades' ghosts walk behind me
> A rebel I came, and I'm still the same
> On the cold winds of night you will find me
> Oh oh oh oh, I wish I was back home in Derry.[1]

It was the week before Seville. Seville, of course, being shorthand for the UEFA Cup final of 2003 between Porto and Celtic. The newsroom of The Herald in Glasgow was unaccustomedly serene. Suddenly a familiar flash of green and white caught my eye. A reporter was showing his colleagues the Celtic strip he had bought for the trip to Spain.

It was a significant moment for me. Three decades previously a Celtic supporter in The Herald newsroom would be somewhat conspicuous. I know. I was that soldier. The situation has, thankfully, changed dramatically over the years. This has put me in a grandstand seat to examine the perceptions of Celtic that are accepted, even promulgated by the media: in particular, the Scottish media.

When I joined the national media as a 20-year-old in the early 1970s, I was unusual on the sub-editors' desk in that I was a Celtic supporter who saw no need to keep

Notes

1 From 'Back home in Derry' Bobby Sands

this information to himself. In that, I do not mean that I circled the newsroom at edition time belting out the 'Soldier's Song' (frankly, I haven't the voice for it). But if the conversation turned to football, I would talk about Celtic. These chats were hardly common on the sub-editors' desk where the correct spelling of Azerbaijan would produce animated debate or a split infinitive would prompt an explosion. Football was, however, the fundamental topic in the caseroom where the newspaper was made up in type and where as a sub-editor I ventured to cut the overmatter, check the proofs and be the butt of what I have done my best to see as essentially good-natured banter over my allegiance to the green section of Glasgow. My Catholic education and upbringing amongst other things has taught me to approach life in a way that tried to see such experiences positively and throw negativity to the wind.

It could be uncomfortable, particularly after an Old Firm defeat, when compositors and linotype operators would form an orderly queue to appraise me of their views. But it could have been worse. I could have been a caseroom employee who supported Celtic. And there was one. Just the one. Despite being a significant concern, The Herald, then (as The Glasgow Herald) was a newspaper where football wasn't much mentioned in polite society and where Celtic supporters could comfortably meet in a phone box.

Football was strictly enclosed in the sports pages, escaping only on to the news pages in times of disaster or extreme triumph. The Glasgow Herald of a May morning of 1967 would carry a brief report on the front page of Celtic's victory in the European Cup final with a curt cross-reference to the sports pages. In contrast, The Herald led on coverage of Seville 2003 with several news pages devoted to reaction and comment. So what has changed? And why?

The first, simple declaration is that football has become sexy. Media owners, from Sky to the broadsheet quality press, have recognised its importance to viewers and readers. However, the specific Celtic conundrum with the media is more difficult to explain or explore. From the inception of the club, it was perceived in the media as the 'work's team' of Irish Catholicism. This was by no means viewed as a good thing. Cartoons from the earliest years of the past century present the Irish as almost sub-human with outlandish features, hairy faces and dull, simple stares.[2] Language that would now be condemned as fiercely racist was routine in Scottish and British societies.

Later, Celtic was embroiled in controversies, particularly the flying of the Irish flag and the subsequent stand-off with the SFA, where much of the Scottish media was less than sympathetic. But in the latter half of the twentieth century and early into the millennium, two factors mark media coverage. Both concern a corrupted notion of neutrality.

The first is to define Celtic and Rangers, the 'Old Firm', as essentially the one coin with two sides. The other is to be suspicious of commentators wearing colours. The former is deeply ingrained in media mentality. It can be summed up in the banal statement routinely articulated that 'one lot are as bad as the other'. Thus Rangers' discriminatory employment practices were dismissed by the counter-accusation that Celtic's board was full of Catholics and the club flew an Irish flag. The flying of the flag of a friendly nation (one that has signed numerous accords with the British government and one from where much of the Celtic support originate) is still routinely trotted out in the face of any 'examination' of sectarianism.

This welding together of the Old Firm is useful to journalists because it defines the problem as a conflict and battles are easy to report. But the first casualty of war is, of course, the truth. Celtic fans' stubborn adherence to Irish symbolism and values in song and chant have been seen as part of the problem rather than as a means to understand 'difference'. This recognition of Irish roots and a reflection of a varied perception of history and its

> This welding together of the Old Firm is useful to journalists because it defines the problem as a conflict and battles are easy to report. But the first casualty of war is, of course, the truth.

2 See Curtis, L, 1988 'Nothing But The Same Old Story: The roots of Anti-Irish Racism' Published by Information on Ireland, 5th edition

meaningfulness has been described as a provocation when tolerance would simply eradicate any strife.

The media seem simply unable to deal with Celtic and Rangers in isolation. For example, any condemnation of the playing at Ibrox of 'Simply the Best', which invites a raucous insult to the Pope, must, it seems, be countered by the derision of a song that recalls the great Irish Famine which, after all, sent so many Irish to Scotland and which provides the context for the birth and development of Celtic Football Club. This, of course, is not to state that Celtic or their fans are blameless in every action, word or song. But they should be judged and, if guilty, condemned on their own actions, not as a counterpoint to Rangers or indeed any other team. This last point is important when we consider football in Scotland as a reflection of huge elements of society rather than as just a reflection of these two clubs.

Journalists, though, seem loath to do this, primarily because they adhere to a corrupted 'neutrality'. There is a deep, ingrained suspicion of writers professing allegiance to Rangers or Celtic. Newspapers subsequently fear being labelled as pro-Rangers or anti-Celtic, or vice versa. The Daily Record, for example, would hardly have done its falling circulation any good by its portrayal of Celtic players as thugs and thieves at the turn of 2002/03. [3]

Sports journalists, it seems, are all Clyde, Partick Thistle, St Mirren, Motherwell and St Johnstone fans. All well and good. But if this bias was reflected in the general population, Rangers and Celtic would be playing to empty stadiums. They are not. So what is going on?

Again, corrupted neutrality raises its pock-marked face. For a sports journalist to declare a prejudice for either team has been considered as professional suicide. How could he (it was always a he) retain his integrity if he was revealed as a supporter of either? It was never asked how he could retain his integrity while indulging in the shameful and frankly embarrassing and dishonest pretence of

3 Daily Record 19/12/03

supporting another team. This also says something about Scottish society.

Thus when I was approached (by a Rangers supporter, incidentally) to write a sports column for The Herald, we came to an agreement. I would write it as a Celtic supporter. It's what I am. He would judge the copy on its merits and publish or spike. It's what a sports editor does. More than ninety-per cent of my columns do not address Celtic. To my recollection, only one column has been spiked in almost 10 years. It was binned because it wasn't funny, perceptive or entertaining (these negatives being an accurate description of my work, I would have thought), not because it said anything pro-Celtic or anti-Rangers.

The reaction in the newspaper to my witterings has thus been strictly professional. The reaction from readers has been instructive. There has been predictable, relentless abuse from extreme elements of the anti-Celtic brigade whenever I display my allegiances, even when I have been critical of the Parkhead board. A straightforward piece on why a section of society brought up in the face of discriminatory employment practices might feel, well, a bit paranoid, prompted a surge of anonymous mail that did little to alleviate my, well, perceived paranoia. The most interesting reaction, though, has been that of fellow Celtic supporters. They vehemently disagree or agree with my opinions and tell me so. But some display an attitude that would be strange in any other city in the world where a columnist would be expected to support one of the big clubs in the metropolis and write about that.

How does he get away with it? my brother is regularly asked by those who know the poor guy is related to me. Get away with what? Is it impossible to write about Celtic in a national newspaper from the viewpoint of a fan? Obviously not. Again, I am that soldier. But it is instructive to gauge the reactions, particularly those born of fear. The virulent anti-Celtic sentiment is easily explained. The cautious, almost apprehensive attitude of the quiet Celtic man who agrees but is surprised to see the sentiment in print offers a testament to a repressed past and possibly present and of fearful assimilation. But it perhaps can offer a lesson for a better future.

Why, in print or in casual conversation, should Celtic supporters be afraid of who they, we are? Surely as Scotland strives towards an all-inclusive, multicultural society there is room for a club and supporters that celebrate Irishness (the very thing that makes Celtic special and unique to its support) and articulate a shared experience honestly and with malice towards none? For didn't someone once say the truth would set us free?

'Shut Up' and 'Trouble': the nonsense over 'sectarianism'

WILLY MALEY

> This land is your land
> This land is my land
> From the northern highlands to the western islands
> From the hills of Kerry, to the streets of Derry
> This land was made for you and me.[1]

I'm a Celtic supporter, faithful through and through, a season ticket holder, and a columnist in the 'View'. I knew my name had a ring to it from an early age. Folk would ask: 'Any relation?' I wasn't, but I've always supported the 'Tic. Tim's my middle name, and my surname's Irish, but that's about as obvious as it gets. I'm not a Catholic, and never was, so I didn't have the luxury of lapsing. I could have played for Ireland, if I'd been any good at football, since I had an Irish-born grandfather – Ned O'Malley from Mayo – but I'm quite happy to see myself as Scottish and be done with it.

I grew up, like a lot of people, in a mixed housing scheme, the product of a mixed marriage. I'd get asked if I was a Billy or a Tim, but it was more of a tease than a threat. I went to Ibrox a few times with a pal of mine, Hank (his mother was a big Country and Western fan).

Notes

1 From 'This land is your land' Woody Guthrie, adapted by The Barleycorn

195

Hank was a red-hot bluenose, still is. The one time I persuaded Hank to come to Parkhead – we must have been around twelve – he managed to get all the Bhoys' autographs for me, something I was too shy to do. Hank wasn't awestruck by Billy McNeill, so he had no problem with pestering him and his team-mates.

There's an old gag about two Glasgow kids called 'Shut Up and Trouble', playing Hide-and-Seek. Stopped by a cop, Shut Up is asked his name. When he gives it, the cop says 'Are you looking for Trouble?' and Shut Up replies, 'No, Trouble's looking for me'. That bad joke sums up the present state of the so-called sectarianism debate in Scotland, so-called because it's nothing to do with sectarianism and there's no debate. Shut up or there'll be trouble, that's about the size and simplicity of it.

What's the Hampden roar? Is it a storm in a Bovril cup? A couple of years ago, John Reid, Northern Ireland Secretary and Lanarkshire Labour MP, speaking on BBC Radio Ulster's Talkback, happened to mention in passing that Ulster Protestants follow Rangers, while Celtic is buoyed up by Irish Catholics, and that both sets of faithful fans, scattered worldwide, would like to see their teams in a big league, competing with Europe's elite. So what? It rains a lot in Glasgow, and some say there's snow in the Cairngorms.

Controversial? You should get out more. Read all about it, but say nothing. The way the words 'row' and 'controversy' attach themselves to any mention of Ireland in relation to Scotland, including the Irish connections of grassroots supporters of Celtic or Rangers Football Clubs, suggests that sensationalism and censorship are the real problems. Why should a nothing remark by a politician make the front page as the first foot-in-mouth of the year?

Denial isn't a river in Egypt. It's a backwater in Scotland. Whatever you say, say nothing. Zip it or stitch it. That's the motto not only of the anti-bigotry organisation, Nil By Mouth, but our national press and most politicians, judging by the reaction to John Reid's innocuous, and merely descriptive, remarks. It appears that for journalists, sectarianism is a handy mix of embarrassment and excitement, tingly but also tinged with guilt. No immigrant community should be asked to check its cultural baggage at customs. Their rights to roots are as vital as their rights of residence.

The wider denial within Scottish culture is the denial of anti-Irish feeling, denied while it goes on behind the scenes, below stairs, or in the cheap seats, where it can be smugly dismissed as the last resort of 'scum', the usual epithet applied to football hooligans. Although a matter of some dubiety, according to the Oxford English Dictionary, the word 'hooligan' probably derives from a 'ruffian' Irish family who lived in south-east London in the late nineteenth century, perhaps a corruption of 'Houlihan'. Whether this is true or not, isn't it ironic that a word associated with football violence is an anti-Irish expression, already aimed at criminalising a poor Irish family?

> The wider denial within Scottish culture is the denial of anti-Irish feeling, denied while it goes on behind the scenes, below stairs, or in the cheap seats,

It's not Irishness but intolerance that's the source of Scotland's shame.[2] No sectarianism please, we're Irish, and Scottish, and any damn thing we like to call ourselves. What politicians and papers should be doing is lifting the embargo on debating what it means to be Scottish, rather than implying that to talk about Irish input into Scottish life on any level is to stir the pot of prejudice – try the unveiling of the Carfin Famine monument in 2001 as an example.[3] On the contrary, to admit there's a problem is the first step on the road to recovery. Why should a community that helped build the bridges, canals, houses, roads, railways and schools of Scotland, among other things, be expected to 'haud its wheesht' about its origins?

Sectarianism might be no more than a flag of convenience for a form of discrimination so ingrained and institutionalised that it is easier not to address it, except in the hand-wringing manner of Uriah Heep or the hand-washing manner of Pontius Pilate. You can't speak out

2 See The Herald 7/12/02 for report on First Minister's view of religious bigotry as 'Scotland's secret shame'

3 See The Herald 9/2/01 pp.6-7, Scotland on Sunday 11/2/01 p.19 and Sunday Herald 11/2/01 pp.12-13

against bigotry without being seen to be biased, or predisposed towards the community discriminated against.

There's only one thing worse than paranoia, and that's the prejudice it conceals. Keep quiet about something for long enough and it eats away at you. Chic Young, the Scottish football presenter, was spot on when he said sectarianism is a cancer. However, you don't deal with cancer by taking a 'quietie'. There may be no cure, but there's treatment, and everyone agrees that investigating the causes will aid prevention. Whose interests are served by tarring the troubled history of Irish-Scottish relations with the broad brush of sectarianism, painting into a corner anyone who wants to celebrate 'Celtic Connections', as a highly successful annual Glasgow festival does? Scotland's shame isn't sectarianism, but the embargo on free speech, an enforced silence on which bigotry feeds.

Post-Devolution, one might expect the denials of the past to be discussed, but the debate about sectarianism marred the first year of the new Scottish Parliament. James MacMillan's 1999 Edinburgh Festival lecture on 'Scotland's Shame' stated the obvious for at least one section of the population in Scotland: there's some unfinished business around anti-Catholic discrimination. MacMillan's was a plea for tolerance, but also attention. Thanks to Professor Tom Devine, whose edited collection of essays (Scotland's Shame? Bigotry and Sectarianism in Modern Scotland)[4] brought together a range of informed opinion on the topic, this scar on the face of Scottish culture was stitched up a treat. But too few people have read this important volume, naming and shaming the stiflingly singular Scotland that refuses to acknowledge its mixed and multiple origins. Sectarianism remains a source of shame rather than shared experience. In the wake of the book's publication, a letter to a newspaper let the cat out of the bag, exclaiming that in serialising the volume, 'The Herald too has become the victim of Irish tribalism!'[5]

4 T M Devine (ed) 'Scotland's Shame? Bigotry and Sectarianism in Modern Scotland' Mainstream Press, Edinburgh 2000

5 The Herald 29/3/00

In the essay that gave the book its name, James MacMillan identified 'a very Scottish trait – a desire to narrow and to restrict the definition of what it means to be Scottish'. More to the point, MacMillan put his finger on the racialised character of 'sectarianism':

> The obsessive attempts, historically and contemporaneously, to peripheralise and trivialise the Catholic experience in Scotland (and in particular the Irish Catholic experience) is a self-defeating tendency. It represents the very opposite of the enriching multicultural pluralism which I crave for this country.[6]

The Irish character of the Catholic experience in Scotland is crucial. There are Scottish Catholics who aren't Irish, and Irish in Scotland who aren't Catholic, but where Irishness and Catholicism meet, 'sectarianism' is seldom far away as far as the protagonists are concerned.

Ironically, the debate around anti-Catholicism in Scotland, and with it a resistance to an Irish identity viewed by some as anti-Scottish, occurs at a time when Ireland and Scotland are moving closer together. Devolution in Scotland offered a model for the new Northern Ireland Assembly, and the emergence of new (or renewed) political institutions went hand-in-hand with the opening of an Irish Consulate in Edinburgh. This process of institutional innovation found an echo, culturally, in the establishment of the Irish-Scottish Academic Initiative (ISAI), a scheme involving the universities of Aberdeen and Strathclyde in Scotland, and Queen's Belfast and Trinity College Dublin in Ireland.

In his contribution to 'Scotland's Shame?', Andrew O'Hagan defended James MacMillan as a fellow artist opposed to bigotry. He said:

> There is something wrong with Scotland's institutional bigotry: and down, and down, with their customary blunt instruments, came the great and dispirited doctors of the Scottish media, filling the air with their oaths and denials, their idiot charts, their poxy prescriptions. . .

6 Ibid, p.16

religion is everything in Scotland. The women in the wash-house could tell you that.[7]

As an atheist, I can't accept that religion is everything – what about race and class and gender? – but O'Hagan, like MacMillan, is right to see denial as the real issue.

Bernard Aspinwall sounds a salutary note of caution when he observes that the Irish connection cuts both ways: 'Ireland equals Catholic is a useful tool for interested parties on both sides'. By claiming affinity with Ireland, Catholics in Scotland enlarge their constituency and lean back for support on a nation to which they can comfortably belong from a safe distance. Meanwhile Scottish Protestants can say 'I told you so!' and reinforce their arguments about the 'un-Scottish' nature, the foreignness, of Catholicism. Aspinwall is less convincing when he goes on to talk of 'the Irish in Scotland' as 'a tiny minority', and to imply that Catholics in Scotland are merely suffering from a lingering Hibernian hangover. Yes, there is cultural baggage, but at what point do they become Scots or does Scotland absorb their positive values? Can they remain Irish, be recognised as such and, be viewed, without feeling under threat, as part of the modern Irish diaspora? These are crucial questions, but they can't be answered by airbrushing Irishness from the national landscape, particularly in the west-central belt. For some of the Irish diaspora, and especially for many Celtic supporters in Scotland, one question eats at them, 'why aren't they allowed to be Irish in Scotland the way the Irish can be Irish in Canada, the USA and Australia?'

Glasgow Rangers and Celtic stand accused of embodying everything that's wrong with Scottish culture. Scottish Socialist Party spokesperson and Hibee, Kevin Williamson, has complained about the stranglehold that the 'Big Two' have on Scottish football. Tommy Sheridan, leader of the SSP, used to be a Parkhead regular, but gave up the ghost allegedly because of the notoriously divisive nature of the Glasgow rivalry. This 'curse on both your

7 Ibid, p.25

houses mentality' ignores the different traditions of the two clubs, and blames them for problems that have a history that goes back further than either team. It blames them too for the very poverty and prejudice from which they provide an escape. I don't have any problem with calling myself a socialist and a Celtic supporter. I don't feel guilty about not being a Catholic. I've had my share of abuse hurled at me in the past because of my Irish name.

John Thomson memorial plaque at Celtic Park

I've never been one for slogans, but it's good to talk, and if we must have one, I prefer 'Sense Over Sectarianism' to 'Nil By Mouth'. The former sends out an SOS, and appeals for sense where there's so much nonsense spoken. The other calls for quietness. A low profile is better than no profile, but speechlessness may in the end be part of the problem rather than part of the solution. If we shut up about sectarianism we might just be looking for trouble. The way out of the cul-de-sac of sectarianism might be twofold. To stop pretending that it's about religion and start accepting that it's about ethnicity and identity or 'race' as it used to be called before we found out there is no such thing. The campaign that I'd subscribe to is 'Show Racism the Red Card' – and that includes anti-Irish racism, one of the longest lasting and most lamentable prejudices afflicting modern Scotland. History has given Scotland its national flower in the thistle and few Celtic supporters, Irish or Catholics, have a problem with that. Celtic and its support have the shamrock and wear it with pride. In a similar sense to the call of a famous black activist in 1960s America, in the society that I crave, the metaphorical shamrock takes its place alongside the metaphorical thistle, distinctive, but in friendship, and the reality is the blooming of a hundred flowers.

FAITH AND SOCIAL CONSCIOUSNESS

Jimmy McGrory

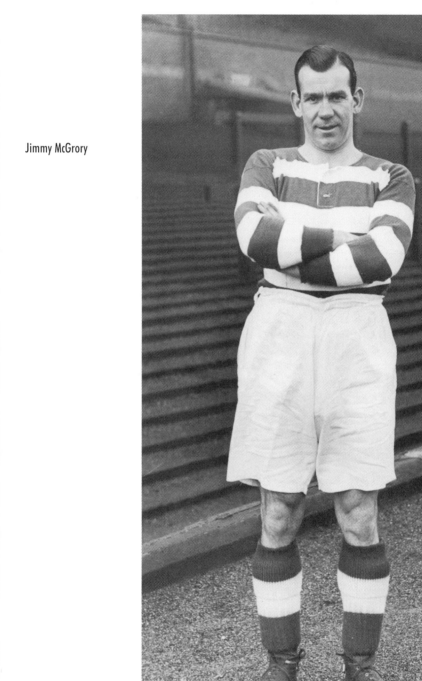

Celtic and Catholicism

Patrick Reilly

> Hail glorious Saint Patrick, dear saint of our isle
> On us thy poor children bestow a sweet smile
> And now thou art high in thy mansions above,
> On Erin's green valleys look down in thy love
> Thy people, now exiles on many a shore
> Shall love and revere thee till time be no more
> And the fire thou hast kindled shall ever burn bright
> Its warmth undiminished, undying its light.[1]

Let us start with a truism: not all Celtic supporters are Catholics, nor are all Catholics Celtic supporters. The relationship between Celtic and Catholicism is much more oblique and complicated than anything so simplistic as that. Nevertheless, there is an undeniable historical and contemporary connection between the two, despite the reluctance of most commentators to mention it, describe it accurately or address it. It is as if the origins and heritage of Celtic F.C. were something shameful and discreditable, a sordid secret best forgotten, a scandal to be stifled and concealed. Listening to the critics in Scotland, one is never quite sure if the Church should be ashamed of Celtic or if Celtic should be ashamed of the Church or, if they should both be ashamed of each other.

Periodically, voices are raised within the Church denouncing football in general and Celtic in particular as a kind of debased, ersatz religion in which the support of

Notes

1 From 'Hail Glorious Saint Patrick'

2 See Sunday Herald, 'Bishops' PR calls for break between Catholic Church and Celtic FC' 23/3/03

a football team is inanely elevated to the level of a faith commitment.[2] This is, of course, both absurd and blasphemous and the critics are totally correct in lambasting so imbecilic an outlook. But the fact that some people are idiotic enough to regard loyalty to a football team as a valid substitute for religious commitment does not entitle us to cultivate a deliberately willed amnesia with regard to Celtic's origins and heritage. It is perhaps pertinent to remember that when the cry first resounded throughout the west of Scotland for a team to beat the Irishmen, this was partly a code for a team to beat the Catholics – the terms were at the time synonymous and there would surely have been no similar clamour had the intruders been men from the Shankill Road. Like it or not, it is historically undeniable that Celtic F.C. was born from the misery and afflictions of a dispossessed, deprived and exiled people.

'So what?' is one modern response emanating from some within, and from many more outside, the Catholic community today. Forget the history, it is surely long past time (so runs the argument) for Celtic as a twenty first century organisation to shed its embarrassing traditions and adjust to the modern world. In that world, religion is a purely private, individual affair which has no rightful place outside centres of worship. Celtic should, Celtic must, sever the cord that continues to bind it to this anachronistic, discreditable past. Some traces of this mindset were discernible in the rationalising tenure of Fergus McCann with its clear predilection in favour of business efficiency at the expense of tradition and sentiment. Revelatory of this mindset was his snub to an Taoiseach as well as his tendency to refer to second, third and fourth Irish generation followers of the team as 'customers', without even realising how grotesquely inappropriate (and offensive to many) this importation of the jargon of commerce was in such a context.[3]

Yet even from a strictly balance-sheet point of view, it is far from obvious that Celtic's best interests would be served by jettisoning its Irish-Catholic heritage in order

3 See The Herald, 'Celtic snub Ahern on glory day' 11/5/98

to reshape its identity as a purely west of Scotland team. It is, of course, a west of Scotland team, as surely as Manchester United is a north-west of England team, but this has not prevented the latter from acquiring massive support from other parts of the country or the world, including, most conspicuously, Asia. Nor have I heard anyone reprimand Manchester United for encouraging the growth of this support or say that they should be ashamed of doing so. Why, then, should Celtic shun the support they receive from Irish and Irish-Scottish communities throughout the world, most strikingly North America and the Antipodes? Why is it all right for many Asians to support Manchester United and all wrong for many Irish Catholics worldwide to support Celtic? Why is the one team to be envied and congratulated for having a mass following beyond its locale, while the other is to be abused and rebuked for having the same?

> It is historically undeniable that Celtic F.C. was born from the misery and afflictions of a dispossessed, deprived and exiled people.

The only explanation is the assumption that there is something inherently disgraceful in Catholic people supporting a team that had its raison d'etre in the horrendous social conditions of their immigrant families and forebears over the past hundred or so years. But this is one of Celtic's great strengths and, leaving anti-Catholic prejudice aside, there seems no valid reason for treating it as something sordid or defiled. The fighting Irish of Notre Dame experience no difficulty in being accepted for what they are by the rest of American society. Why is it only here in Scotland that the word 'Catholic' is a provocation and an affront: that the only way of Catholics avoiding giving offence is for them to go about on tiptoe and in whispers like the Christians under Nero? It is not we, after all, who are a secret society.

Who seriously believes that the vast exodus to Seville of 80,000 supporters (whose conduct was so exemplary as to be honoured by UEFA and FIFA in 2003)[4] would have taken place had Celtic overtly decided in the past to sever all historical links with Ireland and Catholicism and to proscribe any allusion to the circumstance in which

4 See The Scotsman, 'Larsson faces painful past' 29/8/03 and The Celtic View 17/12/03

the club was born and reared? Although, it might be argued that some Celtic employees and custodians have indeed attempted this in the recent past.

The club, to its credit, has, almost from the beginning, welcomed players and supporters from every faith and from none: but, given its origins, it would be perverse indeed if it became a requirement to forego one's Catholicism when following the team. No Catholic need apply: it would be a strange sign to find hanging over the doors of Celtic supporters' clubs.

Regrettably, however, one cannot discuss Celtic's 'Catholicism' without simultaneously discussing Scotland's anti-Catholicism. Rangers have never suffered (self-inflicted wounds apart) and may well have benefited from being regarded as 'the' Scottish Protestant team, the team to beat the Irishmen: this has been their elected role and vocation for a century and more. Celtic has clearly gained in terms of support from being tagged as the 'Catholic' team, but, given the nature of Scottish sectarianism, they have just as surely also lost out. It is, after all, what we would naturally expect. Scotland is undeniably a sectarian society. The latest research has deprived the ostriches of whatever sand they chose to hide their heads in. Thirteen per cent of people in Scotland say that they have personally suffered from religious discrimination, with four times as many Catholics as non-Catholics believing themselves the victims.[5] Many will find this a completely credible proposition, fitting in well as it does with the actuality of our surroundings as we regularly experience them. It would be remarkable indeed if football was somehow immune from this contagion and, of course, it isn't. Football is, indeed, a kind of litmus test that exhibits the bile and the bitterness as most visibly, unmistakably present – its sociological value consists in supplying illuminating insights into the nastier corners of our society. It is where we are at our most naked and open.

The cry for a team to beat the Irishmen (aka Catholics) may not be so vociferous today, but the sentiment is still

5 Sectarianism in Glasgow – Final Report, prepared for Glasgow City Council by NFO Social Research, January 2003

there, strong as ever. In recent times Rangers' financial plight has clearly stemmed from an obsessive resolve to match Celtic's feat in winning the European Cup. This was reflected in Glasgow Rangers Chairman David Murray's comment that if Celtic spent five pounds to progress then he and his club would spend ten pounds.[6] It has often been felt by many as intolerable that a team representing immigrant Irish Catholics should succeed where a team of Scottish Presbyterians consistently fail: it means that Rangers have defaulted upon their historic mission. One irony among many is the fact that not one of the Lisbon Lions was Irish born and almost half of them, together with the manager, were Scots Protestants.

Season 2002/03 contributed its own striking additions to the evidence of anti-Celtic sentiment in Scottish football. When the Scottish Premier League clubs voted unanimously for the Old Firm game to take place a mere forty-eight hours after Celtic's strenuous UEFA semi-final in Portugal, they did so with vehement denials that their decision was in any way biased. But as Martin O'Neill asked so cogently at the time, can anyone imagine them ever doing this to Rangers after a European semi-final? Certainly not Hearts, who, several years before, had leaned over backwards to accommodate Rangers in a parallel situation when Hearts themselves were the opposition and might have directly profited from insisting that Rangers fulfil their obligations. They agreed instead to 'switch the tie'. Yet, with nothing to gain themselves, the Scottish Premier League (ie, other clubs in Scotland) inconsistently insisted that an exhausted Celtic should travel to Ibrox on the date arranged, regardless of how this might disadvantage one team and benefit the other. A stranger might have thought that the other clubs would have signalled their gratitude to Celtic for enhancing the profile of Scottish football by granting them this one small favour of a few days' grace (and gratitude and encouragement in raising Scotland's co-efficient in European football) – but a stranger is necessarily ignorant of the unspoken, underlying realities of Scottish football.[7]

6 See Sunday Mail, 'Take the money and win: O'Neill won't lift title without plc cash' 3/12/00

7 In December 2003, Lyon, Celtic's French opponents in the Champions League, 'were given extra help' by being 'allowed to postpone a midweek game' and bring forward another fixture to suit their preparation for a vital tie against Celtic. A Lyon spokesperson reported that this was 'down to the French league routinely re-organising the match calendar to help all our Champions League contenders'. See Daily Mail, 'O'Neill jealous of Lyon' 29/11/03

Which is why he would have been startled by the extraordinary scenes on the terracings at Rugby Park at the final game of the season during the home team's crushing 4-0 defeat by Celtic. Were the home fans, as one might have expected, upset at the drubbing? Not a bit. Many were too busy deliriously cheering the news of every goal from Ibrox. What mattered if their own team was being hammered provided the championship was not going to Parkhead? For those ninety minutes they seemed to many Celtic supporters to become Rangers fans. All the bitter bile of our sectarian society was concentrated in the joyous singing as they taunted the visitors, players and fans alike: 'you're gonna win f___ all' – a prediction bellowed more in unconfined elation rather than in sober assessment. Never has a support been more ecstatic in humiliating defeat. Our hypothetical stranger might have been puzzled, but it is what every Celtic supporter has come to expect. For Kilmarnock are not singularly guilty in this respect.

Towards the close of season 2002/03, at every away ground visited by Celtic, the same taunting chorus was heard. Why this delight in Celtic's discomfiture? Certainly, the fans of these teams want to beat Rangers too, but it is undeniable that, given a choice between Rangers and Celtic, almost all of these 'neutrals' will instinctively, enthusiastically plump for the team to beat the Irishmen. There is no unfathomable mystery here – the solution is clearly related to the fact that when the Celtic players run out as these provincial grounds they are greeted with similar chants and certainly the sentiments that they hear at Ibrox. It is the price Celtic pays in this country. It explains why some Rangers supporters include attacks upon Catholic churches[8] as part of their victory celebrations after winning the league. It is what incited them to barrack their own player Shota Adverladze for imprudently blessing himself in a friendly against Linfield at Windsor Park in 2002.[9] That Adverladze is not a Catholic but a member of the Eastern Orthodox Church did not seem to matter in this incident. Such people care little for fine

8 Daily Record, 'Gers yobs in sick attack on Church' 25/5/03

9 Sunday Mail, 'Gers must get Shota this game' 3/8/02

distinctions when such blatantly offensive gestures are performed.

There is loss as well as gain in being regarded as 'the' Catholic team, however ludicrous some people may find that title. But, short of wholesale apostasy (or taking the soup?)[10] or sacking everyone with an Irish name, there seems little that any recent past or future prospective custodians of Celtic can do about it – these things were ineluctably decided many years ago when Brother Walfrid called his momentous first meeting in the east end of Glasgow in 1887.

Despite the difficulties, despite the labelling, despite the frequent experience of 'keeping one's head down', there is nothing to be ashamed of in this history, nothing to be ashamed of in Celtic's Catholic meaningfulness. Many Celtic supporters feel a deep sense of pride in this part of their history and heritage and it's one of the elements in the club's identity that makes it different. It's one of the things that makes the club what it is, unique and distinguished. Its one of the things that makes people 'Celtic Minded'.

10 See Mark Burke's chapter in this book

Worthy is the Lamb
that was slain

JAMES MACMILLAN

Have you learnt to love your neighbors?
Of all colors, creeds and kinds?
Are you washed in the blood of the lamb?
I've learnt to love my peoples
Of all colors, creeds and kinds.
I'm all washed in that blood of that lamb.[1]

'There's a sheep loose on Dumbrochan Road!' the cry went up around the Barshare estate, and dozens of teenage and pre-teenage boys rushed to take in the spectacle. Although Cumnock is in rural Ayrshire, there was sufficient separation between the bustling mining town and the rolling farmlands around for such an event to be rare and incongruous. Although everyone seemed to be running with great purpose, Angus and I had no idea what we would do when we got there. Others did have ideas or would allow the moment to develop naturally.

A crowd had gathered at the far end of 'The Flush' – a badly maintained football pitch provided for the kids in the new houses and flats at that side of town. The animal had fallen into a ditch and the bigger boys had brought their dogs. When Angus and I eventually glimpsed it through a small forest of limbs we could see it was more of a lamb than a sheep, crazy with fear, and had already

Notes

1 'Blood of the Lamb'
  Woody Guthrie

damaged a leg. The bigger boys could not believe their luck. Their dogs – a sexually aroused alsatian and assorted mongrels – were let loose. Jaws and teeth went scything into belly and throat. The lamb looked up at us, eyes black, first with terror then blacker with despair. The alsatian was most persistent and determined – vein or artery was burst and the victim's gaze turned blacker still with resignation.

Mouth wide open, I recoiled as the beast was torn apart. The boys' faces were radiant and engorged with a primal pleasure. Angus turned one way without a word and ran full-pelt back to his mum in River View, I turned the other and rushed home to mine in Bank Avenue.

The Irish site at Carfin Grotto, Lanarkshire

A few weeks previous to this incident, my mum had been feeling sorry for herself because I thought I was too old to need a mother's cuddles. I was a big boy now, and a ten-year-old didn't need all that sissy stuff. She was flabbergasted, therefore, when this lightning bolt came through the front door, flying into her arms, clinging on for grim death, and apparently very reluctant to let go.

I was grateful for my mother at moments like this. There had been a veritable accumulation of these frightening incidents at that time. A craze had developed for pulling legs off frogs. I thought I was going to set a new world sprint record when I first saw that. And the catching of fish in the burn – not to eat, but to smash off rocks. Another one I had forgotten, understandably until now, was the hunt for bird's nests – not to steal the eggs – but to drop nails down the fledglings' throats as they opened, expecting worms from their mothers. Hilarious.

Cumnock had a thriving working-class culture in the 1960s – I remember the Berlin Octet giving a concert at the local music club, and there was great community pride in local amateur operatic and oratorio societies – performances of Handel to Gilbert and Sullivan being fondly remembered. However, there was another side to life there, dominated by machismo, hard-drinking and sporadic violence. I once witnessed a hapless motorist who had strayed unintentionally into the slipstream of an Orange Walk, catching one of the fife-players with his front bumper and bringing him crashing to the ground. The marchers fell on the driver with an excited malevolence and began to wrench him from the car. He was seconds from the same fate as the Dumbrochan sheep, but the police turned up visibly terrified, and spirited him away.

As a fledgling composer the musical dimension of these demented scenarios left an enduring impact. Turning away in fright from the sheep in the ditch I had just discovered what being knee-deep in blood actually looked like. But one of the most celebrated 'folk-songs' sung in places like Cumnock, and belted out with gusto in a number of other popular locations and environments, wallows in the image of being 'knee-deep in Fenian blood' – that's the blood of people like me – Catholics with Irish ancestry. We had our battle-songs too of course – not as raw or nakedly sectarian – recalling the victories and defeats of seemingly endless wars. These were also sung with visceral energy in yet other locations and environments in parts of the west of Scotland. This was the musical soundtrack to the disturbing testosterone-charged context of growing up in Cumnock.

In the midst of all this, my dad seemed strangely out of place. He didn't drink (much), and was quiet, thoughtful and sensitive. He preferred the company of his family to that of hard-drinking men. One of my earliest memories of him is observing him on his knees before a statue of Mary, lost in a distant humble introspection. The first time I saw him weep was on the death of Sister Clarissa, a feisty, eccentric Sacred Heart nun who had taught him in Primary One and me a generation later. These moments

letter pages of the press and were echoed throughout other media organs.

In 1999, in response to yet another incident of perceived anti-Catholic bigotry with the capturing on video of Glasgow Rangers vice-chair Donald Findlay singing about being up to his knees in Fenian blood and other supporters' songs, a Sunday Herald article asserted that:

> there is still this a strong victim mentality among many of the descendants of those early immigrants
> . . . if you're not discriminated against then you're not truly Irish, not a faithful Catholic. And **the need to be a victim** [my emphasis] leaves them open to taking offence if a nice but tipsy man sings a folk song that doesn't quite reflect admiration for them and their kind. . . He [Donald Findlay] is not and never has been a bigot. . . Neither is he prejudiced against Catholics – only Celtic football club, and that's not quite the same thing.[3]

Outside of the omnipresent Catholic schools debate, the issue of whether or not sectarianism affects modern Scottish society has only been raised in recent years because people like James MacMillan has been prepared to challenge what, for many Catholics of Irish descent, has been a prominent aspect of their experience in Scotland. Likewise, a debate ensued because Donald Findlay was 'caught'. In practising or, being complicit in, the creation and sustenance of bigotry and narrow-mindedness, much of Scottish society has remained silent over sectarianism. In such episodes one, an individual of unquestionable talent and profile, dared to state publicly the unspoken and unmentionable – namely, Scotland has a problem perhaps every bit as bitter, poisonous and debilitating as that which infests Northern Ireland – and two, a high profile individual was caught on video singing anti-Catholic songs.[4] In both instances sectarianism was forcibly brought into the realms of public debate.

Nevertheless, the degree to which Scottish society has fallen into a comfortable state of blissful unconsciousness can be seen by the initial decision of the Scottish Executive

3 Sunday Herald 'In defence of Donald' 13/6/99

4 Ibid

to exclude religion as a category for consideration in the Census (Scotland) Order 2000. It was only after a series of interventions by those such as the Medical Research Council in Glasgow, the Equal Opportunities Committee and 'some' academics, politicians and lobby groups, who pointed out the wealth of research material evidencing Catholic and Irish health and employment disadvantage, that the 2001 Census in Scotland was amended to include questions on religion, ethnicity and language spoken at home. Scotland has a wound, and it festers.

SECTARIANISM, CATHOLIC SCHOOLS AND CELTIC

The debate sparked by MacMillan's address did not pressurise the authorities in Scotland to engage in deep soul-searching to identify and tackle the roots of sectarianism. Befitting of a society that is engulfed by 'sleep-walking bigotry', the drive to 'do something' is directed at those institutions and social elements deemed divisive by those who claim to espouse tolerance and pluralism. Suspicion has, once again, fallen on the usual suspects – the Catholic Church, especially its schools, and Celtic Football Club. Much of the Scottish media's long-standing view of Catholic schools as 'the' principal source of division is typical of the received wisdom in Scotland that goes something like, 'if only the Catholic Church would give up its anachronistic, socially divisive and sectarian schooling system and send its children to integrated schools then we would have an inclusive, pluralist, respectful and tolerant society'.[5] Rather peculiar reasoning? Let's celebrate diversity, promote respect for all traditions and build an inclusive society. . . 'by closing Catholic schools'?

That a wealth of research exists extolling the positive benefits of Catholic education for both the student and the wider community seems of no consequence to today's critics of denominational schools. The American sociologist, Andrew Greeley, has pointed out that Catholic schools:

5 See The Herald 'Only pupils can decide if the supercampus passes the test' 4/11/03 and Daily Record 'School fury at bigots' split' 23/12/02

by every imaginable (academic) measure. . . are superior to their public counterparts. . . are strongest (and most successful) among disadvantaged students. . . irrespective of race and background. . . not because of rigid discipline but because they make greater academic demands, provide stronger community support, and give more personal attention to students.[6]

Nor is Greeley a lone voice in proclaiming the value of Catholic schools. The late Dan Murphy, for example, points out that a wide range of research from the USA, Australia, Canada, Great Britain and Ireland demonstrates that, using standard universally accepted educational criteria, Catholic schools substantially outperform their secular/public counterparts.[7] Furthermore, and of crucial importance in the context of divided societies such as Scotland and Northern Ireland, Murphy states that research suggests pupils in Catholic schools are less prejudiced in religious matters than those who attend public (or secular) schools.[8]

One further characteristic that distinguishes and defines the secular-liberals in modern society is a breathtaking arrogance that allows every pundit to hold and espouse an expert opinion on any aspect of religious practice and teachings of the Catholic Church with the absolute certainty of any secular or anti-Christian zealot.[9] One might expect that no reputable newspaper editor would send his cricket columnist to cover a flower show, nor would he ask an economist to write a report on a football game. Yet when it comes to commentating on any issue concerning the Catholic Church everyone – including those who have never entered a Chapel or read a single Church teaching – is an expert and should not feel constrained by ignorance, lack of knowledge or even humility.

The same blindness and faulty reasoning is similarly applied to the second area of attention for those striving to overcome sectarian division and bitterness in Scotland, namely the 'Old Firm'. After all, is this not the clearest and most publicly visible manifestation of sectarianism in

Let's celebrate diversity, promote respect for all traditions and build an inclusive society . . . 'by closing Catholic schools'?

6 A. Greeley 'Catholic Schools at the Crossroads: an American Perspective' in J.M. Feheny (ed) 'From Ideal to Action: The Inner Nature of a Catholic school Today' Dublin 1998 p.182

7 D. Murphy 'International Trends in Denominational schooling' in 'Parent and Teacher Magazine, Dublin Oct/Nov 1998 p.19

8 Ibid. p.20

9 See for example numerous articles by Muriel Gray in Sunday Herald including 22/6/03, 10/8/03, 30/11/03

Scotland? Indeed, for some, this is the last remaining relic of sectarianism that prevents Scotland from finally becoming the pluralist and tolerant society that surely all decent right-thinking people crave?[10] Solve the sectarian undercurrents that underpin this rivalry and you remove the last cancerous and poisonous element that has blighted and embarrassed Scottish society for more than a century. So goes the mantra of modern liberal Scotland uttered with all the self-confidence of an unchallengeable self-evident truth.

Voices in the media, in political life and in wider civil society in general have almost exclusively focused on overt symbols and expressions of ethno-religious-cultural identity associated with Celtic and Rangers, especially with their fan bases. Without examination or discussion (or as a reflection of their own bias?) an unquestioning appearance of equivalence of respective expressions of identity has been established and it is on this basis that the attempt to eradicate sectarianism has recently been taking place in Scotland. Very quickly attention has been directed at some of the songs sung by both sets of fans.

In relation to Celtic supporters' long established tradition of singing Irish ballads, whatever their merits or lack of them, they are not 'sectarian'. There would be a much greater degree of honesty in the debate if those who object to such songs of Celtic supporters state that, in reality, they oppose the singing of Irish songs in Scotland, particularly rebel and political songs – including some that recall the events associated with those such as Michael Davitt, a leading member of the revolutionary Irish Fenian Brotherhood and one of the club's original patrons, the great Irish Famine, as well as invoking a history of opposition to British hegemony in Ireland and over Irish people generally.[11]

However, their arguments might have a degree of integrity if they also applied the same logic to the anthem officially endorsed by the Scottish Football Association (as well as other Scottish sporting and non-sporting bodies

10 For example, see numerous publications by Steve Bruce including 'Catholic Schools in Scotland: a rejoinder to Conroy' in Oxford Review of Education Vol 29, No 2, 2003, pp.269-277 (also see Conroy's original article and reply to Bruce in Oxford Review of Education Vol 27, No 4, 2001 and Vol 29, No 3, 2003) and 'Social divisions and the social impact of Catholic schools' in Scottish Affairs No 29, 1999 pp.1-8

11 On the subject of the early years of Celtic and Irish politics see T. Campbell and P. Woods 'The Glory and the Dream: the History of Celtic F.C. 1887-1986' Edinburgh 1986 pp.15-20

and millions of Scots in Scotland and around world) and sung before all Scotland international matches. The song, 'Flower of Scotland', celebrates the victory of the Scots over the English at the Battle of Bannockburn in 1314 and, while few seem to object to that in terms of it being sectarian, socially divisive, narrow-minded, harking back to times long irrelevant, triumphalist or militaristic (debatably the case or not), it seems inconsistent that Irish songs of freedom – including the Irish national anthem – are condemned as such.

CELTIC'S RESPONSE

Unfortunately, the response of those who officially and publicly represent Celtic Football Club, especially in recent years, to these issues, has often tended to accept the received wisdom or analysis of the problem of sectarianism and bigotry. This has resulted in an approach by some of the authorities at Celtic Park distinctly lacking in courage and vision. Indeed, maybe these responses have indicated that some recent Celtic employees have even lacked in knowledge about the club itself? They certainly seem to be socially, culturally and politically lacking in relation to Celtic and its supporting community's history.[12]

Many Celtic officials (and some supporters?) in recent years have bought into the limiting, conditioned and self-evidently politically correct world vision of the self-appointed guardians of tolerance and pluralism that does nothing to either analyse or genuinely reduce the problem of sectarianism in Scottish society. This is akin to the arguments and standpoints of so-called anti-sectarian bodies that, sadly, often seem to adopt the priggish 'one side's as bad as the other' standpoint or, those who see the real problem as the expression/existence of an overt Irish Catholic identity in Scotland. These responses have severely hampered those who truly wish to tackle the roots of sectarianism and bigotry. Fergus McCann's 'Bhoys Against Bigotry' campaign of the mid-1990s was the opening salvo in what many believe was an attempt to re-

12 See Daily Record 'The Guest Slot' 5/10/02 and The Times 'First Minister backs ban on sale of sectarian items' 17/10/02, for references to Celtic employee's Ian McLeod's letter to Celtic season ticket holders, an outstanding example of this lack of understanding, appreciation and empathy.

write Celtic's history and re-define in terms more attuned to the PLC ethic and a post-modern vision of football than a genuine reflection and articulation of the identity of Celtic Football Club and its relationship to the Irish Catholic community in Scotland.

This campaign – created and endorsed by a few employees of Celtic, but ultimately at the behest of anti-Catholic and anti-Irish forces in Scottish society, without any consultation on the origin or meaning of Celtic supporter's songs – explicitly linked the singing of any Irish political song with 'sectarianism'. The 'Celtic Social Charter' is also indicative of this trend.[13] The Charter consciously defines Celtic in the most minimalistic terms imaginable – given Celtic's Irish Catholic history – as 'a Scottish club proud of its Irish roots'. For some, this desire to mark Celtic as a Scottish club has almost taken on the status of a quest for 'the Holy Grail'. Like Norman Tebbit's 'cricket test' on whether Asian immigrants could really be acceptable to British society on the basis of whether they supported India/Pakistan or England,[14] many Scots and media people in Scotland 'test' Celtic fans in Scotland by looking for sights of a Lion Rampant or a Cross of St Andrew amongst the crowd in order to confirm Celtic and its supporters acceptable inclusion in Scottish society.[15]

This might also be viewed as a campaign to coax Celtic supporters to carry these more acceptable banners in Scotland, thus encouraging them to actually become Scottish or at least, more Scottish and less Irish when supporting Celtic. This is actually about socialising the Irish in Scotland out of one identity and edging them towards another. In other words, enforce the second, third and fourth generation Irish in Scotland to become Scottish and reject their Irish identities. How many have felt the need to do this to be 'accepted', to feel, 'included'? How many have become 'Scots' or acceptable 'Scots' because of these pressures?

13 Possibly the brainchild of Fergus McCann and Peter McLean and launched on 10th January 1996

14 See Michael Ignatieff's article in The Observer 16/9/90 for reference

15 See Scotland on Sunday, Sport 24/3/02 (p.20) for reference

CELEBRATING DIVERSITY

Celtic is – and always has been – an inclusive and open club. Some of its greatest heroes – at managerial and playing level – number, and proudly so, numerous non-Catholics; Thomson, Peacock, Stein, Gemmell, McGrain, Dalglish, Lambert: the list is endless. Celtic never went down the sectarian road – and rightly so. From its very first days, Celtic resisted any temptation to follow the 'Catholic only' line. Indeed, in 1895 the committee of Celtic rejected a resolution placed before it proposing that no more than three Protestants be selected for the side adopting in its place a resolution authorising the club to sign and play whoever it desired irrespective of race, class or creed.[16] To some this may seem unusual given Celtic's undeniable Irish Catholic roots. After all the club was formed by the Marist Brother, its first patron was His Grace Charles Eyre, Archbishop of Glasgow, while a list of its players, officials, members and supporters would not look out of place in an Irish telephone directory. And yet, its openness in no ways denies its Irish Catholic roots: in fact the sense of inclusion, tolerance and pluralism – as well as its social solidarity with the disadvantaged and its charity work for needy causes of all description – is a manifestation and outworking of a Catholic ethos and world vision.

To misunderstand and misrepresent Celtic as sectarian is to misunderstand and misrepresent Catholicism. This idea is crucial to understanding real 'sectarianism' in Scottish society, especially in the media. The Catholic Church is not a ghetto church – insular, exclusive or predestining. At the heart of Catholic theology is the notion that **every** person is created by the Father, redeemed by the sacrifice of the Son and confirmed by the Spirit, that they are, in the words of the mediaeval philosopher, Thomas Aquinas, 'God's reflections'. This means that Catholics have an inescapable and unconditional duty to respect and care for all of our fellow beings, from conception until death, and that we must reach out to others in a spirit of love, solidarity, truthfulness and respect

16 See Campbell and Woods, 1986 p.18

to create a community based on mutual affirmation, tolerance and, above all else, justice.[17] For Scotland to reawaken from its state of 'sleepwalking bigotry' it might consider the words of Christ in Matthew's gospel:

> Why behold thou the mote that is in thy brother's eye but consider not the beam that is in your own eye? Wilt thou say to thy brother, 'let me pull the mote of your eye'; and behold a beam in your own eye? You hypocrite, first cast out the beam out of your own eye: and then shalt thou see clearly to cast out the mote out of thy brother's eye.   [Mt. 7:3-5]

Then, and only then, will Scotland come to be a healed, genuinely pluralist and tolerant society. Only then will it be able to celebrate diversity, to acknowledge the existence, presence and contribution of the Irish community to Scottish society and, allow Celtic Football Club and this supporting community to confidently and unapologetically assert its identity as a social institution that carries many of the hopes, aspirations and values of the Irish diaspora in Scotland.

17 On this see the Catholic Bishops of Northern Ireland, Proclaiming the Mission, Dublin 2001 pp.6-8

Home, School and Church: for it's a grand old team?

ROISÍN COLL & ROBERT A. DAVIS

> And they gave us James McGrory and Paul McStay.
> They gave us Johnstone, Tully, Murdoch, Auld and Hay.
> And most of the football greats, have passed through Parkhead gates
> Just to play football, the Glasgow Celtic way.[1]

Celtic fanlore frequently revolves around key or defining episodes in the Club's history; in recent years the European Cup win of 1967; the Centenary double of 1988; the last-gasp win of the 1998 League thwarting the 10-in-a-row ambitions of Rangers. Common to all these episodes, though only rarely acknowledged, is the wider role of the social, religious and cultural environment in shaping the experience of following and supporting the team.[2] The vernacular tradition of the Celtic support is rich in narratives that illustrate these connections. There are the many supporters' buses that announce their association with particular parish churches and major fixtures affecting the timings of church liturgies. Most especially, there is the experience of Seville in 2003, when teachers played truant from Catholic schools with the tacit approval of their superiors, where women left behind in towns and villages created their own support groups for the evening of the game, and where the sense of a genuinely inter-

Notes

1 From 'The Willie Maley Song' by David Cameron. The original song includes the relation of Paul McStay's, James, instead of Paul, while other verses have been added since the song was first penned to the tune of 'Matchstalk Men and Matchstalk Cats and Dogs', a British chart hit for Brian and Michael in 1978. See Celtic View 4/11/03

2 J.M. Bradley 'Ethnic and Religious Identity in Modern Scotland' Aldershot, Ashgate Publishing Ltd (1995) p.183

national fanbase, based on the Irish diaspora, suddenly became a felt reality.

The recent growth in the sociology of football has seen much greater attention devoted to the interaction between attachments to football clubs and involvement in a range of other social institutions. Celtic remains exceptional in the extent to which the attachment to the football club is, for a great many fans, inextricably bound up with the experience and practice of the Catholic faith. The role of Catholicism in the founding of Celtic football club is well documented, but the continuing interactions between Catholicism in the west of Scotland and the support of Celtic are often in general a source of embarrassment or even disapproval for both scholarly opinion and the mass media.[3] Indeed, detaching Catholicism in Scotland from its affiliations with Celtic is seen by many to be a moral undertaking, even a mission, aiming to rid the club of unacceptably tribal and supposedly outdated allegiances with no place in modern, tolerant, secular Scotland.[4]

The undeniably negative tone of much of this discussion fails completely to understand the true nature and ethos of the community from which Celtic springs and obstructs deeper understanding of the character of Catholic life in much of Scotland as it is reflected in support for the club. Involvement in the fortunes of Celtic is not an accidental or regrettable accretion to Catholicism in Scotland, but a central element in the formation and expression of Catholic cultural identity as it has evolved over the last hundred years in Scotland.

Historically, the club has provided a despised and marginalised Irish immigrant community with esteem, prestige and the celebration of success. As these positive experiences derived from association football – an indigenous British sport – the community has been able to reinforce its solidarity while participating in mainstream working class cultural life. The institutional infrastructure for the promotion of Celtic was from the outset provided

3 See 'Bishops' PR calls for break between Catholic Church and Celtic FC' Sunday Herald 23/3/03

4 M. Rosie and D. McCrone 'The Past is History: Catholics in Modern Scotland' in T.M.Devine (ed) 'Scotland's Shame: Bigotry and Sectarianism in Modern Scotland' Edinburgh, Mainstream Publishing 2000 p.200

by the triangle of home, school and Church[5] and this arrangement has remained pivotal in sustaining and developing the club and its support.

How do these three elements interrelate today? The triangle of home, school and Church represents a powerful and influential model of the Catholic community operating in society worldwide precisely because it embraces the full life of the community including every aspect of its cultural, political and spiritual existence. It therefore makes perfect sense to locate the passionate support of Celtic Football Club firmly within the synergy of this triangle where each element serves to reinforce the others. Family influence is of course decisive in stimulating and nurturing the sense of belonging to most football clubs. In Catholic families in the west of Scotland where the support of Celtic is part of a larger narrative of Irish Catholic struggle and achievement at home and abroad, the levels of emotional investment in the successes and disappointments of the club are, arguably, correspondingly higher than at most football clubs. The Catholic family lies at the centre of a chain of associations that extend beyond the immediate confines of the family itself to encompass ancestral affiliations and pride in the achievements of the wider community to which the family belongs.

In this context, support for Celtic functions as a validating sign of cultural and religious recognition. It derives in the main from the 'male line', where loyalty to and knowledge of the club and its achievements are passed down from father to son (and often daughter and even from mother to son) in the form of heroic stories and initiation ceremonies such as attendance at a first game. It can therefore be understood as part of the pattern of meaning and purpose binding together the generations and unifying the extended family. In an era where families of all kinds come under increasing pressure from the forces of fragmentation and dispersal, within Catholicism and at Celtic this influence is to be celebrated. This especially since it has shown itself to be readily adaptable to the

> The institutional infrastructure for the promotion of Celtic was from the outset provided by the triangle of home, school and Church and this arrangement has remained pivotal in sustaining and developing the club and its support.

5 G. McColl 'Celtic: The official illustrated history, 1888 – 1995' London, Reed International 1995 p.10

more positive aspects of modern social change such as the increased visibility of women in traditionally male domains. Without question the central role of families in the support of Celtic is shaped by the influence of Church teaching on the importance of family life in the maintenance and transmission of the faith, an influence that continues to be felt even where levels of formal religious observance have declined.[6]

The other key location where faith, football and the support of Celtic come together is, by implication, the Catholic school. This proposition may at first seem problematic, since for several decades some Catholic schools in Scotland have endeavored to distance themselves from any kind of explicit association with Celtic for fear of the accusation of sectarianism. In its Scottish context, while the anxieties informing this view may be understandable, the effort to deny or suppress the pervasive influence of support for Celtic on the culture of Catholic schools suggests that it is misguided. Even the attempt to break the link serves only to highlight the enduring connections between school and club that continue to be revealed in a range of recognisable forms. Involvement with Celtic is a rich and active feature of the recreational life of many staff and pupils at a Catholic school – particularly in the west central belt where most of them are located.

In this sense, because of these interactions as well as their historical legacies, Celtic often (unofficially) represents a powerful motif in the cultural identity of the Catholic school, particularly in the west of Scotland, and figures prominently in the hidden curriculum of playground, corridor and informal exchange between teacher and pupil. As with any other football club or contemporary event or institution, day-to-day discussion of the fortunes of Celtic can be an important source of communication between many staff and pupils, strengthening and humanising relationships and often embracing those pupils (especially boys) otherwise

6 R. Boyle 'Crisis? What Crisis?' in R. Boyle and P. Lynch 'Out of the Ghetto? The Catholic Community in Modern Scotland' Edinburgh, John Donald Publishers 1998 p.136

disaffected from formal education. Even those pupils not actively supporting the club, or with loyalties to other teams, can be caught up in the celebratory sentiment. Properly affirming the place of Celtic in the cultural experience of the Catholic school can actually contribute positively to the reinforcement of an inclusive, caring ethos. Similarly, the unacceptable aspects of football support in Scotland, such as hooliganism and sectarian violence, can also be addressed, moderated and neutralised, if appropriate recognition is accorded to genuine football and cultural enthusiasm. If this enthusiasm is then integrated into the broader system of values, mutual respect and social responsibility for which Catholic schools in Scotland are repeatedly commended,[7] then Celtic can be viewed as remaining important to this basic strand of Catholic life in Scotland.

Modern Catholic educationalists' understandings of the Catholic school see it as an expression of the mission of the Church and this mission depends critically on the relations between school and parish.[8] It is therefore inevitable that the support of Celtic, which finds such a keen covert and overt expression in the cultural life of the Catholic school, also manifests itself significantly in the life of the parish.

Celtic Cross, Ireland

Historically, Catholic parishes were the centres of the distinctive communities that they served and in consequence strove to provide all-embracing care for the spiritual, moral and material needs of their parishioners. Involvement in the recreational and sporting life of the community, culminating in the wholesale affirmation of Celtic Football Club and the principles for which it stood, originated in a desire to influence the frequently potent emotions associated with working class pastimes such as football. In Scotland, the adoption of football by the Catholic Church amounted to an endorsement of a sport that reflected specific values and ideals and that impacted on the community in a variety of positive ways. The response of parishioners to this ratification of their leisure

7 K. Sinclair 'Catholic Schools give our children true values' The Herald 13 January 2003 p.4

8 'Gravissimum Educationis' Chapters 5–9 in W.M.Abbot 'The Documents of Vatican II' 1996, London, Geoffrey Chapman Publishing pp.637-651

pursuits was to increase the sense of identification between football and religion. The attachment to Celtic within parishes in the west of Scotland can therefore be seen not as extraneous to religious practice but as implicitly legitimated by it.

This observation helps to explain the widespread impression that support for Celtic seems often to involve levels of feeling normally associated with religious devotion. However, the connection with the parish shows that this convergence does not trivialise or compromise religious practice but serves rather to extend its meaning beyond the confines of the church building and formal parish life out into everything that matters to the Catholic faithful. Family, community, memory, story-telling, sharing, emotion, joy and sadness, are just some of the factors involved.

In a time of change all of the institutions of religious belief have come under pressure from the forces of secularisation. Celtic Football Club has also felt the effect of these forces and this has resulted in a loosening of the official ties between the club and the Catholic Church. Since the late twentieth century it might be argued that it has become uncommon for the club to make any explicit connection, other than a historical one, with the Church. This may (or may not) be viewed as an understandable position for a major football team operating on the international sporting stage and in a 'pluralist society'.

However, such a response may also be seen as the club succumbing to the forces of secularisation and, as evidence of the pressures that have been experienced to conform to the more dominant and acceptable ways of Scottish life, rather than as an expression of a plural Scotland that gives due recognition to Catholics and their cultural, spiritual and often differing ethnic values. From the perspective of the Catholic community, particularly in the west of Scotland, their overwhelmingly abiding loyalty to Celtic represents a form of continuity, unity of purpose and cultural validation of undiminished significance. For many Catholics who follow Celtic, the Club remains an integral and unmistakably positive influence within the Catholic community of the west of Scotland.

Henrik Larrson

Contributors

Dr Joseph M Bradley, the editor of this collection of essays, is the author of 'Ethnic and Religious Identity in modern Scotland' (Avebury 1995), 'Sport, Culture, Politics and Scottish Society: Irish Immigrants and the Gaelic Athletic Association' (John Donald 1998) and joint author of 'Sport Worlds: a sociological perspective' (Human Kinetics 2002). Dr Bradley has published widely on sporting matters in relation to religion, ethnicity, diaspora and politics. His publications include works on Orangeism in Scotland, Scotland's international support, politics in Scottish football and the Irish diaspora in Scotland. He is currently exploring the culture of football in Scotland with a view to a published book in 2005. He is lecturer in Sports Studies at the University of Stirling.

Mark Burke was born and bred in Dublin and was a founder member (in 1987) and chairperson of the Naomh Padraig Celtic Supporter's Club in Ireland's capital city. Since 1998 he has also been the Assistant General Secretary of the Celtic Supporter's Association based in Glasgow. His first game was in December 1984 in the controversial UEFA ordered replay of the Cup Winners' Cup second round tie against Rapid Vienna in Manchester, when Celtic were beaten 1-0 in front of 51,500.

Roisín Coll graduated with BEd (Hons) from St Andrew's College/ University of Glasgow in 1995 and with a Masters in Education in 1999. Roisìn lectures in religious education at the University of Glasgow. She is currently engaged in doctoral research on the continuing professional development needs of Catholic teachers and has published on the relationship between the Catholic Church and the State in Scotland. Her other interests include performing Irish folk and traditional music. Her first Celtic game was in May 1987 when Falkirk won 2-1 at Celtic Park. 14,238 attended the match.

Dr Robert A Davis graduated from the University of Strathclyde with a BA and from the University of Stirling with an MLitt in English Literature and Anthropology. He is a senior lecturer in religious education at the University of Glasgow and has taught and written widely on many aspects of Scottish education, childhood and literature. His first Celtic game was in October 1966 in the league against Airdrie when Celtic won 3-0 in front of 41,000.

Frank Devine graduated with a degree in Economic and Social History and Politics from the University of Strathclyde in 1997. His 'Honours' dissertation examined working class culture and Irish identity in Scottish society. Frank comes from Mossend in Lanarkshire and now lives in Blantyre. He is employed as a Client Development Worker with Careers Scotland. He attended his first Celtic game v St Johnstone in 1968. Celtic won 2-1 and 37,000 attended the match.

Des Dillon is an award-winning writer. Born 1960 and brought up in Coatbridge, he studied English at the University of Strathclyde, taught English at High School and was Writer in Residence in Castlemilk during 1998-2000. Poet, short story writer, novelist and dramatist for film, television and stage, he was TAPS Writer of The Year 2000, and won a Scottish Arts Council Writers' award 2000 and the International Playwriting Festival Award 2001. His novel 'Me an Ma Gal', was voted the book that best evokes contemporary Scotland on World Book Day 2003. He lives in Galloway. First Celtic match v Kokkola (Finland) in the European Cup in 1970. Celtic won 9-0 and 41,000 attended the match.

Dr Aidan Donaldson is a teacher of Religious Education at St Mary's Christian Brothers Grammar School, Belfast. Has published widely on the subject of Catholic schools and on the philosophy and vision of Catholic education. His work with the Christian Brothers involves him taking students from Belfast to Misisi Township in Lusaka (Zambia) where they live and work with some of the most marginalised people in Africa including AIDS victims, orphans, the handicapped and poverty-stricken. He has represented the Republic of Ireland at international level on several occasions at marathon running. He attended his first Celtic match at Celtic Park in November 1980 when Aberdeen won 2-0 in front of 29,000.

Patricia Ferns was born and brought up in the Glasgow area. Her life now is a reflection of 'Faith', 'Family' and 'Football' that was inherent in her early upbringing. Her love of Ireland and Celtic are evident in her music and have earned her the nom de plume 'Celtic's first lady of song'. Her earliest memories of watching Celtic are from the late sixties and early seventies, when Jimmy Johnstone was every Celtic fan's hero. Married with two young children, along with her husband Martin, all are season ticket holders at Celtic Park.

Stephen Ferrie is a communications professional working in the financial services industry in Scotland. He is married with two teenage children and lives in Coatbridge where his love of Celtic has been carefully nurtured since the 1960s. This is his first contribution to a published work. Stephen attended his first Celtic match in a league game versus Raith Rovers in November 1968. Celtic won 2-0 and 31,000 attended.

Tommy Gemmell was born in October 1943 and brought up in the Motherwell and Wishaw areas. Attended Craignuik Primary and achieved the dux medal before going to Wishaw High. While at Wishaw in the late 1950s, Tommy played against future Celtic players John Cushley and Bobby Murdoch who played with Our Lady's High, Motherwell. Served his apprenticeship at the local Ravenscraig works as an electrician. Played for Scotland twenty-three times including the 1967 victory over England at Wembley. Scored in both Celtic's European Cup Finals in 1967 and 1970.

Tom Grant was born in 1952 and lived his early life in the mining village of Cardowan on the outskirts of Glasgow. Attended St Patrick's High School Coatbridge before entering architecture. Became a director of club for ten years from 1985. Was stadium director during the rebuilding of the new stadium under Fergus McCann. Attended first Celtic game v Third Lanark in a Scottish Cup quarter final tie in March 1962. The game ended 4-4 (Celtic won the replay 4-0) and was attended by 42,500.

James Greenan works as an electrical contractor in County Monaghan. A founding member in 1992 of the Paul Johnson CSC in Monaghan, he was first chair of the Association of Irish Celtic Supporters Clubs on its foundation in 1998. In July 1975, Jim attended his first Celtic match, a friendly game in Dundalk, fourteen miles from his home town of Castleblayney.

Willy Maley is Professor of English Literature at Glasgow University. Together with Ian Auld, Bertie's brother, he wrote 'The Lions of Lisbon' (1992), a play celebrating the silver anniversary of Celtic's European Cup victory, which filled the Arches, the Pavilion and the Tron Theatres. His first game was Hibs at home (probably January 1971 when 38,500 attended the match). Evan Williams was in goal but all Willy really remembers is the rush going up the stairs into the stadium, forgetting his feet as he floated to the surface.

Joseph McAleer was brought up in the Garngad in the east end of Glasgow. Attended Saint Roch's Primary and Secondary Schools. A self-employed builder, Joe was a member of the Garngad Millburn CSC before joining the Sons of Donegal in the early 1980s. He was one of the main organisers of the street parties in Garngad when Celtic won the league in 1998 under Wim Jansen and later when the treble was won in 2001 under Martin O'Neill. Joe's first visits to Celtic Park included the major European games of the early 1970s as well as some of the Cup Finals against Hibernian at Hampden in the same period.

Hugh MacDonald was born in 1955 and was brought up in Possil, St George's Cross and then Busby when, in the sporting event surely of 1967, he captained the local St Joseph's primary school. He spent a year at St Mungo's in Duke Street, Glasgow, before joining the Xaverian Fathers in Coatbridge as a seminarian. He joined the newspaper industry in 1972, completing a journalism course at the then Napier College, and has worked with many newspapers in a variey of roles. He is currently a sports columnist for The Herald. His first Celtic match was in the late fifties or perhaps 1960 against Airdrie at Parkhead.

Dr James MacMillan is a composer whose music is played all over the world. He studied as an undergraduate in music at the University of Edinburgh, and completed his doctoral studies at the University of Durham. He has numerous honorary doctorates and fellowships from various British universities and colleges. He was awarded a CBE in 2004. His Edinburgh Festival speech 'Scotland's Shame: anti-Catholicism as a barrier to genuine pluralism', was delivered in 1999 provoking a bout of national soul-searching. While alienating him from many of the Scottish commentariat, it has attracted much more objective and thoughtful reflection elsewhere. His first Celtic game was the Scottish League Cup Final in April 1969 v Hibernian at Hampden. Celtic won 6-2 and 74,000 attended the match.

Dr Francis J O'Hagan graduated from the Open University with a BA and from the University of Glasgow with an MEd. He is a lecturer in History and Environmental Studies in the Faculty of Education at the University of Glasgow. His published work has been predominantly on the achievements of the religious orders to education and their contributions to social amelioration in the city of Glasgow in the nineteenth and twentieth centuries. Attended his first Celtic match against Third Lanark in the Scottish Cup at Hampden Park in 1961. Celtic won 4-0 in front of 51,518 after a 4-4 draw at Celtic Park.

Edward O'Neil was born in Glasgow and brought up in Easterhouse. He graduated with a BA in English Studies from the University of Strathclyde in 1988. He now lives in Coatbridge and teaches English in a secondary school in Cumbernauld. The first match he

remembers distinctly was the May 1972 Scottish Cup Final against Hibs when Dixie Deans scored for fun and rosettes were very much the fashion. Celtic won 6-1 and 106,102 attended the match.

Patrick Reilly was educated at the University of Glasgow and the University of Oxford where he completed his research degree on Jonathan Swift. Head of Department of English at the University of Glasgow before retiring as Emiritus Professor in 1997. Journalist and broadcaster, has published seven books on literary criticism including studies of Swift, Orwell, Golding, Fielding, Conrad and Joyce. Patrick lives in Glasgow. The first game he remembers attending was a wartime league match (southern) against Albion Rovers in Coatbridge in November 1941. The match ended 4-4 and Jock Stein, playing centre-half, either made his debut or played as a trialist for Rovers. This was also a time when the Celtic forwards were affectionately referred to as the 'Five Sorrowful Mysteries'.

James Rooney is an inventory manager for a large North American bakery and currently working towards his CPIM university designation. Originally from Faifley in Clydebank, attended St Joseph's Primary and St Columba's High School in the area. Has lived in Canada since the early 1980s. He has been involved with two CSCs in the suburbs of Toronto and until 2002 held various positions with North America's largest CSC in Bramalea. Aged three, he attended his first Celtic game v St Johnstone in October 1968 when 37,000 were present.

Heiko Schlesselmann was born in 1972 in Hamburg and has been supporter of FC St Pauli since 1984. Employed as a social worker with the club's supporters and contributes to the various fanzines of St Pauli. Since his first Celtic game he has been fascinated by the supporters and culture of Celtic. Has followed the club around Europe with the highlights being a friendly game between Celtic and St Pauli in Hamburg in 1995. First Celtic match attended was a UEFA Cup match v Dortmund in 1992 when Celtic lost 1-0 in front of 31,578.

Brendan Sweeney was born in Clydebank in 1967. He attended St Joseph's Primary and St Columba's High School. He was a founding member of 'Celts for Change', that helped oust 'The Old Board' at Celtic Park in 1994. Member of the Linnvale Shamrock CSC in Clydebank and Executive Committee member of the Celtic Supporters Association. Currently employed with Scotrail in Glasgow. Earliest Celtic memory was listening to Celtic songs whilst sitting on his dad's knee. Attended first Celtic match at the Scottish Cup Final v Hibernian in 1972. Celtic won 6-1 and the game was attended by 106,102.

Edward Toner was born in 1963 in the east end of Glasgow. First Celtic game attended in the late 1960s. Attended the 1970 European Cup Semi Final v Leeds United at Hampden Park. Joined his first Celtic Supporters Club as a teenager and has been a member of the Dennistoun No1 CSC since 1983. Has been active member of the Celtic FC Supporters Association for many years. Was elected as General Secretary of the CSA in October 1999. In 2003 he represented Celtic supporters in receiving the FIFA 'Fair Play' Award in Switzerland. Has lived and worked all his life in the east end of Glasgow. Currently employed as a Welfare Rights Officer.

Andrew Walker was born in 1965 and enjoyed sixteen years as a professional footballer, six of which were spent as a Celtic player. One of eleven children, Andy is married with four children of his own. Retired from playing in 2000, Andy has since been active in the media writing columns for newspapers and appearing regularly on both radio and television. Andy's first game as a fan was a league game in September 1971 when his dad took him to see Celtic beat Clyde 9-1 in front 30,000.

The huddle, Cup Final 2001

Bibliography

Allison L. 'The Politics of Sport' Manchester University Press 1986

Anderson B. 'Imagined Communities: Reflections on the Origins and Spread of Nationalisms' Verso, London 1991

Archer I. & Royle T. (Eds) 'We'll Support You Evermore: The Impertinent Saga of Scottish 'Fitba' ' London: Souvenir Press 1976

Armstrong G. and Giulionotti R. (Eds) 'Entering the Field: New Perspectives in World Football' Oxford: Berg, 1997

Audrey S. 'Multiculturalism in Practice: Irish, Jewish, Italian and Pakistani migration to Scotland' Ashgate, Aldershot 2000

Bairner A. Football and the idea of Scotland, in G Jarvie and G Walker (Eds), 'Scottish Sport in the Making of the Nation' Leicester: Leicester University Press, 9-26, 1994

Beresford D. 'Ten Men Dead' Grafton Books, London 1987

Billig M. 'Banal Nationalism' London: Sage 1995

Black I. 'Tales of the Tartan Army' Edinburgh: Mainstream Publishing 1997

Blain N. and Boyle R. Battling along the boundaries: The marking of Scottish identity in sports journalism, in G. Jarvie and G. Walker (Eds) 'Scottish Sport in the Making of the Nation' Leicester: Leicester University Press, 125-141, 1994

Boyle R. and Haynes R. 'The Grand old game': football, media and identity in Scotland, in Media, Culture and Society Vol.18, No.4, pp.549-564, 1996

Boyle R. and Haynes R. 'Power Play: Sport, the Media and Popular Culture' London, Longman 2000

Bradley J.M. 'Ethnic and Religious Identity in Scotland: Politics, Culture and Football' Aldershot: Avebury 1995

Bradley J.M. 'Intermarriage, Education, and Discrimination' in T. M. Devine (ed) 'St Mary's Hamilton: A Social History 1846-1996' John Donald, Edinburgh, pp.83-94 1995

Bradley J.M. 'Profile of a Roman Catholic Parish in Scotland' in Scottish Affairs No 14, Winter, pp.123-139 1996

Bradley J.M. 'Identity, Politics and Culture: Orangeism in Scotland' in Scottish Affairs No 16, Summer, pp.104-128 1996

Bradley J.M. 'Facets of the Irish Diaspora: 'Irishness' in 20th Century Scotland' in Irish Journal of Sociology Vol.6 1996

Bradley J.M. ' 'We Shall Not Be Moved'! Mere Sport, Mere Songs?: a tale of Scottish Football' in 'Fanatics' London: Routledge, pp.203-218 1998

Bradley J.M. 'Sport, Culture, Politics and Scottish Society: Irish immigrants and the Gaelic Athletic Association in Scotland' John Donald, Edinburgh 1998

Bradley J.M. 'Imagining Scotland: nationality, cultural identities, football and discourses of Scottishness' Stirling Research Papers in Sports Studies, University of Stirling 2001

Bradley J.M., Maguire J., Jarvie, Mansfield L. 'Sport Worlds: A sociological perspective' Human Kinetics, USA 2002

Bradley J M, 'Images of Scottishness and Otherness in International Football' Social Identities: Journal for the Study of Race, Nation and Culture, 9, 1, pp.7-23 2003

Brah A., Hickman M.J., and Mac an Ghaill M. 'Thinking Identities: Ethnicity, Racism and Culture' London: MacMillan Press 1999

Brown A. (Ed) 'Fanatics: Power, Identity and Fandom in Football' London: Routledge, 1998

Brown A., McCrone D., Paterson L., and Surridge P. 'The Scottish Electorate: The 1997 General Election and Beyond' London: Macmillan Press 1999

Brown C. 'The Social History of Religion in Scotland Since 1730' Methuen, London 1987

Brown C. 'Did Urbanisation Secularize Britain' Urban History Yearbook 1988

Brown C. 'Religion and Society in Scotland since 1707' Edinburgh: Edinburgh University Press 1997

Brown S.J. 'Outside the Covenant: The Scottish Presbyterian Churches and Irish Immigration 1922-1938' in The Innes Review, Vol.XLII, No.1, Spring pp.19-45 1991

Brubaker R. 'The return of assimilation? Changing perspectives on immigration and its sequels in France, Germany, and the United States' in Ethnic and Racial Studies, 24, 4, pp.531-548 2001

Bruce S. 'No Pope Of Rome: Anti-Catholicism In Modern Scotland' Mainstream Publishing, Edinburgh 1985

Bruce S. 'Out of the ghetto: the ironies of acceptance' The Innes Review, Vol.XLIII, No.2, pp.145-154 1992

Bruce S. 'Comparing Scotland and Northern Ireland' in 'Scotland's Shame: Bigotry and sectarianism in modern Scotland' Mainstream, Edinburgh 2000, pp.135-142

Bruce S. 'Catholic Schools in Scotland: a rejoinder to Conroy' in Oxford Review of Education, vol 29, no 2, pp.269-277 2003

Buckley M. 'Sitting on your politics: the Irish amongst the British and the women among the Irish' in J. McLaughlin (ed) 'Location and Dislocation in Contemporary Irish Society' Cork University Press, Cork, pp.94-132 1997

Burdsey D and Chappell R, ' "And If You Know Your History. . ." An Examination of the formation of football clubs in Scotland and their role in the construction of social identity' in The Sports Historian, No.21, pp.94-106, 2001

Campbell T. and Woods P. 'The Glory and The Dream, The History of Celtic FC, 1887-1986' Mainstream Publishing 1986

Canning Rev B.J. 'Padraig H Pearse and Scotland' Published by Padraig Pearse Centenary Commemoration Committee, Glasgow 1979

Cassidy L. 'Faded Pictures from Irish Town' in Causeway, pp.34-38, Autumn, 1996

Coakley J.J. 'Sport in Society: Issues and Controversies' Mosby, Colerado 1990

Coakley J.J. 'Sport in Society: Issues and Controversies' USA, Irwin, McGraw-Hill 1998

Cooney J. 'Scotland and the Papacy' Paul Harris, Edinburgh 1982

Conroy J. ' "Yet I Live Here. . ." A Reply to Bruce on Catholic Education in Scotland' Oxford Review of Education Vol.29, No.3, Sept pp.403-412, 2003

Curtis L. 'Ireland The Propaganda War' Pluto Press 1984

Curtis L. 'Nothing But The Same Old Story: The roots of Anti-Irish Racism' Published by Information on Ireland, 5th edition 1988

Curtice, J. & Seawright, D. 'The Decline of the Scottish Conservatives and Unionist Party 1950-1992: Religion, Ideology or Economics?' in Journal of Contemporary History, 2, 2, pp.319-342 1995

Davis G. 'The Irish In Britain 1815-1914' Gill and Macmillan 1991

Devine T.M. (ed) 'Irish Immigrants and Scottish Society in the Nineteenth and Twentieth Centuries; Proceedings of the Scottish Historical Studies Seminar: University of Strathclyde, 1989/90' John Donald Publishers Ltd 1991

Devine T.M. 'Scotland's Shame: Bigotry and Sectarianism in Modern Scotland' Edinburgh: Mainstream 2000

Devine T.M. (ed) 'St Mary's Hamilton: A Social History, 1846-1996' John Donald, Edinburgh 1995

Devine T.M. & Mitchison R. 'People and Society in Scotland: Vol.1, 1760-1830' John Donald, Edinburgh 1988

Dickson T. (ed) 'Capital and Class in Scotland' John Donald Publishers 1982

Docherty D. 'The Celtic Football Companion' John Donald, Edinburgh 1986

Donovan R. 'Voices of Distrust: The Expression of Anti-Catholic Feeling in Scotland 1778-1781', in The Innes Review Vol.XXIX, 2, pp.111-139, 1978

Doyle A. 'Ethnocentrism and History Textbooks: representation of the Irish Famine 1845-49 in history textbooks in English secondary schools' Intercultural Education, Vol.13, No.3 2002

Dunning E. 'Sport Matters: sociological studies of sport, violence and civilization' London, Routledge pp.130-158 1999

Eitzen D. Stanley and Sage, George H. 'Sociology of North American Sport' 5th ed. Dubuque I.A., Brown and Benchmark 1993

Esplin R. 'Down the Copland Road' Argyll: Argyll Publishing 2000

Feehan J.M. 'Bobby Sands and the Tragedy of Northern Ireland' Mercier Press, Dublin and Cork 1984

Finley R.J. 'Nationalism, Race, Religion and The Irish Question in Inter-War Scotland' in The Innes Review, Vol.XLII, No.1, Spring, pp.46-67 1991

Finn, G.P.T. 'Racism, Religion and Social Prejudice: Irish Catholic Clubs, Soccer and Scottish Society – I The Historical Roots of Prejudice' in The International Journal of the History of Sport, 8, 1, pp.72-95 1991

Finn G.P.T. 'Racism, Religion and Social Prejudice: Irish Catholic Clubs, Soccer and Scottish Society - II Social Identities and Conspiracy Theories' in The International Journal of the History of Sport 8, 3, pp.370-397 1991

Finn G.P.T. 'Faith, Hope and Bigotry: Case Studies of Anti-Catholic Prejudice in Scottish Soccer and Society' in 'Scottish Sport in the Making of the Nation: Ninety-Minute Patriots' Leicester University Press 1994

Finn G.P.T. 'Sporting Symbols, Sporting Identities: Soccer and Intergroup Conflict in Scotland and Northern Ireland' pp.33-55 in 'Scotland and Ulster' I.S. Wood (ed), Mercat Press, Edinburgh 1994

Finn G.P.T. Series of papers lodged with Jordanhill Library, Strathclyde University on the role of conspiracy in anti-Catholicism in Scotland and Northern Ireland, 1990-1994

Forgacs D. 'The Antonio Gramsci Reader' Lawrence and Wishart, London 1999

Forsyth R. in Linklater M. and Denniston R. (eds) 'Anatomy of Scotland: how Scotland works' Edinburgh: Chambers, pp.334-353, 1992

Fraser T.G. (ed) 'The Irish Parading Tradition: Following the Drum' Macmillan Press, London, 2000

Gallagher D.J. 'Neutrality as a Moral Standpoint, Conceptual Confusion and the Full Inclusion Debate' Disability & Society Vol.16, No.5, pp637-654 2001

Gallagher T. 'Glasgow The Uneasy Peace' Manchester University Press 1987

Gallagher T. 'The Catholic Irish in Scotland: In Search of Identity' in T.M.Devine (ed) 'Irish Immigrants and Scottish Society in the Nineteenth and Twentieth Centuries' John Donald Publishers Limited 1991

Gilley S. and Swift R. eds 'The Irish in the Victorian City' Croom Helm, London 1985

Giulianotti R. 'Scoring away from Home: A Statistical Study of Scotland Football Fans at International Matches in Romania and Sweden' International Review for Sociology of Sport 29/2, pp.172-200 1994

Giulianotti R. 'Football and the Politics of Carnival: An Ethnographic Study of Scottish Fans in Sweden' in International Review for Sociology of Sport 30/2 1995, pp.191-223 1995

Giulianotti, R. 'Taking Liberties: Hibs casuals and Scottish law' pp.229-261, in 'Football, Violence and Social Identity' R. Giulianotti, N. Bonney & M. Hepworth (eds), London, Routledge, 1994

Giulianotti, R. Game Without Frontiers: Football, Identity and Modernity, Aldershot, Arena Ashgate 1994

Giulianotti R. 'Built by the Two Varelas: The Rise and Fall of Football Culture and National Identity in Uruguay' in Finn G.P.T. and Giulianotti R. 'Football Culture: Local Contests, Global Visions' Frank Cass, London (originally from Galeano E. (1997) 'Football: in Sun and Shadow' London p.42 2000

Gramsci A. 'Selections from prison notebooks of Antonio Gramsci' New York, International Publishers 1971

Greely A.M. McCready 'Does Ethnicity Matter' in Ethnicity Vol.1, No.1, April, pp.91-108 1974

Gruneau R. & Whitson D. 'Hockey Night in Canada' Toronto, Canada, Garamond Press 1993

Handley J.E. 'The Irish in Scotland' John S Burns & Sons, Glasgow (this book incorporates both 'The Irish in Scotland 1798-1845' and 'The Irish in Modern Scotland' 1943 & 1947, Cork University Press) 1964

Handley J.E. 'The Celtic Story' Stanley Paul, London 1960

Hargreaves J. 'Sport, Power and Culture – A Social and Historical Analysis of Popular Sports in Britain' Cambridge, Polity Press 1986

Hargreaves J. (ed) 'Sport, Culture and Ideology' Routledge, pp.30-61 1982

Hargreaves J. & McDonald I. 'Cultural Studies and the Sociology of Sport' in J. Coakley & E. Dunning 'Handbook of Sports Studies' Sage, pp.49-60 2000

Hickman M. 'A study of the incorporation of the Irish in Britain with special reference to Catholic state education: involving a comparison of the attitudes of pupils and teachers in selected

Catholic schools in London and Liverpool' unpublished PhD, University of London 1990

Hickman M. 'Religion, Class and Identity: The State, the Catholic Church and the Education of the Irish in Britain' Avebury, Aldershot 1995

Hickman M. 'Reconstructing deconstructing 'race': British political discourses about the Irish in Britain' Ethnic and Racial Studies, Vol.21, No.2, pp.289-305 1998

Hoberman J. 'Sport and Political Ideology' Heinemann, London 1984

Hobsbawm E. 'Nations and Nationalism Since 1780: Programme, Myth, Reality' Cambridge: Cambridge University Press 1990

Holmes M. 'Symbols of National Identity: The Case of the Irish National Football Team' in Irish Political Studies 9, pp.81-98 1994

Holt R. 'Sport and History: The State of the Subject in Britain' in Twentieth Century British History Vol.7, No.2, pp.231-252 1996

Horne J. 'Racism, Sectarianism and Football in Scotland' in Scottish Affairs 12, pp.27-51 1995

Horne J, Tomlinson A, Whannel G. 'Understanding Sport' London, E&FN Spon 1999

Inglis J 'The Irish In Britain: A Question Of Identity' in Irish Studies in Britain No.3, Spring/Summer 1982

Isajiw W. W. 'Definitions of Ethnicity' in Ethnicity Vol.1, No.2, July, pp.111-124 1974

Jarvie G. & Maguire J. 'Sport and Leisure in Social Thought' London, Routledge 1994

Jarvie G. & Reid I. 'Sport, Nationalism and Culture in Scotland' in The Sports Historian, 19, 1, pp.97-124 1999

Jarvie G. Walker G. (eds) 'Scottish Sport in the Making of the Nation: Ninety Minute Patriots' Leicester University Press 1994

Jenkins R. 'The thistle and the grail' MacDonald & Co, Glasgow 1983

Kendrick S. 'Scotland, Social Change and Politics' in 'The Making of Scotland: Nation, Culture and Social Change' D. McCrone, D. Kendrick & P. Straw (eds), Edinburgh University Press 1989

Kelly E. 'Challenging Sectarianism in Scotland: The Prism of Racism' in Scottish Affairs, No.42, Winter, pp.32-56 2003

King C.R., Staurowsky E.J., Davis L.R., Pewewardy C. 'Of Polls And Race Prejudice: Sports Illustrated Errant Indian Wars' in Vol.26, No.4, pp.381-402 2002 Journal of Sports and Social Issues

Kircaldy J. 'Irish Jokes: No Cause For Laughter' Irish Studies in Britain, No.2, Autumn/Winter 1981

Kinealy C. 'This Great Calamity: The Irish Famine 1845-52' Gill & Macmillan Ltd 1994

Logue P. (ed) 'Being Irish: Personal reflections of being Irish today'
Oak Tree Press, Dublin 2000

McCaffrey J. 'Roman Catholics in Scotland in the nineteenth and
twentieth centuries', Records of the Scottish Church History
Society, 21, 2, 1983

McCrone D. 'The Sociology of Nationalism' London: Routledge 1998

McCrone D. Rosie M. 'Left and Liberal: Catholics in modern
Scotland' in Boyle R. & Lynch P. (eds) 'Out of the Ghetto: The
Catholic Community in Modern Scotland' Edinburgh: John
Donald, 67-94 1998

McCrone D. 'Understanding Scotland: the sociology of a nation' 2nd
edition, Routledge, London 2001

McDevitt R. 'A Life in the Tartan Army' Glasgow: Zipo Publishing
1999

MacDonald C.M.M. 'Unionist Scotland 1800-1997' Edinburgh: John
Donald 1998

McFarland E.W. 'Protestants First: Orangeism in 19th Century
Scotland' Edinburgh University Press 1990

McKenna Y. 'Forgotten Migrants: Irish Women Religious in England,
1930s-1960s' International Journal of Population Geography, 9,
pp.295-308 2003

MacLaughlin J. 'Pestilence on their backs, famine in their stomachs:
the racial construction of Irishness and the Irish in Victorian
Britain' in 'Ireland and Cultural Theory, The Mechanics of
Authenticity' C. Graham, R. Kirkland (eds), Macmillan

McPherson B.D., Curtis J.E. & Loy J.W. 'The Social Significance of
Sport' Human Kinetics, Illinois 1989

Maver I. 'The Catholic Community in Scotland in the 20th Century'
in T.M. Devine & R.J. Finley (eds) Edinburgh University Press,
Edinburgh, pp.269-284 1996

Miller D. (ed) 'Rethinking Northern Ireland, Culture, Ideology and
Colonialism' Addison Wesley Longman, Essex 1998

Mitchell J. 'Religion and Politics in Scotland' unpublished paper
presented to Seminar on Religion and Scottish politics,
University of Edinburgh 1992

Miles R. & Muirhead L. 'Racism in Scotland: a matter for further
investigation?' in Scottish Government Yearbook, pp.108-136
1986

Miles R. 'Racism' Routledge, London 1989

Mitchell M.J. 'The Irish in the West of Scotland 1797-1848: Trade
unions, strikes and political movements' John Donald,
Edinburgh 1998

Moorhouse B. 'Professional Football and working class culture:
English Theories and Scottish evidence' in Sociological Review,
32, 285-315 1984

Moorhouse B. 'Scotland Against England: Football and Popular

Culture' in International Journal of the History of Sport, 4, 189-202 1987

Morley D. & Chen K.H. (eds) Stuart Hall: Critical dialogues in cultural studies, Routledge, London 1996

Morrow S. 'The People's Game?: Football, Finance and Society' Palgrave Macmillan, Basingstoke 2003

Muirhead Rev. I.A. 'Catholic Emancipation: Scottish Reactions in 1829' Innes Review, 24, 1, Spring 1973

Muirhead Rev. I.A. 'Catholic Emancipation in Scotland: the debate and the aftermath' Innes Review, 24, 2, Autumn 1973

Murray B. 'The Old Firm: Sectarianism, sport and society in Scotland' John Donald, Edinburgh 1984

Murray B. 'Glasgow's Giants: 100 years of the Old Firm' Mainstream, Edinburgh 1988

Murray B. 'Bhoys, Bears and Bigotry: The Old Firm in the New Age' Mainstream, Edinburgh 2003

Nixon H.L. & Frey J.H. 'A Sociology of Sport' London, Wadsworth 1996

O'Conner K. 'The Irish in Britain' Torc, Dublin 1970

O Tuathaigh M.A.G. 'The Irish in Nineteenth Century Britain: Problems of Integration' pp.13-36, in Gilley and Swift 'The Irish in the Victorian City' 1985

Reid I. 'Nationalism, Sport and Scotland's Culture' in Scottish Centre Research Papers in Sport, Leisure and Society, Vol.2 1997

Rosie M. & McCrone D. 'The Past is History: Catholics in Modern Scotland' in 'Scotland's Shame: Bigotry and sectarianism in Modern Scotland' Mainstream, Edinburgh, pp199-217 2000

Rowe D. & Wood N. (eds) Editorial of Media, Culture and Society, Vol.18, No.4 1996

Schlesinger P. 'Media, the Political Order and National Identity' in Media, Culture and Society, Vol.13, No.3, pp.297-308 1991

Sugden J. & Bairner A. 'Northern Ireland; Sport in a Divided Society' in Allison L. 'The Politics Of Sport' pp.90-117, Manchester University Press 1986

Sugden J. & Bairner A. 'Sport, Sectarianism and Society in a Divided Ireland' Leicester University Press, Leicester 1993

Sugden J. & Tomlinson A. (eds) 'Hosts and Champions: Soccer Cultures, National Identities and the USA World Cup' Aldershot: Arena, Ashgate 1994

Walker G. 'There's not a team like the Glasgow Rangers: football and religious identity in Scotland' in G. Walker &

T. Gallagher (eds) 'Sermons and Battle Hymns: Protestant Culture in Modern Scotland' Edinburgh: Edinburgh University Press 1990

Walls P. & Williams R. 'Sectarianism at work: Accounts of employment discrimination against Irish Catholics in Scotland' in Ethnic and Racial Studies, Vol.26, No.4, pp.632-662 2003

Walter B., Morgan S., Hickman M.J. & Bradley J.M. 'Family Stories, public silence: Irish identity construction amongst the second-generation Irish in England' Scottish Geographical Journal, Special Edition on 'The Fate of 'Nations' in a Globalised World', Vol.118, No.3, pp.201-218, 2002

Walvin J. 'The People's Game: The History of Football Revisited' Edinburgh, Mainstream 1994

Wilson B. 'Celtic, A Century with Honour' Willow Books, William Collins Publications, Glasgow 1988

To all my friends I leave kind thoughts,
To my enemies the fullest possible forgiveness,
And to Ireland the undying prayer
For the absolute freedom and independence
which it was my life's ambition to try and obtain for her

Michael Davitt
1846-1906

Seville 2003

Match tickets from Celtic's three European Finals to date:
Lisbon 1967; Milan 1970; and Seville 2003

Estadio Olímpico
21 May 20:45
SEVILLA 2003

CELTIC FC

Official Programme
Price: 5 euros

FC PORTO

The Celtic starting XI at the UEFA Cup Final vs Porto, 2003

Other Books from Argyll Publishing

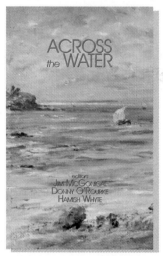

Across the Water
– Irishness in modern Scottish writing
editors Jim McGonigal, Donny O'Rourke & Hamish Whyte
1 902831 15 2 £10.99 382 pages

Across the Water is an anthology of Irishness in modern Scottish writing. Issued at an important time in the revising of the Scottish nation's identity, this book is both an enjoyable read as well as a document of immigration and the often humorous and sometimes painful process of integration. All of the 41 contributors reflect on their experience of Irishness in Scotland.

Contributors include **Patrick MacGill** Edward Gaitens *Freddie Anderson* Matt McGinn **Joan Lingard** William McIlvanney *Stephen Mulrine* Anne Downie **John Byrne** Tom McGrath *Bernard MacLaverty* Hayden Murphy **Alan Spence** Theresa Breslin *Brian McCabe* Gerald Mangan **Danny Boyle** Christopher Whyte *John Burnside* Anne Donovan **William Hershaw** Chris Dolan *Susie Maguire* Danny McCahon **Gerry Cambridge** Rody Gorman **Willy Maley** Angela McSeveney *Andrew O'Hagan*

"large, ambitious and timely" **Sunday Herald**
"enjoyable, sometimes polemical" **Scotland on Sunday**
"vibrant exploration of a culture" **Scotsman**
"a fine book" **Irish Times**
"excellent" **Irish Post**
"shows the depth of feeling that still remains on both sides of the religious divide" **Irish World**

**Available direct from Argyll Publishing, Glendaruel Argyll
PA22 3AE Scotland tel 01369 820229
email argyll.publishing@virgin.net   www.skoobe.biz**